T0316464

VALUE

The Representation of Labour in Capitalism

Essays Edited by
Diane Elson

VALUE

The Representation of Labour in Capitalism

Essays Edited by
Diane Elson

VERSO

London • New York

This edition published by Verso 2015
First published by CSE Books 1979
The Collection © Verso Books 2015
The Contributions © The Contributors 1979, 2015

1 3 5 7 9 10 8 6 4 2

Verso
UK: 6 Meard Street, London W1F 0EG
US: 388 Atlantic Ave, Brooklyn, NY 11217
www.versobooks.com

Verso is the imprint of New Left Books

ISBN-13: 978-1-78478-229-0 (PB)
eISBN-13: 978-1-78478-231-3 (US)
eISBN-13: 978-1-78478-230-6 (UK)

British Library Cataloguing in Publication Data
A catalogue record for this book is available from the British Library

Library of Congress Cataloging-in-Publication Data
A catalog record for this book is available from the Library of Congress
Printed in the United States

CONTENTS

Notes on Contributors

Chris Arthur teaches philosophy at Sussex University, and has contributed to *Radical Philosophy, Critique* and *CSE Bulletin*.

Aboo Aumeeruddy is currently working at the Institute of Development Studies, Sussex University. He is a member of the Editorial Committee of *Capital and Class.*

Jairus Banaji lives and works in Bombay, and has contributed to *Capital and Class*.

Diane Elson teaches economics at the University of Manchester. She was formerly a member of the Editorial Committee of *Capital and Class* and of the Brighton Labour Process Group.

Athar Hussain teaches economics at the University of Keele and is a member of the CSE Money Group. He has contributed to the *CSE Bulletin* and *Economy and Society*.

Makoto Itoh teaches economics at the University of Tokyo and has contributed to *CSE Bulletin, Capital and Class* and *Science and Society*.

Geoff Kay teaches economics at the City University, London, and is a member of the Editorial Board of *Critique*. He has contributed to the *CSE Bulletin*.

Ramon Tortajada works in the University of Grenoble, France, and has contributed to *Capital and Class*.

Nobuharu Yokokawa is carrying out research on the work of Ricardo and Marx at the Universities of Tokyo and Cambridge.

INTRODUCTION

To some readers, the publication by CSE Books of a collection of essays on Marx's theory of value will simply be an indication of the unwillingness (or inability) of Marxist intellectuals to leave the realms of high theory and produce some politically useful, concrete analysis of the accumulation of capital today. To others it will signify a mystifying refusal to jettison a theory which, it is claimed, has now been shown to be at best redundant, at worst incoherent and without foundations in real social relations. Yet others may expect one more, incomprehensible round in a debate which obsesses 'Marxist economists' but has little significance for those interested in Marx's theory of class or the state or the mode of production. So why has CSE Books chosen to put together this volume? Why is Marx's theory of value important?

It is important because Marx's theory of value is the *foundation* of his attempt to understand capitalism in a way that is politically useful to socialists. It is not some small and dispensable part of Marx's investigation of capital; it constitutes the basis on which that investigation takes place. If we decide to reject that theory, we are at the same time rejecting precisely those tools of analysis which are Marx's distinctive contribution to socialist thought on the workings of capital. The debate about Marx's value theory is, in fact, a debate about the appropriate method of analysis, about the validity of the concepts which are specific to, and constitute the method of, historical materialism. The outcome of this debate therefore has implications far beyond the way in which we understand prices and profit in the capitalist economy. It has implications for the question of how we should carry out our empirical investigations today of the international restructuring of capital accumulation; of new forms of class struggle, of the capitalist state; and of the possibilities for socialism. It has implications for the fundamental question of whether what is distinctive about Marx's method of analysis is really of any use to socialists today.

Accordingly this collection of essays concentrates on investigating and evaluating the method of analysis instantiated in Marx's theory of value, a method which Marx claimed in his Preface to the French Edition of *Capital*, I, had not been previously applied to economic subjects. It is not a premise of this book that every word which Marx wrote must inevitably be 'correct', and that the task is simply to propagate them. But it is a premise that much recent debate over Marx's theory of value has been hampered by a mutual incomprehension on matters of method; on the meaning to be attached to terms like 'determination', 'substance', 'measure', 'abstraction', 'form', 'transformation', 'law', 'equivalence', etc.; and on the question of what Marx's theory of value is a theory of, what is its object. Marx himself wrote in the Postface to the Second German Edition of *Capital* I,

> 'That the method employed in *Capital* has been little understood is shown by the various mutually contradictory conceptions that have been formed of it.'

The essays in this book attempt to explore and to resolve some of the differences that exist in current interpretations of Marx's theory of value, recognising that the cause of misunderstandings may lie in inadequacies in Marx's texts, as well as the preconceptions that readers have brought to those texts.

The essays have been written by CSE members from France, India and Japan, as well as from Britain, reflecting the international membership of the CSE. They are not all written from exactly the same perspective; nor do they all reach exactly the same kind of conclusion. But what they have in common is an awareness of the question of method of analysis, raised above. Two of them, the ones by Kay and Hussain, have already appeared in print, in *Critique* and *Theoretical Practice* respectively. The rest have been written specially for this collection.

Recognising that there are always readers to whom the topics under discussion are quite new, readers who perhaps are just beginning to read *Capital*, the first essay in this collection is an annotated guide to reading what Marx wrote on value, prepared by Aboo Aumeeruddy and Ramon Tortajada. They stress the complexity of the relation between Marx's texts and those of classical political economy, in particular of Ricardo, arguing that in Marx's texts there is both a deepening of the analysis begun by classical political economy, and a break with it. Readers with no previous knowledge of Marx's theory of value might find it helpful to begin with this short discussion of Marx's texts, and then turn to the last essay, by Diane Elson, which among other things discusses the various interpretations of Marx's theory of value which have been prominent in CSE debates. This should provide sufficient background for following the more detailed consideration of different aspects of Marx's theory of value presented in the other essays.

The second essay in the collection, by Jairus Banaji, draws our attention to Lenin's well known conclusion that,

> 'It is impossible completely to understand Marx's *Capital*, and especially its first chapter, without having thoroughly studied and understood the whole of Hegel's *Logic*',

and explores the relation between Hegel's dialectic and Marx's theory of value. In the course of this, Banaji argues that it is quite wrong to suppose that Marx's theory of value is first elaborated for a pre-capitalist economy of simple commodity producers. Rather, the capitalist mode of production is assumed from the very first sentence of *Capital*. Banaji also shows that Marx was as concerned with appearance as he was with essence, as much with money as with the abstract and reified form of social labour. Most importantly, Banaji shows that the development of the theory of value at the beginning of *Capital* embodies a dialectical method decomposable into two phases. First is a phase of analysis which begins from an immediate appearance, an historically determinate abstraction, the commodity. By analysing the commodity Marx arrives at the concept of value as the abstract-reified form of social labour. Value then forms the point of departure for the second, synthetic phase, of the investigation which returns to the level of appearance, to the commodity, showing it to be a representation of social relations not immediately apparent.

Geoffrey Kay, in the third essay, replies to some of the criticisms that bourgeois economics makes of Marx's method of analysis in his theory of value. He does so in the form of a discussion of the criticism advanced by Bohm-Bawerk in 1896 which he argues 'remains ahead in its field as the most coherent and systematic challenge to Marxism by any bourgeois economist'. In particular, Kay takes up the challenge that Marx's method of analysis is formalist, a 'purely logical method of deduction' not rooted in a consideration of real social relations. His argument is that this belief arises from a misunderstanding of the method of abstraction that Marx used. The same kind of misunderstanding creates confusion about the form of existence that Marx postulated for value: this was, argues Kay, not a type of labour, but money. Finally Kay considers Bohm-Bawerk's conviction that Marx's theory of value implies that commodities must in practice exchange in ratios proportionate to their relative values, and argues that in fact the possibility of a discrepancy between the two is an essential feature of Marx's analysis, right from the beginning of *Capital*, I.

A neglected aspect of Marx's theory of value is the subject of the fourth essay by Chris Arthur. This discusses the argument of the third section of *Capital*, I, Chapter 1, on the value-form, or form of appearance of value. As Arthur comments

> 'From the point of view of formal thinking nothing is going on here except the complication of a tautology –' 'a value is a value is a value!';

and this is perhaps why this section, with its important distinction between the relative and the equivalent forms of value, has been largely ignored. Arthur shows, however, that Marx's method of argument here is not one of formal abstraction, but a dialectical method, which Arthur calls 'the logic of the concrete'. It draws attention to material characteristics of the relation of exchange between commodities which cannot be captured by the methods of formal logic; and its achievement is to lead to an understanding of money as the form of appearance of value, not as a mere numeraire.

The fifth essay by Athar Hussain discusses the way in which Marx's theory of value has been read as a theory of price, in the context of a consideration of Marx's Marginal Notes on Wagner. Wagner overlooked the difference between Marx and Ricardo, and so, suggests Hussain, have many later economists themselves Marxists, or sympathetic to Marxism. This essay originally appeared in 1972 in *Theoretical Practice*, and since then Hussain has changed his evaluation of Marx's value theory itself. But his comments on the way that other questions have been substituted for Marx's question, in the reading of the theory of value, retain their pertinence. Of particular interest is his treatment of the distinction between concrete and abstract labour, including the controversial view that the latter is not specific to the capitalist mode of production.

The sixth essay, by Makoto Itoh and Nobuharu Yokokawa, discusses the theory of the market process in Marx's theory of value. Its starting point lies in Japanese debates about the status of Marx's discussion of market-value i.e. the determination of value in cases where there are differences in conditions of production for the same kind of commodity. The authors argue that the social value cannot simply be deduced statically and technically as an average of the individual labour-times associated with the different production conditions. In a commodity economy the social value is only made apparent through the process of market competition, which reveals which of the individual conditions of production is the regulative one for that sector.

The authors go on to discuss the nature of the additional profit that accrues to producers with conditions of production superior to the regulative condition, and the particular form this takes when land is one of the conditions of production.

The final essay, by Diane Elson, argues that the object of Marx's theory of value is not prices but labour. She suggests it is the traditional interpretation of Marx's theory as a labour theory of value which has been shown to be redundant; but not the value theory of labour which Marx presents in *Capital*. There are various ambiguities and incompletenesses in Marx's presentation, but nevertheless the core of his argument is a coherent and decidedly non-redundant exploration of the contradictions of the capitalist form of the determination of labour. Its political importance lies not in providing the foundation for a proof that capital exploits labour; but rather in providing the foundation for an analysis of the material basis for overcoming that exploitation.

Acknowledgements

I am grateful to the Editorial Board of *Critique* for permission to reprint the essay by Geoff Kay; and to Dave Smart for translating the essay by Aboo Aumeeruddy and Ramon Tortajada.

Special thanks to Sylvia Worsencroft for helping with the typing; and to John Gaffney of CSE Books for encouraging me to try to meet deadlines, being patient and re-arranging schedules when I didn't, and overseeing the transformation from manuscript to book.

Diane Elson,
Manchester, April 1979.

READING MARX ON VALUE: A NOTE ON THE BASIC TEXTS

A Aumeeruddy and R Tortajada

Introduction

Marxist theory (and, in particular, the theory of value) has been, and remains, a source of much controversy. On the one hand, the ruling class ceaselessly and systematically attacks 'marxists', at the same time attempting to recuperate, if not co-opt, Marxist theory by stripping it if its revolutionary content. On the other hand, some Marxists themselves try to turn Marxism into an 'improved political economy'.

If an 'economistic' reading of Marxism has proved possible, this is because there exist certain texts by Marx which admit this reading, while at the same time other of Marx's texts criticise such an approach; Marx's relationship with political economy is consequently very complex, and there can be no question of a key or set of instructions for reading Marx's works.

The reader can, in fact, begin with any text. Nevertheless, two works can be recommended as a starting point — the two series of lectures which Marx prepared for workers' organisations, and which directly address political and social struggles, both against capital and within these organisations themselves.

The first series — subsequently collated by Engels under the title *Wage Labour and Capital* — dates from August 1847 and was written for the German Workers' Association of Brussels as a contribution to these workers' 'political education'.

The second series of lectures was considered by Marx himself to form a 'course in political economy', although he emphasised 'that it isn't easy to explain all economic questions to the uneducated' (Letter to Engels of 20th May 1865). It dates from June 1865, and was written for the General Council of the International Working-Men's Association. Subsequently published under the title *Wages, Price and Profit*, it enjoyed massive circulation in pamphlet form, like the first series.

The advantage of starting with these texts lies not only in the fact that they are short, in plentiful supply, cheap, and thus readily available, but also in that Marx himself gave them a pedagogic character:

they formed, and continue to form, a model of how to spread Marxist theory within the working class.

There is, however, the apparent paradox that these texts leave relatively obscure – or rather, deal in summary fashion – with certain aspects which are today at the centre of debate on Marx's theory, in particular the notions of value, of value-form, of magnitude of value, of the existence of the commodity, etc.

This is because Marx's principal intention in these lectures is not in fact to make a break with political economy but to call attention to capital itself, or rather to the social relation which appears in machinery as 'accumulated labour'. In doing so, Marx frequently bases himself on political economy, and in particular, as regards the concept of value, on Smith and Ricardo, while at the same time attacking and denouncing the 'Vulgar Economy' that superseded Ricardo's thought in the 1830s. (See 'Afterword' to the Second German Edition of *Capital*, I.)

In order to understand Marx's relationship with political economy more deeply, it is essential to refer to other texts. The purpose of this note is to present a selection of these. This selection can obviously be neither neutral nor complete, particularly since Marxist theory is itself neither neutral nor finished except, that is, when transformed into its opposite – dogma. The texts which we put forward are thus those which seem to us the most adequate for understanding Marx's relationship with political economy, and are one way or another at the centre of the current discussion on this relationship.

It is common, particularly among 'economists', to start with Volume One of *Capital*, or in some cases with its forerunners, the *Contribution to the Critique of Political Economy*, or the *Grundrisse* or even the *Theories of Surplus Value*, often neglecting the works of 'the young Marx' which are considered to belong to the field of 'philosophy'. This kind of approach in fact reflects the academic separation of the 'social sciences', and it is consequently not surprising to see an academic like Schumpeter distinguishing a 'sociologist' Marx, a 'philosopher' Marx, an 'economist' Marx, etc. However, Marx's very procedure invites us to reject this separation and not to see *Capital* as a work of political economy (albeit a 'left-wing' one), nor even as the culmination of a system of thought but as a moment in the development of a theory which sets out to challenge the existing order.

The order in which these texts are presented in no way seeks to define the best order for reading them, nor even to place them chronologically in order of writing or publication. As has been said above there is no 'key' to reading Marx. The *Marginal Notes on Adolph Wagner's 'Lehrbuch der politischen Okonomie'* have been placed first not because these notes are Marx's least known work on political economy, but simply because this is one of the rare texts in which Marx replies directly to an economist who ventured to criticise his theory of value.

I. Marginal Notes on Adolph Wagner's 'Lehrbuch der politischen Okonomie'

This was written in 1881-82 (or 1879-80) and first published in 1932 as an appendix to the Moscow Marx-Engels-Lenin Institute edition of *Capital*. There are the following translations in English:
1) In *Theoretical Practice*, No. 5, London, 1972, pp. 40-64;
2) Translated by Terrell Carver under the title *Notes on Adolph Wagner* in K Marx, *Texts on Method*, Oxford, Basil Blackwell, 1975, pp. 179-219.
3) Translated by Albert Dragstedt under the title *Marginal Notes to A Wagner's 'Textbook on Political Economy'* in *Value: studies by Karl Marx*, London, New Park Publications, 1976, pp. 197-229.

   Marx here recalls his analysis of the relations between value, use-value and exchange-value. He emphasises:
a) that exchange-value and value must not be confused, *exchange-value* merely being the 'phenomenal form' or 'necessary mode of expression' of *value*;
b) that he does not do away with *use-value*, unlike classical political economy: 'The *value* of a commodity is expressed in the use-value, that is to say the natural form of the other commodity';
c) that value, use-value and exchange-value are not alternative concepts, in logical opposition to one another, but are the *forms* in which the commodity presents itself: in other words, three forms which co-exist.

   It is in this text that Marx repeatedly emphasises that he does not set out from 'value', but from the 'commodity', that is to say, 'the simplest social form in which the product of labour presents itself in contemporary society'. And it will be recalled that the first chapters of both the *Contribution to the Critique of Political Economy* (1859) and the first volume of *Capital* (1867) are in fact entitled 'The Commodity'.

II. The different versions of Chapter 1 of *Capital*, Volume I

The first edition of *Capital* Volume I, was published in German in 1867 under the supervision of Marx. A French edition prepared by Marx himself, was published in instalments from 1872-75, and a second German edition also prepared by Marx was published in 1873. The first edition in English was published in 1887, a translation by Samuel Moore and Edward Aveling of the third German edition, prepared by Engels, in 1883, with the assistance of notes left by Marx, indicating the passages of the second German edition which were to be replaced by designated passages from the French edition. There are textual differences between all these four editions, but the most important difference is that between Chapter 1 of the first and subsequent editions.

The versions currently most widely available in English are:
1) The Moore-Aveling translation of the Third German edition, incorporating amendments made by Engels for the Fourth German edition, published by Lawrence and Wishart, London, various dates;
2) The new translation of Volume I by Ben Fowkes published by Penguin Books, London, 1976;
3) The text of the Appendix to Chapter 1 of the First German edition, translated by M Roth and W Suchting in *Capital & Class* No. 4, Spring 1978, pp. 134-150. This deals with the value form.

In reading *Capital* it is necessary to bear in mind the *Introduction* sketched out by Marx in August 1857 for *A Contribution to the Critique of Political Economy*. In this 'Introduction'—which was not in fact published with the *Critique* but can be found in the edition of the *Grundrisse* prepared by M Nicolaus and published by Penguin Books, 1973, pp. 81-111—Marx shows that in presenting an exposition of his theory, it was in fact necessary to reverse the order in which it was constituted, a reversal which represents a significant formal aspect of *Capital*. It must also be remembered that the texts published posthumously under the title *Capital* Volumes II and III and the analyses collected in the *Theories of Surplus Value* were, as regards essentials, already in existence *before* Marx wrote the first volume of *Capital*.

Consequently, neither Volumes II or III of *Capital* nor the *Theories of Surplus Value* are intended to 'complement' or 'make specific' the 'abstractions' of the first volume of *Capital*. On the contrary, it is on the basis of reading this latter, and more particularly Chapter 1 that certain of the questions raised in Volumes II, III and in *Theories of Surplus Value* can be analysed. This does not mean that these works are not worthy of attention. On the contrary, study of them is an integral part of research-work aimed at clarifying the relations between Marx and political economy.

The questions which today appear central to numerous debates relating to Marxist theory are posed from the first chapter of *Capital*, (a chapter which, as Marx himself wrote in his Preface to the First Edition of *Capital* presents 'the greatest difficulty'.) Among them are: the primacy of the category 'commodity' for the comprehension of capitalist relations; value and its forms; the magnitude and measurement of value; the status of labour and abstraction; the relationship between Marxist theory and Ricardian theory; and the fetishism of commodities.

However, two of the questions raised seem to us to require particular attention insofar as one led Marx to rewrite the beginning of *Capital* Volume I, and the other defines a certain mode of reading not only this work, but Marxist theory as well.

The first concerns the relation between the study of value and of the forms which it assumes. It is important firstly because the relationship between the '*value*' of a commodity and its phenomenal form '*exchange-value*' is at the centre of the debates on Marx's relationship with political economy. Moreover, understanding of the 'general equivalent' and hence of money derives, in Marx's view, from an understanding of the forms of value. Finally, it is this same question which is at the root of the profound reworking of *Capital* Volume I by Marx between the first and second editions of *Capital*, a reworking retained in subsequent editions.

In the first edition, Chapter 1 was in fact devoted to the 'commodity' and to 'money', and was divided into three sections: The Commodity, The Process of Commodity-Exchange, Money and Commodity-Circulation. Analysis of the forms of value was consigned to an Appendix at the end of the work, in which Marx analysed these forms systematically and in detail. The three sections became the first three chapters of subsequent editions and the appendix was reintegrated into the first of them.

The second question concerns the process of abstraction. In *Capital*, and in the first chapter in particular, there is not one single process of abstraction, but two processes of abstraction profoundly *different* in character. It is therefore worth distinguishing very precisely between them, if only to avoid the very common *confusion* by which

a) *Capital* Volume I is seen as an 'abstract' construction (in the sense of being estranged from reality by the adoption of extremely restrictive hypotheses, often cited examples of which are identical organic composition between the various branches of production, and homogeneous labour);

b) Volumes II and III are seen as Marx's attempts to relate his 'abstract' theory to some reality, thus characterising Karl Marx as a 'builder' of economic models to be tested against 'reality'.

On the one hand there is a process of *thought* or *reasoned abstraction*, to use the terms Marx himself employs in the *Introduction*, and on the other hand, on an entirely different level, a process of *real abstraction*.

Reasoned abstraction is to do with the discovery of categories which permit bourgeois social relations to be understood. As Marx emphasised in his pamphlet against Proudhon, 'Economic categories are only the theoretical expression, the abstractions of the social relations of production' (*The Poverty of Philosophy*, (1846-47), Lawrence & Wishart, n.d., Chapter II, Second Observation, p. 105). At the same time, he makes it clear that these abstractions are not to be confused with the social relations themselves. Later, in writing the Preface to the first edition of *Capital*, he returns to this aspect of abstraction, pointing out that 'In the analysis of economic forms moreover, neither micro-scopes nor chemical reagents are of use. The force of abstraction must replace both.'; and that within bourgeois society this leads one to set out from the simplest and, it would seem, most immediate form, the commodity. Study of the commodity is thus the corner-stone of the analysis of a society characterised by the generalisation of commodity relations to include the labourer himself.

Real abstraction, on the other hand, is not the result of analy-tical effort, but the consequence of a real process which is at the heart of bourgeois social relations – commodity-exchange.

In bourgeois society, where the private division of social labour prevails, products are the result of private, isolated processes of pro-duction operating independently of one another. It is only when pro-duction has been completed, that is to say when the labour mobilised has been objectified in a determinate good, that producers' respective acts of production encounter one another on the market, as products offered in exchange for money. And the producers will only know that their products effectively answered a social need if they succeed in ex-changing them. Commodity-exchange is the social mode of recognition of the different products, and it is *via* this exchange that they cease to be products and become commodities, or rather that the commodity which is potential when the product is present on the market becomes real – is realised. It is thus as commodities that the different acts of labour privately carried out in separation from one another become fractions of social labour.

But commodity-exchange is only conceivable if there exists a relation of equivalence between different commodities. From the point of view of their use-values – the physical characteristics of the products – commodities are of course different, hence non-equivalent, and it is precisely this difference which is the motive force of exchange. But in the course of exchange, the use-value of the commodities is abstracted from, and only the social capacity of the commodities to be exchanged is recognised. According to Marx's terms, this 'abstraction' entails ab-straction from the specific characteristics of the acts of labour objectified in the commodities. This leaves the commodities as nothing but the result of human labour, without regard to the particular form it takes, in other words of labour 'full stop'. This is abstract labour.

It is because all products participate in this process of abstraction when they become commodities and are therefore recognised as fractions of abstract social labour that one can conceive of establishing a relation of equivalence between them; they belong to the same sphere.

In order to avoid any ambiguity, it is worth emphasising that the process whereby different acts of labour are reduced to abstract labour has nothing whatever to do with the process whereby 'complex labour' is reduced to 'simple labour'. Whereas the first process is involved in the *founding* of value, the second belongs to a different logic: it relates to the *measurement of magnitudes already constituted*.

III. Results of the Immediate Process of Production

Sometimes known as the 'lost chapter' of *Capital*, this was written between June 1863 and December 1866 and was first published in 1933, simultaneously in German and Russian. An English translation has recently been made by Rodney Livingstone, and appears as an Appendix to the new Fowkes translation of *Capital*, I, Penguin Books, 1976, pp. 948-1084.

It was originally planned as a transitional chapter between Volume I and Volume II of *Capital*, as it is not definitely known why Marx discarded it. It contains both a synthesis of the argument of Volume I, and a further development of the relations between 'value' and 'use-value' in terms of the subsumption of labour to capital. It completes the argument of Volume I by investigating commodities not only as the *premise* of the formation of capital but also as the *result* of capitalist production. 'Only on the basis of Capitalist production does the commodity actually become the *universal elementary form of wealth*'. (Op. cit., p. 951).

IV. Introduction drafted for a Contribution to the Critique of Political Economy

Written in 1857 (dated 29th August), it was first published in *Die Neue Zeit*, 1903 (?); and republished in 1939 by the Moscow Marx-Engels-Lenin Institute. The following English versions are available:
1) Translated by Martin Nicolaus in *Grundrisse*, Penguin edition, 1973, pp. 81-111;
2) Translated by David McLellan in Marx's *Grundrisse*, Paladin edition, 1973, pp. 26-57;

3) In *Texts on Method*, ed Terrell Carver, Oxford, Basil Blackwell, 1975.

Although Marx did not publish this 'Introduction' on the grounds that it anticipated too much the ideas developed in the work itself, it is of fundamental importance both to understanding Marx's 'methods' and to his critique of economic analysis which began from the isolated 'individual' and considered 'production', 'distribution', 'exchange' and 'consumption' only as separate economic 'moments' not as interpenetrating processes.

V. A Contribution to the Critique of Political Economy

Written in 1858-9, it was first published in Berlin in 1859 under the title *Zur Kritik der Politischen Okonomie*. An English translation, edited by Maurice Dobb, was published by Lawrence & Wishart in 1971. The most famous section of it is the Preface, but more relevant to the question of value is the first chapter, entitled *The Commodity*. It is one of the few works published during his lifetime by Marx himself.

VI. Letters on Capital

Marx and Engels carried on a voluminous correspondence. A selection of this was published by Progress Publishers, Moscow, and distributed by Lawrence & Wishart. The following three letters are of particular interest. (Page references to Marx-Engels, *Selected Correspondence*, Progress Publishers, Moscow, n.d.)

(a) Letters from Marx to Engels, 2nd and 9th August, 1862. (pp. 157-161; 164-165).

It was in connection with Ricardo's theory of ground-rent that Marx, for the first time, came to make the relations between 'value' and 'price' explicit, doing so in terms very close to those used in what would later form *Capital*, Volume III, Part VI.

From the outset, Marx emphasises that 'Competition does not therefore equate commodities to their value, but to cost prices which are higher than, lower than or equal to their values according to the organic composition of the capitals.' It would seem that Marx is rediscovering the difficulty previously encountered by Ricardo: exchange is not based on the labour-time incorporated if the prices incorporate the general rate of profit.

This difficulty results in two kinds of development. On the one hand, the analysis of the forms of value, which manifests itself in the successive versions of *Capital*, I, Chapter 1 (Cf. Section II above). On the other hand, the well-known 'transformation of values into prices'.

Besides this first formulation of the analysis of the relationship between value and price, we can see Marx's concern to establish as quickly as possible the connections between the development of theory and the practice or struggle in which he was taking part. In this case, it is analysis of the contradictions of a certain practical solidarity between capitalists and landed proprietors.

It is in fact this concern which leads him: firstly, unlike Ricardo, to distinguish the possibility of 'absolute' rent independently of 'differential' rent; secondly, to base the existence of ground-rent on comparison of values with 'cost prices' (which he confused, at the time, with 'production prices'). This procedure made possible an *identification* of the spheres of 'value' and 'exchange-value' with one another. Marx himself elsewhere criticised this identification which arises again in the problem of 'transformation'. (Cf. Sections I and VIII in this note).

(b) Letter to Kugelmann, 11th July 1868, (pp. 250-253)

This letter has been quoted and referred to so often that it must, if only because of this, be read in its entirety. May we repeat, however, that like all the other of Marx's texts cited here, it cannot form a key or method for the reading of *Capital*. It certainly raises the question of Marx's complex relationship with political economy – in which Marx simultaneously deepened, and broke with, the latter's analysis.

We would emphasise three points about this letter:

(i) As in his *Marginal Notes on Adolph Wagner's 'Lehrbuch der politischen Okonomie'*, Marx distances himself from the 'theory' of value, indicating that the *concept* of value takes second place, in his work, to the analysis of real relations. 'The unfortunate fellow (author of a review of *Capital*, I) does not see that, even if there were no chapter on 'value' in my book, the analysis of the real relations which I give would contain the proof and demonstration of the real value-relation.' (op. cit. p. 251).

(ii) The second point concerns the relation between the magnitudes of values and exchange-relations. Rebutting the vulgar economists, Marx emphasises that there cannot be *immediate* identity between 'the real relations of day-to-day exchange' and the 'magnitudes of values' in bourgeois society. But if there is no immediate identity, Marx nevertheless leaves room for a certain ambiguity on the possibility of *mediations*. The 'blindly operating mean' has in fact been interpreted in an 'economistic sense' to form the basis for the 'transformation' approach.

(iii) Finally, this letter leaves open the possibility of a naturalist interpretation of the concept of 'law': 'No natural laws can be done away with. What can change in historically different circumstances is only the *form* in which these laws assert themselves'. (op. cit. p. 251). Consequently, it seems that Marx is here considering 'value' to be an ahistorical concept, and that it is only the form in which it manifests itself, exchange-value, that is historically determined.

VII. The 1844 Manuscripts

Written in 1844, these manuscripts were not published until 1932. The following versions are available in English:
1) 'Excerpts from James Mill's Elements of Political Economy', translated by Rodney Livingstone in Marx, *Early Writings*, Penguin, 1975, pp. 259-278.
2) 'Economic and Philosophical Manuscripts', translated by Gregor Benton in *Early Writings*, Penguin, 1975, pp. 280-400.
3) In *Economic and Philosophical Manuscripts*, translated by Martin Milligan, Lawrence & Wishart, 1959.
4) In Marx, *Early Writings*, ed. T Bottomore, London, 1963.

At the end of 1843, Marx began serious study of the works of the principal economists. The first writings explicitly dealing with political economy were subsequently known by the title of the *1844 Manuscripts*: comprising the *Notes on James Mill* and, more importantly, the *Economic and Philosophical Manuscripts*.

'Economistic' interpretation of Marxism has neglected the works of Marx's 'youth' and continues to do so. We do not propose to enter into the debate over the 'continuity' (Meszaros, Colletti) or the 'break' (Althusser) between the 'young' and the 'mature' Marx here, but simply to emphasise that, in so far as they constitute a 'turning point' between the critique of philosophy, law and the state (in the writings of 1843, in particular the *Critique of Hegel's Doctrine of the State*, the *Jewish Question*, and the *Introduction to the Critique of Hegel's Philosophy of Right*) and the critique of political economy, it is essential to *read* the *1844 Manuscripts*. This is not so as to arrive at the 'correct'(!) interpretation of Marx's thought—there is obviously no *single* interpretation of the *1844 Manuscripts*—but in order to consider such questions as that of the relationship between the 'abstraction of labour' elaborated in the *1844 Manuscripts* and the concept of 'abstract labour'—the substance and measure of value—elaborated in *Capital*. On this the most useful passages are the section on Estranged Labour in the first of the *Economic and Philosophical Manuscripts*, and in *Excerpts from James Mill's Elements of Political Economy*, op. cit. pp. 265-278. See, for example, the following passage from the latter:

'Thus private property as such is a *surrogate*, an *equivalent*. Its

immediate unity with itself has given way to a relation to
another. As an *equivalent* its existence is no longer peculiar to it.
It thus becomes a *value*, in fact an immediate *exchange-value*. Its
existence as *value* is a determination of itself diverging from its
immediate nature, external to it, alienated from it, a merely
relative existence. The problem of defining this *value* more precisely, as well as showing how it becomes price, must be dealt
with elsewhere. In a situation based on *exchange*, labour immediately becomes wage-labour.' (Op. cit, p. 268.)

VIII. Theories of Surplus Value, Parts One, Two, Three

Written in 1862-63, this massive examination and critique of the
development of economic thought is often referred to as the Fourth
Volume of *Capital*. An edition was first published between 1905 and
1910 by Kautsky, but the arrangement of the text differed in various
ways from that of the manuscript. A German edition was published in
Berlin in 1956-1966 on the basis of the German original kept in the
Institute of Marxism-Leninism in Moscow. The English edition published by Lawrence and Wishart, 1969-1972, is a translation of the
Berlin edition.

In so far as the manuscripts are devoted to the theory of value
and surplus-value in their entirety, it is difficult to pick out particular
passages. Nevertheless, in the context of current debates on the theory
of value, it seems useful to consider in particular the chapters which
Marx devotes to a critical examination of the theories of Smith and
Ricardo. In Part One, Chapter III is devoted to Smith. In Part Two, the
relevant passages are Chapter X, where Marx compares Smith and
Ricardo's theories of cost price; and Chapter XV and XVI, which are
devoted to Ricardo's theory of surplus value and of profit. These
passages throw light on Marx's analysis of 'classical' theories of value,
but only illuminate indirectly his own theory. Consequently, they leave
the door open for an 'economistic' reading of Marx's position.

Note also the criticism Marx makes of the 'vulgar economists', in
particular that of S Bailey and the (unknown) author of *Observations
on Certain Verbal Disputes in Political Economy*, where Marx is led to
tackle the problem of the relations between 'invariable measure' and
'value' (see Part III, Chapter XX, pp. 124-168; cf. also pp. 110-117).
We would emphasise three points in this critique:
(i) First of all, there is the question of the relationship between the
 search for an 'invariable measure' and Marx's theory of value. As far
 as Marx is concerned, the search for an 'invariable measure' falls outside the problematic of value. The object of the theory of value is

not to constitute an 'invariable measure' of the exchange-relations of commodities. A 'measure' of this kind can only be conceived, in Marx's view, if a theory of value has *first* been constituted. For commodities to be compared with one another in exchange, in terms of exchange-value, it is necessary for the various commodities to be expressions of the same substance. 'The commodities must *already be identical as values*'. (Op. cit. p. 134).

It is in so far as they are fractions of abstract social labour that commodities are expressions of the same substance. The abstraction here has nothing to do with any kind of mental process, but is the social mode whereby men's different acts of labour are recognised in a society in which commodity-exchange prevails.

(ii) Although Marx repeatedly emphasises the difference between the status of value and that of the forms which it is liable to assume, and also the difference between the status of labour in Ricardian theory and in his own theory of value, he nevertheless uses ambiguous formulations on these two points. These ambiguities are, moreover, only very partially resolved when he takes up the question again in *Capital*, Volume One. The first ambiguity arises from the fact that Marx, on occasion, attributes to Political Economy aims which it was not pursuing, for example, the formulation of a theory of 'value' or of 'surplus-value' whereas its objective, as Marx himself often emphasises, was principally the analysis of exchange-value or the forms of surplus-value. In this particular passage, Marx implies that the search for an 'invariable measure' coincides with the search for the 'value' of commodities:

> 'The problem of an 'invariable measure of value' was simply a spurious name for the quest for the concept, the nature of *value* itself, the definition of which could not be another value, and consequently could not be subject to variation of value'. (Op. cit. p. 134.)

A second ambiguity, which follows on from the first, concerns the status of labour. Marx's main reproach to Ricardo is not so much that he is oblivious of 'abstract labour', but that he 'continually confuses' it (op. cit. p. 139) with the labour which is represented in use-value.

(iii) Finally, it is in elaborating his criticism with respect to Bailey that Marx emphasises with particular clarity why the determination of the exchange-relation cannot be based solely on the exchange-relation itself.

This critique, which is aimed directly at Bailey, also forms the corner-stone of the criticism directed at the various theories which do base the theory of value solely on the exchange-relation – viz. supply and demand.

IX. Grundrisse: Foundations of the Critique of Political Economy

This is a series of seven notebooks rough-drafted by Marx, chiefly for the purpose of self clarification, during the winter 1857-8. The manuscript became lost under circumstances still unknown and was first effectively published in the German original in Berlin in 1953.

The following versions are available in English:
1) A full version translated by Martin Nicolaus, Penguin, 1973.
2) Extracts in David McLellan, *Marx's Grundrisse*, MacMillan, 1971, Paladin, 1973.
3) Extracts in Karl Marx, *Precapitalist Economic Formations*, ed. E Hobsbawm, Lawrence & Wishart, 1964.

In these 'jottings' Marx tackles a number of points which subsequently receive only sketchy treatment; in particular, with respect to value, the relationship of money to value, (in particular Penguin ed. pp. 136-172) and the relationship between exchange-value and private property (previously dealt with in the *1844 Manuscripts*). Note also the passages relating to 'Forms preceding capitalist production' (Penguin, pp. 471-514); not only because these passages have been much discussed (and criticised), but also because they contain in germinal form an analysis of the historical genesis of value and of the 'abstraction of labour', a problem which lies at the heart of our preoccupations.

FROM THE COMMODITY TO CAPITAL: HEGEL'S DIALECTIC IN MARX'S 'CAPITAL'

Jairus Banaji

THE DIALECTIC IN LENIN AND MARX

Lenin

It is well known that on reading Hegel's *Logic* late in 1914 Lenin was so profoundly impressed by the impact which he now discovered it had made on Marx that he wrote,

'It is impossible completely to understand Marx's *Capital*, and especially its first chapter, without having thoroughly studied and understood the whole of Hegel's *Logic*.'

Then a startling conclusion: 'Consequently, half a century later none of the Marxists understood Marx!!' (Lenin, 1972, p. 180).

Today, over a century later, this statement has a special significance. In Lenin's day, the Second International had more or less explicitly shifted the philosophical and scientific premises of Marxism in directions quite distant from its Hegelian origins — towards biological evolutionism (Kautsky), varieties of neo-Kantianism (Bernstein among others), and even, through Max Adler, the positivism of Comte (cf. Goldmann, 1959, pp. 280-302). In our own, contemporary period the publication of Della Volpe's *Logica come scienza positiva* (its original title of the fifties) inaugurated a roughly similar reaction. Conscious repudiation of the dialectic, of the enormous weight of Hegel's method in Marx's development and thus in the formation of Marx's theory, became a fundamental and unifying characteristic of postwar 'Western Marxism'. As in the nascent period of reformism, late in the nineteenth century, so now, in its declining phase, in the sixties, this critique of 'metaphysics' (Della Volpe, 1969) or of 'illusion' (Althusser, 1969) *could only* take the form of a bizarre philosophical eclecticism ranging across the most divergent and logically incompatible tendencies: from forms of empiricism more (Colletti) or less (Della Volpe) sympathetic to Kant, or simply reflecting the hostility of Positivists to any philosophical connection (Timpanaro), to a revitalised Spinozist rationalism (Althusser). As Althusser's own acknowledgment suggests (1969, pp. 37-38), Della Volpe was the *major* figure in this belated movement of reaction. The most serious specific consequence of Della Volpe's attack on Hegel was its 'experimentalist' recasting of the dialectic into a conception of science, and of scientific method, strikingly close to Popper's neo-empiricism.[1] When he turned to *Capital* with this under-lying conception of the 'reciprocity of fact and theory', or of induction and deduction, or of reason and experience, Della Volpe would not only ascribe to Marx a *labour* theory of value, but see in the latter a scientific 'hypothesis' which the real development of 'monopoly capitalism' had finally confirmed as true (Della Volpe, 1969, p. 201). Of course, it was with a similar philosophy of science and from similar premises that Popper himself set out to argue the precise opposite.[2]

Lenin's statement thus takes on a special importance today. The *Logic*, he says, is fundamental to a correct understanding of Marx's *Capital*, and 'especially of its first chapter' which contains the theory of value.

On the other hand, how well did Lenin himself understand the *Logic*? His *Notebooks* are full of question-marks, of doubts, for Lenin is actually reading Hegel for the first time, with a philosophical past of his own, dominated by a form of empiricism. One group of passages in particular reveals a quite incomplete penetration of the movement of the dialectic. For example, in the concluding sentence of his summary of Hegel's small *Logic*, Lenin writes,

'Cf. concerning the question of Essence versus Appearance
—price and value
—demand and supply versus *Wert (= krystallisierte Arbeit)*
—wages and the price of labour-power' (Lenin, 1972, p. 320).

This says, value = 'essence', price = 'appearance'. Now in the price-form value appears either as pure contingency or as a merely imaginary relationship (cf. *Capital*, I, p. 197) so that the equations suggested identify appearance with *contingency*. A passage from the essay on 'Dialectics' shows that this is in fact how Lenin understood the matter. In any proposition of language,

'already we have the contingent and the necessary, the appear-ance and the essence; for when we say: John is a man, Fido is a dog. . . we *disregard* a number of attributes as *contingent*; we separate the essence from the appearance, and counterpose the one to the other.' (Lenin, 1972, p. 361.)

In his 'Conspectus' of the *Logic,* in the summary of Hegel's section on Appearance (in the major *Logic* this starts with a very short sentence, 'Essence must appear', *Science of Logic,* p. 479), Lenin criticises Hegel in the following terms:

> 'The shifting of the world in itself further and further *from* the world of appearances – that is what is so far still not to be seen in Hegel.' (1972, p. 153. All emphases Lenin's.)

And this makes sense. If the world of appearances is a world of pure contingency, if we arrive at the 'essence' of the matter by 'disregarding' its contingent attributes, then it follows that it is the task of scientific cognition to carry through this 'separation', to *'shift* the world in itself *further and further from* the world of appearances'. As Lenin correctly notes, Hegel *does not do this*.

The conception that Lenin holds to has two consequences. Firstly, it sees the dialectic as a study of the *opposition* of essence and appearance. In his own words,

> 'Dialectics is the study of the opposition of the thing-in-itself, of the essence . . . from the appearance.' (1972, p. 253.)

Secondly, this false conception of the dialectic implies something quite specific for the *method* of scientific cognition, and this too is quite plain from the *Notebooks*.

> 'Hegel is completely right as against Kant. Thought proceeding from the concrete to the abstract – provided it is correct . . . does not get away from the truth but comes closer to it. The abstraction of matter, of a law of nature, *the abstraction of value*, etc., in short *all scientific* (correct, serious, not absurd) *abstractions reflect nature more deeply, truly and completely*. From living perception to *abstract* thought, and *from this* to practice – such is the dialectical path of the cognition of truth. . .' (1972, p. 171) (Emphasis mine)

But how from *abstract* thought or from the 'abstraction of value' does one move straight to practice? This is not a question Lenin asks himself at this point. On the other hand, in *Hegel*, he finds a more subtle, more complex movement, and this puzzles him:

> 'it is strikingly evident that *Hegel sometimes passes from the abstract to the concrete . . . and sometimes the other way round . . .*

Is not this the inconsistency of an idealist? . . .Or are there deeper reasons?' (1972, p. 318.)

The 'inconsistency' lies not in Hegel, but in Lenin. For on the one hand, as the *Notebooks* show, he realises that for Hegel essence 'must appear', that appearance itself is essential (cf. 1972, p. 148, p. 253), but on the other hand, he regards appearances as pure contingency, as that from which we 'abstract' so as to arrive at 'essence', as a world apart from and opposed, or counterposable to essence.

Hegel in Marx

There are countless references to problems of scientific method scattered across the pages of Marx's later work. To draw some of these together here in a form that recapitulates their underlying conceptions: *firstly*, there is a methodological reference that is basic to any understanding of the architecture of *Capital*, namely, the distinction Marx repeatedly draws between 'capital in general' and 'many capitals' (cf. Rosdolsky, 1968, Volume 1, p. 61 ff.). The former refers to the 'inner nature of capital', to its *essential* character' (*Grundrisse*, p. 414), and is also called 'the simple concept of capital' (ibid.); by contrast, 'many capitals or competition of capitals, entails a study of capital 'in its *reality*' (*Grundrisse*, p. 684 note), or in its 'concrete' aspects as they appear reflected on the *surface of society*, in the *'actual* movement' of capitals (*Capital*, III, p. 25). So in the first place the investigation of capitalist economy is broadly stratified into two levels which contrapose the 'essential character' of capital to its 'concrete' or 'actual' superficial movements. But *secondly*, the investigation itself is a *movement* from one level to the other, from essence to concreteness. In the Preface to the first edition (1867) of *Capital* I, , Marx writes that in the analysis of 'economic forms', i.e. of social phenomena as such, the 'power of abstraction' must replace a directly experimental, hence empirical, relation to the object. In what does the power of abstraction consist, however? About this the passage in question leaves no room for doubt. It consists in our ability to identify a *point of departure* for the movement from one level to the other, and a point of departure which will be simultaneously the *foundation* of that movement. For Marx here introduces the notion of a 'cell-form' (*Capital*, I, p. 90), which he identifies with Hegel's 'in itself' (*An-sich*, or essence) in the first edition form of Chapter One (cf. Zeleny, 1973, p. 78, n. 8, for the passage). The movement from the cell-form to the concrete is logically continuous, so that, in approaching the concrete forms in which capital appears on the surface of society, we do not abandon the sphere of essential

R.I. C

relations as if we were moving across into new territory; rather, we now investigate those very relations in 'their' forms of appearance, i.e. in the forms determined within their own logical movement, as part of this movement.

These intermediate levels of the logical process, which connect abstract and concrete, are as essential as essence in its abstract and simple cell-form. Marx's constant reference to these intermediate levels or 'terms' or 'stages', or to the 'connecting links' (*Theories*, 3, p. 453, 2, p. 174, *Capital*, I, p. 421), implies a *logic of derivation* (of 'deduction' in the broad sense) which is distinct from the pure deductive method of axiomatic systems (on this see Zeleny, 1973, p. 75 ff., p. 141 ff.). The concrete is derived by stages, from the abstract. Where this process of dialectical-logical derivation collapses, as it does in Classical Economy, Marx refers to 'forced abstractions', to the direct subordination of the concrete to the abstract (*Theories*, 1, p. 89, p. 92; 2, p. 164 f., p. 437; 3, p. 87).

Thirdly, in the famous introduction of 1857 (*Grundrisse*, p. 100 ff.), the movement of essence from abstract to concrete is also described as a journey from the simple to the combined. The movement of derivation of forms within a framework defined by its logical continuity is thus also a process of 'combination', of the 'concentration' of many 'determinations' into a 'rich totality' which reproduces the concreteness of reality no longer simply as something that impinges confusedly on perception but as something rationally comprehended. These 'determinations' are only the forms derived in the movement of essence as the *form-determinations of essence* (cf. Rubin, 1972, p. 37 ff.).

Finally, the entire process by which the concrete is reproduced in thought as something rationally comprehended is described in places by Marx as the 'dialectical development' of the 'concept' of capital, and all moments within this movement which are derivable as essential determinations, including, of course, the forms of appearance, no matter how illusory they may be, count as moments (forms, relations) 'corresponding to their concept' (e.g. *Capital*, III, p. 141). (This is why, despite its illusory and deceptive character, Marx can call the wage-form 'one of the *essential* mediating forms of capitalist relations of production', *Results*, p. 1064.)

It is obvious that the methodological references express a consistent and internally unified conception which it is impossible to grasp without reference to the dialectic, that is, to what can now be formally defined as a specific, *non-classical logical type* of scientific thought, a form of scientific reasoning and proof distinct from generalising inductivism, deductive-axiomatic methods, or any combination of these supposedly characteristic of a 'scientific method in general', e.g. Della Volpe's hypothetico-deductive method.

The point can also be put in these terms: it is impossible to grasp Marx's conception of scientific method outside the framework of Hegel's *Logic*. This is not to claim that, like Lassalle, he simply 'applied an abstract ready-made system of logic' (*Selected Correspondence*, p. 123) to the phenomena of capitalist economy. The claim is a different one: the method that Marx followed was a method 'which *Hegel* discovered' (*Selected Correspondence*, p. 121). It was Hegel who first enunciated the conception of a point of departure which is simultaneously the foundation of the movement which it initiates (*Science of Logic*, p. 71). For Hegel this was only conceivable because the principle that forms the beginning is not something 'dead', something fixed and static, but something 'self-moving' (Hegel, 1966, p. 104). Hegel's great announcement in the 'Preface' to the *Phenomenology* is the conception of 'substance' as 'subject', or the conception of a 'self-developing, self-evolving substance', where the term 'substance' can be taken in its classical, Cartesian sense to mean 'that which requires only itself for its existence'. (The importance of this idea for Hegel's work and for its relation to Marx is drawn out by Zeleny, 1973, p. 47 f., p. 98 f.)

As the 'process that engenders its own moments and runs through them' (Hegel, 1966, p. 108) this substance-subject is what Hegel calls *das Wesen*, essence. Essence cannot be said to be something '*before* or *in* its movement', and this movement 'has no substrate on which it runs its course' (*Science of Logic*, p. 448). Rather, essence is the movement through which it 'posits itself', 'reflects itself into itself', as the totalising unity of 'essence and form' (*Science of Logic*, p. 449). Conversely,

'the question cannot therefore be asked, *how form is added to essence*, for it is only the reflection of essence into essence itself . . .' (*Science of Logic*, p. 449-50)

Moreover, if form is *immanent*, or

'if form is taken as equal to essence, then it is a misunderstanding to suppose that cognition can be satisfied with the 'in itself' or with essence, that it can dispense with form, that the basic principle from which we start (*Grundsatz*) renders superfluous the *realisation of essence* or the *development of form*. Precisely because *form is as essential to essence* as essence to itself, essence must not be grasped and expressed merely as essence . . . but as form also, and with the entire wealth of developed form. Only then is it grasped and expressed as something *real*.' (Hegel, 1966, p. 50)

In this decisive passage Hegel says essence must realise itself, or 'work itself out', and this it can only do through the 'activity of form' (*Science of Logic*, p. 453). Only as this self-totalising unity of itself and form does it become something 'real' (*wirkliches*). Otherwise, as immediate substance, substance not mediated through its self-movement, essence remains something abstract and so one-sided and incomplete. It remains something basically *untrue*, for, as Hegel goes on to say, in the passage cited above, 'the truth is *totality*' (Hegel, 1966, p. 50), a fusion of essence and form, universal and particular, or the universal drawing out of itself the wealth of particularity.

It is interesting that in a terminology that is almost indistinguishable from Hegel's, Marx articulates an identical conception as early as his *Dissertation*. For Hegel's argument can be summarised in his own words as follows: '*Appearance is itself essential to essence*' (Hegel, 1970, p. 21). Now in the *Dissertation* Marx argues that although they shared the same general principles (Atomist), Democritus and Epicurus evolved diametrically opposed conceptions of knowledge and attitudes towards it. Democritus maintained that 'sensuous appearance does not belong to the Atoms themselves. It is not *objective appearance* but *subjective semblance (Schein)*. The true principles are the atom and the void. . . ' (Marx, 1975, p. 39). So for Democritus 'the principle *does not enter into the appearance*, remains without reality and existence', and the real world, the world he perceives, is then '*torn away from the principle*, left in its own independent reality' (Marx, 1975, p. 40). In Hegel's terms, for Democritus the Atom is devoid of form, has no form of appearance, so that the world of appearances (*Erscheinungen*) necessarily degenerates into a world of pure illusion (*Schein*). 'The Atom remains for Democritus a *pure and abstract category, a hypothesis*' (Marx, 1975, p. 73. All emphases in this paragraph mine). Or, 'in Democritus there is no *realisation of the principle itself* (Marx, 1975, p. 56 ff.). On the other hand, if Democritus transforms the world we perceive into pure illusion, Epicurus regards it as 'objective appearance'.

'Epicurus was the first to grasp appearance as appearance that is, as alienation of the essence' (Marx, 1975, p. 64).

'In Epicurus the consequence of the principle itself will be presented' (id. p. 56).

Or for Epicurus the Atom is not a simply abstract and hypothetical determination, it is something 'active', a principle that 'realises itself'.

The Dialectic as Critique of Bourgeois Economy

The conception of Democritus is dominated by the following contradiction: what is true, the principle, remains devoid of any form of appearance, hence something purely abstract and hypothetical; on the other hand, the world of appearances, divorced from any principle, is left as an independent reality. It is not difficult to see that in the critique which Marx developed many years later, classical and vulgar economy emerged as the transfigured expressions of the poles of this contradiction. So Marx would write,

'By classical political economy I mean all the economists who . . . have investigated the real internal relations of bourgeois economy as opposed to the vulgar economists who only flounder around within their forms of appearance' (*Capital*, I, p. 174. Translation modified).

'Vulgar economy feels especially at home in the alienated external appearances of economic relations' (*Capital*, III, p. 796. Translation modified),

whereas classical economy, which investigates those relations themselves, seeks to grasp them '*in opposition to their different forms of appearance*'. Classical economy says, the appearances are pure semblance (*Schein*), only the principles are true. So

'it is not interested in evolving the different forms through their inner genesis (*die verschiednen Formen genetisch zu entwickeln*) but tries to reduce them to their unity by the analytic method' (*Theories*, 3, p. 500. Translation modified).

Again, classical economy 'holds instinctively to the law', 'it tries to rescue the law from the contradictions of appearance', from 'experience based on immediate appearance', while vulgar economy relies here 'as elsewhere on the mere semblance as against the law of appearance (*gegen das Gesetz der Erscheinung*)' (*Capital*, I, p. 421 f.), that is, as against the notion of appearances as 'essential' (*Science of Logic*, p. 500 ff.).

In short, as in the atomism of Democritus, so in bourgeois economy essence and appearance *fall apart*. It follows that classical economy which 'holds to the law', the principle or essence or inner relations, comprehends this only abstractly as a principle that remains 'without reality and existence', as an essence without form, as dead substance or *hypothesis*. In Hegel's terms, its 'principle', the Ricardian labour theory of value, forms an Abstract Identity incapable of passing over into a Concrete Totality, hence into something true. Ricardo

> 'abstracts from what he considers to be accidental',

or the appearances are of no concern to him, his is an essence that can dispose of form.

> 'Another method would be to present the *real process* in which both what is to Ricardo a merely accidental movement, but what is constant and real, and its law, the average relation, appear as *equally essential*'. (GKP p. 803. Emphasis mine.)

This method is Marx's own, the conception of Epicurus in Antiquity or of Hegel in the modern world.

It follows that the 'abstraction of value' cannot by itself 'reflect nature . . . truly and completely', as Lenin supposes. As the abstract universal, it is something simple and undeveloped, this form of simplicity is its one-sidedness, it remains a principle that has still to 'realise itself', to become 'active'. And this it can only do by 'entering into appearance', determining itself in appearance or in the whole 'wealth of developed form'. For to trace the movement through which the principle (essence) enters into appearance and acquires reality and existence, is precisely to 'evolve the different forms through their inner genesis', it is to develop conceptually the movement which Marx calls 'the real process of acquiring shape' (*Theories*, 3, p. 500, *der wirkliche Gestaltungsprozess*).

But finally, it is just as important to bear in mind that this movement through which the forms emerge is only the 'reflection of essence into itself', essence as a movement of reflection or mediation. Henryk Grossmann's example is a good illustration of this. Both in his major study (Grossmann, 1970) and in his critique of Luxemburg's understanding of the Reproduction Schemes (Grossmann, 1971, pp. 45-74), Grossmann saw in the return to the level of appearances or to the concrete, both the chief task of scientific investigation and the main thrust of the method. (Luxemburg was criticised for allegedly confusing different stages in the process of abstraction, that is, for supposing that a *value*-schema could explain phenomena which presupposed regulation by *prices*.) On the other hand, Grossmann himself proposed an extremely one-sided understanding of Marx's method in *Capital*, precisely in failing to see in the return to the concrete a process defined by logical continuity. Grossmann writes,

'The empirically given world of appearances forms the object of investigation. *This, however, is too complicated to be known directly*. We can approach it only by stages. To this end *numerous simplifying assumptions are made*, and these enable us to grasp the object of knowledge in its inner structure.' (Grossmann, 1970, p. vi. Emphases mine.)

Grossmann thus sees in the dialectic a 'method of approximation to reality' and in doing so he recasts the relation between abstract and concrete as a progressive 'correction' that again 'takes into account the elements of reality which were initially disregarded' (ibid.). Because this completely ignores the law of motion of the enquiry itself, the conception of substance as self-developing or of the essential movement, Grossmann has no means of explaining on what basis other than pure intuition Marx could select the specific assumptions defining a given level of abstraction. If the 'simplifying assumptions' are the main thing, then, through an opposite route, we are back with Lenin's idea that we arrive at the 'essence' as opposed to the ''appearances' by a process of 'abstracting from'. We 'separate' essence from appearance through the series of simplifying assumptions we make, then, reversing the movement, abandon these assumptions step by step so as to arrive at the appearances again. Or, in Hegel's words,

'the procedure of the finite cognition of the understanding here is to take up again, equally externally, what it has left out in its creation of the universal by a process of abstraction.' (*Science of Logic*, p. 830.)

Indeed, the true logic of this conception is evident in one writer (Himmelmann, 1974, pp. 41-50) who, starting with the notion of appearances as the pure 'other' of essence, drives himself into the conclusion that Marx is concerned with *two different* objects of analysis, one 'abstract-sociological' and the other 'concrete-economic'.

COMMODITY AND CAPITAL. THE PROBLEM OF THE BEGINNING OF *CAPITAL*

The 'Beginning' in the Literature on *Capital*.

'Beginnings are always difficult in all sciences. The understanding of the first chapter, especially the section that contains the analysis of commodities, will therefore present the greatest difficulty.' (*Capital*, I, p. 89.)

No section of *Capital* gave Marx as much trouble as its beginning. Why could he not just begin with Part Two, the transformation of money into capital (as Althusser asks the French readers of *Capital* to do)? Quite clearly because the whole understanding of *what capital is*, of its relation to social labour, depends crucially on the exposition of the theory of value. (The sense in which 'value' is used here and throughout this essay will be clarified in the next section.) As Marx says about capital, 'In the concept of value its secret is betrayed' (*Grundrisse*, p. 776).

Before turning to an analysis of the structure of the beginning, it would be useful to look briefly at some of the conceptions current in the literature. The most widespread and manifestly incorrect understanding is the one proposed by Meek. Misinterpreting Engels' remarks on the relation of the 'logical' and 'historical' methods *in the critique of political economy* to be a statement about the relation between the theory and the history *of capitalism as such*, Meek argues that Marx's logical procedure in *Capital* reflects the actual historical process of the coming-into-being of capital. The consequence of this mistaken conception is twofold. On the one hand, Marx is supposed to begin *Capital* with a 'society of simple commodity producers'; however, because the historical existence of a society of this type is problematic, Marx is supposed to start with a *fiction*, in the fictionalist philosophies of science sense (i.e. a sort of device). So Meek writes,

'Marx's postulate of an abstract pre-capitalist society . . . was not a myth, but rather mythodology' (Meek, 1973, p. 303 f.),

not science fiction but scientific fiction. The second consequence may be stated as follows:

'In so far as Marx's logical transition in *Capital* (from the commodity relation as such to the 'capitalistically modified' form of this relation) is presented by him as the 'mirror image' of a historical transition (from 'simple' to 'capitalist' commodity production), *Marx's procedure becomes formally similar to that of Adam Smith and Ricardo*, who also believed that the real essence of capitalism could be revealed by analysing the changes which would take place if capitalism suddenly impinged upon *some kind of abstract pre-capitalist society*.' (Meek, 1973, p. xv. Emphasis mine.)

This is a fairly neat way of reabsorbing *Capital* into the flaccid methodological tradition which Marx himself severely criticised in three whole volumes (the volumes which compose *Theories of Surplus-Value*). We shall see later, from Marx's own statements, how in this conception, and in the disguised form of supposedly valid scientific 'fictions', Meek only ascribes to Marx his own totally fictitious conception of science.[3]

Secondly, passing from the stolid and unshakeable empiricism of the British tradition in philosophy, to the more delicate, but also more hesitant empiricism of the Della Volpe school, there is Colletti who dissolves the dialectic into the 'circle of induction and deduction'. That is, into a twofold process in which the concept is both logically first and empirically or inductively, second. Without explicitly endorsing hypotheticism, Colletti states the conclusion of this conception as follows: 'one must bear in mind that implicit in the logical process is a process of reality which works in the opposite direction' (Colletti, 1973, p. 121) and which makes the concept a *result* of the *observation* of reality.

This conception of the twofold process is translated into an interpretation of the beginning of *Capital* in the following terms – the first moment in the logical process or chain of 'deductive reasoning' forms likewise the last in the real process, or the chain of 'induction'. What is this moment, however? When we turn to the analysis itself, it is a striking fact that no *stable* identification is evolved.

Passage one:

'*Exchange-value* presents itself to us in two different respects: on the one hand, as the most comprehensive and broadest generality from which all the other categories are deduced and from which a scientific exposition must begin; on the other hand, as an objective characteristic, as the last (in the inductive chain) and therefore *most superficial* and abstract characteristic ... of the concrete object in question.' (Colletti, 1973. p. 126. Emphasis mine.)

Passage two:

'The work begins its analysis by studying the '*form of value*', the '*commodity form*'. . .' (Colletti, 1973, p. 126.)

from which the other forms (money, capital) are derived.

Passage three:

'The work develops, together with the deductive process descending from the *commodity* to money, and from the latter to capital, as an inductive process going back from the generic or secondary features of the object in question to its specific or primary ones . . . the expository formula commodity-money-capital, shows itself to be also the exposition best-suited to the procedure by which analysis gradually penetrates the object in question, *departing from the non-essential* or generic aspects and going back to the fundamental or specific ones, *from effects to causes* and (in short) from the most superficial phenomena to the real basis implicit in them.' (Colletti, 1973, p. 127 f.)

Throughout this exposition, in other words, the commodity = the commodity-form and both (individual commodity and commodity-form) are indifferently and variously characterised as 'the most comprehensive generality', 'the universal', 'most superficial aspect', 'secondary feature', 'non-essential aspect', 'effect'. So in Colletti's understanding, the point of departure in a logical (or logico-deductive) process can actually be something 'non-essential' and yet something which *somehow* takes us to that which *is* 'essential' ('fundamental'). As he says, 'departing *from the non-essential*' we arrive at capital. Or what this entire analysis argues is simply this: the essence of capital does not lie in the *commodity-form* (that is, in *value* in the definition to be given later) because the *commodity* is, after all, only a 'phenomenal form' of capital and as such a merely secondary and subordinate aspect.

Finally, even an obvious sympathy for the dialectic is not a sufficient condition for grasping the structure of the beginning, as the case of Nicolaus shows. According to him,

'It is this category, the commodity, which forms the starting point of . . . *Capital* I (1867). It is a beginning which is at once concrete, material, almost tangible',

here note the suggested synonyms for 'concrete',

'as well as historically specific to capitalist production . . . Unlike Hegel's *Logic*, and unlike Marx's own initial attempts earlier, this beginning begins not with a pure, indeterminate, eternal and universal abstraction, but rather with a compound, determinate, delimited and *concrete whole* – '*a concentration of many determinations, hence unity of the diverse'.*' (Nicolaus, 1973, p. 36. Emphasis mine.)

This is really quite strange, for in the very sentence from which Nicolaus quotes Marx, Marx makes it clear that 'the concrete is concrete because it is the concentration of many determinations, hence unity of the diverse. It appears in the process of thinking, therefore, . . . *as a result, not as a point of departure.' (Grundrisse*, p. 101)

The commodity which forms the starting-point is thus by no stretch of one's dialectical imagination, a 'concrete whole' in the sense suggested by Nicolaus. (The underlying confusion here is the same as Colletti's.) Secondly, because Nicolaus somewhat crudely contraposes 'abstract universal' to 'concrete' (Zeleny, 1973, chapter 4, is also prone to this sort of argument), and discerns in the beginning of *Capital* only this 'concrete', he is forced into a conclusion which, *if true*, would render the whole motion of the dialectic something absolutely incomprehensible. This is the conclusion that

'the notion that the path of investigation must proceed from simple, general, abstract relations towards complex, particular wholes *no longer appeared to him* (Marx) . . . as 'obviously the scientifically correct procedure'.' (Nicolaus, 1973, p. 38. Emphasis mine.)

From the fact that Marx does not begin with a *historically indeterminate* abstract, production in general, Nicolaus concludes that Marx does not begin with an abstract at all.

It is obvious from these three examples (Meek, Colletti, Nicolaus) that there is a considerable amount of confusion regarding the beginning, even when everyone agrees that the commodity is the starting-point.

How Marx Begins *Capital*.

'Compared with your earlier form of presentation, the progress in the sharpness of dialectical exposition is quite striking.' (Engels to Marx, 16.6.67.)

(a) A Summary of the Argument.

It would be good to summarise the general argument of the section in advance for the sake of simplicity. The total structure (*Gesamtaufbau*) of *Capital* is best understood in terms of an image that Marx himself uses at one point. Namely, if it is seen as an 'expanding curve' or spiral-movement composed of specific cycles of abstraction. Each cycle of abstraction, and thus the curve as a whole, begins and ends with the Sphere of *Circulation* (the realm of appearances), which is finally, at the end of the entire movement, itself determined specifically as the Sphere of the

Competition of Capitals. The first specific cycle in *Capital*, the one which initiates the entire movement of the curve, starts with Circulation as the *immediate, abstract* appearance of the total process of capital, that is, it starts with 'Simple Circulation'. As an immediate appearance of this process, as its *Schein*, Simple Circulation *presupposes* this process, which is capital in its totality. The first cycle then moves dialectically from Simple Circulation, or what Marx calls the individual commodity, to capital. This movement will be called the 'dialectical-logical derivation of the concept of capital'. Methodologically, it is itself decomposable into specific phases: an initial phase of Analysis which takes us from the individual commodity to the concept of value, and a subsequent phase of Synthesis which, starting from value, derives the concept of capital through the process Hegel called 'the development of form'. Capital then emerges through this movement as 'nothing else but a value-form of the organisation of productive forces' (Ilyenkov, 1977, p. 85). In the return to the Sphere of Circulation which concludes cycle 1, initiates cycle 2, the individual commodity from which we started is now 'posited', that is, established dialectically, as a form of appearance (*Erscheinungsform*) of capital, and Circulation is posited as both presupposition and result of the Immediate Process of Production. The dialectical status of the Sphere of Circulation thus shifts from being the immediate appearance of a process 'behind it' (*Schein*) to being the posited form of appearance (*Erscheinung*) of this process. (Cf. for example, *Grundrisse*, p. 358, *Theories* 3, p. 112, *Results* p. 949 ff.)

(b) Capital as Presupposition of the Commodity.

> 'In the completed bourgeois system . . . everything posited is also a presupposition, this is the case with every organic system.' (*Grundrisse*, p. 278.)

In the *Grundrisse* Marx sketches a series of short anticipatory drafts of the plan of his work as a whole. They are, of course more in the nature of notes which he will revise from time to time. In one of these he writes,

> 'In the first section, where exchange-values, money, prices are looked at, commodities always appear as already present. . . We know that they (commodities) express aspects of social production, but the latter itself is the presupposition. However, they are *not posited* in this character. . .' (*Grundrisse*, p. 227, Nicolaus' translation slightly modified, Marx's emphasis.)

Here Marx says that at the beginning of the entire movement of investigation the commodity already presupposes social production (capital) of which it is only an 'aspect', or determination, but it is not yet posited as such an aspect. That is, it has still to be *established dialectically* or dialectico-logically as a determination of the total process of capital. Secondly, this world of commodities that confronts us on the surface of bourgeois society 'points beyond itself towards the economic relations which are posited as relations of production. The internal structure of production therefore forms the second section. . .' (ibid.). In his original draft of the 1859 *Critique*, reprinted in the German edition of the *Grundrisse*, Marx returns to this idea and develops it more explicitly:

> 'An analysis of the specific form of the division of labour, of the conditions of production which are its basis, or of the economic relations into which those conditions resolve, would show that *the whole system of bourgeois production is presupposed* before exchange-value appears as the simple point of departure on the surface.' (GKP, p. 907. Emphasis mine.)

As the form which confronts us immediately on the surface of society, the commodity *as such* is our point of departure. But this simple commodity, the point of departure, already presupposes a specific form of the social division of labour, it presupposes the bourgeois mode of production in its totality. On the other hand, at the beginning itself, the commodity has still to be posited as only an 'aspect' or form of appearance of the total process of capital.

Because capital in its totality is the presupposition, when he starts Chapter One of *Capital* Marx must explicitly *refer to* this presupposition. And that is exactly what he does. He says,

> 'The wealth of societies *in which the capitalist mode of production prevails* appears as an immense collection of commodities; the individual commodity appears as its elementary form.' (*Capital*, I, p. 125. Emphasis mine.)

So the very first sentence of *Capital* makes it quite clear that *capital* is presupposed.

One consequence of this is obvious. The conceptual regime of Part One, Volume One is not some 'abstract pre-capitalist society' of 'simple commodity producers', it is the Sphere of Simple Circulation, or the circulation of commodities as such, and we start with this as the process that is *'immediately present* on the surface of *bourgeois* society' *(Grundrisse*, p. 255, emphasis mine), we start with it as a reflected sphere of the total process of capital which, however, has still to be determined *as reflected*, i.e. still to be *posited*. When we examine the simple commodity,

or the commodity as such, we only examine *capital* in its most superficial or immediate aspect. As Marx says,

> 'We proceed from the commodity as *capitalist production in its*
> *simplest form.*' (*Results*, p. 1060, emphasis mine.)

Indeed, capital '*must*' form *the starting-point* as well as the finishing
point' (*Grundrisse*, p. 107, emphasis mine), but as the starting-point
capital is taken in its 'immediate being' or as it appears immediately on
the surface of society.

It is, therefore, difficult to understand how anything except the
most shallow and hasty reading of Marx's *Capital* could have led to the
kind of view proposed by Meek and so many other professional ex-
pounders of Marx. The 'abstract pre-capitalist society' that Marx is
supposed to have started with is not a fiction that Marx consciously
uses in the tradition of certain medieval conceptions of science, but a
fiction that 'mythodologists' unconsciously tend to elaborate.

(c) The Structure of Marx's Concept of Value.

Also in the remarkably clear original draft of the *Critique*, Marx
writes,

> 'Simple circulation is an abstract sphere of the total process of
> production of capital which *through its own determinations*
> becomes identifiable as a *moment*, a mere form of appearance of
> a deeper process that underlies it.' (GKP p. 922 f. emphasis mine.)

This means (i) that the individual commodity contains immediately
within itself determinations that can be drawn out of it. 'Our investigation . . . begins with the analysis of the commodity' (*Capital*, I,
p. 125). The individual commodity is a 'concrete' in the specific dialectical sense that it comprises a *relation within itself* (*Science of Logic*,
p. 75). 'As concrete, it is *differentiated within itself*' (*Science of Logic*,
p. 830), hence something analysable. However, (ii) in drawing out the
differentiated determinations that lie within the given object, analysis
only initiates, or sets in motion, a process that allows us to *return to*
the commodity and identify it now as a 'moment', a form of appearance, of capital. The immediacy from which we started then becomes
what Hegel calls 'a *mediated* immediacy' (*Science of Logic*, p. 99).

Through the movement of analysis Marx draws out the inner
determinations of the commodity regarded as a concrete, immediate representation. These determinations are, of course, use-value and exchange-value. *In the first instance* these differentiated determinations

are merely a 'diversity' (*Science of Logic*, p. 830), or in Marx's words, (cited Berger, 1974, p. 102, note 37), use-value and exchange-value are simply 'abstract opposites' that split apart in mutual indifference.

Now to say that 'through its own determinations' the simple commodity must become identifiable as a form of appearance of capital is to say that the analysis of the commodity, the drawing out of its inner determinations, must *establish the dialectical-logical basis* for the derivation of capital, whose own further determination or development will then 'mediate' the immediacy of the commodity as such. *This* the analysis of the commodity can only do if it takes up *specifically that determination* which allows us to pass dialectico-logically to a notion like capital. This 'use-value' does not do, because it is the commodity's 'material side which the *most disparate epochs of production* . . . have in common' (*Grundrisse*, p. 881). Marx begins therefore with 'exchange-value', taking this as the only basis on which he can begin to penetrate the social properties of the commodity.

These properties then appear initially as a sort of 'content' 'hidden within' their 'form of appearance', exchange-value. Insofar as Marx, both in Section 1 and later, calls this 'content' '*value*' (cf. *Capital*, I, p. 139: 'We started from exchange-value . . . in order to track down the value that lay hidden within it'), it is easy to fall into the illusion of supposing that value is something actually contained in the individual commodity. For example, it is easy to suppose that Marx means by value (as quite clearly he did *at one stage*) 'the labour objectified in a commodity', and then from there to proceed to the more general identification of labour with value which I I Rubin quite correctly polemicised *against* (Rubin, 1972, p. 111 ff.). But Marx also makes it clear in Chapter One that this is not how he understands the matter. If value appears initially to be a 'content' concealed within its form of appearance, exchange-value, then this false appearance is plainly contradicted when he writes,

> 'Political economy has indeed analysed value and its magnitude . . . and has uncovered the content concealed *within these forms*. But it has never once asked the question why this content has assumed that particular form, *that is to say, why labour is represented in value* (*warum sich also die Arbeit im Wert . . . darstellt*).' (*Capital*, I, p. 173-74. Translation slightly modified and emphasis mine.)

In this lucid sentence Marx calls value the *social form as such*..Let us look at this a bit more closely.

Outside of the purely vulgar and quite incorrect Ricardian understanding of Marx's theory of value, which identifies value with the labour objectified in commodities, the usual mode of presentation of the theory in the Marxist literature is the one apparently started by F. Petry and typified in the expository accounts of Rubin, Sweezy and others. In this mode of presentation, the crucial architectural distinction within Marx's value theory is its separation of 'quantitative' and 'qualitative' aspects in the problem of value. For example, Sweezy writes,

> 'The great originality of Marx's value theory lies in its recognition of these two elements of the problem.' (Sweezy in Howard and King, 1976, p. 141 f.)

What *is* the *'qualitative'* aspect' of the problem of value, however? No sooner do we pose this question, than it becomes evident that the qualitative/quantitative distinction is *not enough* to render a proper account of Marx's concept of value. Indeed, in the very passages where Marx himself refers to this distinction explicitly, he also says,

> 'Ricardo's mistake is that he is concerned only with the magnitude of value . . . But the labour embodied in (commodities) *must be represented (dargestellt) as social labour* . . . this qualitative aspect of the matter which is contained in the *representation of exchange-value as money (in der Darstellung des Tauschwertes als Geld)* is not elaborated by Ricardo. . .' (*Theories*, 3, p. 131).

Again, some pages later,

> 'This necessity of representing individual labour as general labour is equivalent to the necessity of representing a commodity as money.' (*Theories*, 3, p. 136, translation modified)

In passages such as these Marx isolates two dimensions of the value-process, (a) the representation of the commodity as money, and (b) the representation of (private) individual labour as social labour. The relation between these two dimensions can be described as follows: in the social process of exchange a surface relation, exchange-value, becomes the form of appearance of an inner relation, the relation which connects individual labour to the total social labour. (This connection is, in any case, what we might call a 'material law of society'. Cf. *Selected Correspondence*, p. 239, p. 251, *Theories*, 1, p. 44.) The surface-relation is simultaneously a 'relation among things' and the inner relation a 'relation among persons'. Finally, each of these two dimensions of the value-process is susceptible to the earlier-mentioned distinction into qualitative and quantitative aspects, so that the following structure results:

Dimension	(1) Quantitative	(2) Qualitative
(A) The commodity represented as money. . .	exchange-value as surface appearance (*Section One*)	the money-form as objective appearance (*Section Three*)
(B) Individual labour represented as social labour. . .	socially-necessary labour-time (*Sections One and Two*)	abstract labour (*Sections One and Two*)

When we look at Marx's final presentation of Chapter One, the 'substance of value' and 'magnitude of value' aspects are taken together, investigated without any specific formal separation, in both of the first two Sections. This is so because, although separable as qualitative and quantitative aspects respectively, they belong to the same dimension of the value-process, the dimension of its inner content as a process within which individual labour is connected to and becomes part of total social labour. On the other hand, this 'content' is logically inseparable from its specific 'form'; or to put the same thing differently, it only becomes something real *through its form*, which is the representation of the commodity as money. In its 'immediate being' the commodity is only a use-value, a point which Marx repeatedly makes in the *Critique*. Its immediate being is thus the commodity's relation of self-repulsion, or its 'negative' relation to itself as a commodity (cf. *Science of Logic*, p. 168: 'The negative relation of the one to itself is repulsion'.) The commodity can posit itself as a commodity-*value*, a product of *social* labour, only in a form in which it negates itself in its immediate being, hence only in a *mediated form*. This form is *money*. Only through the representation of the commodity *as money*, or, expressed more concretely, through the individual act of exchange, the transformation of the commodity into money, is individual labour *posited* as social labour. The concept of value in Marx is constructed as the indestructible unity of these two dimensions, so that *logically it is impossible to understand Marx's theory of value except as his theory of money* (cf. Backhaus, 1975).[4] This is the aspect developed explicitly in Section 3, the '*form* of value'. In Section 3, moreover, or in this return to the level of appearances, the contradictory determinations of the commodity, which appeared initially as mutually indifferent, become reabsorbed as a *unity* (money). In Marx's words,

'Use-value or the body of the ócmmodity here plays a new role. It becomes ... the form of appearance of its own opposite. Instead of splitting apart, the contradictory determinations of the commodity here enter into a relation of mutual reflection' (cited Berger, 1974, p. 102, Zeleny, 1973, p. 78).'

The sequence of Marx's presentation is thus: $A(1) \longrightarrow B \longrightarrow A(2)$.

In Section 1 'exchange-value' figures as pure surface appearance (*Schein*), hence as a quantitative relation of commodities. But already within this section Marx accomplishes a transition to dimension B, whose two aspects (socially-necessary labour, and abstract labour) he then investigates, in this and the following section, without formal separation. Finally, in Section 3, Marx 'returns' to exchange-value, to dimension A, to deal with it no longer as the immediate illusory appearance of the exchange-process but as *objective* appearance, or *form, Erscheinung.*

(d) Value (Commodity-form) as the 'Self-evolving Substance'

In short, value is not labour and 'to develop the concept of capital it is necessary to begin not with labour but with value' (*Grundrisse*, p. 259), that is, with the twofold process by which individual labour becomes total labour through the reified appearance-form of the individual act of exchange (transformation of the commodity into money). Regarded as this twofold process of representation, the concept of value can then be formally defined as *the abstract and reified form of social labour*, and the term 'commodity-form of the product of labour' can be taken as its concrete-historical synonym. It is value, the commodity-form, in this definition, just outlined here, that composes the 'self developing substance' of Marx's entire investigation in *Capital*. As Marx says, value is

'the social form as such; its further development is therefore a further development of the social process that brings the commodity out onto the surface of society.' (GKP p. 931)

Or value

'contains the whole secret ... of all the bourgeois forms of the product of labour'. (*Selected Correspondence*, p. 228)

The money-form of value (or money) is 'the first form in which value', social labour in abstract form 'proceeds to the character of capital' (*Grundrisse*, p. 259). So as the abstract-reified form of social labour, value 'determines itself' first as money, then as capital. In its money-form value obtains its sole form of appearance, and through this the moment of actuality. In its capital-form it *posits* itself as 'living substance', as a substance become 'dominant subject' (*Capital*, I, p. 255 f.), or *posits itself* as that totalising process which Hegel calls 'essence'. Or, in the concept of value the analysis of the commodity arrives through its own movement at a basis for the dialectical-logical definition of capital.

At the moment of dialectical-logical derivation, this definintion is only the most simple or abstract definition of capital. 'If we speak here of capital, that is still merely a word (*ein Name*)', Marx says.

'The only aspect in which capital is here posited as distinct from (. . .) value and from money is that of (. . .) value which preserves and perpetuates itself in and through circulation.' (*Grundrisse*, p. 262)

On the other hand, capital is here *posited*, or this moment of the determination of capital as a form of value is the initial moment of its positing, so that the 'internal structure of production' which 'forms the second section' (Part Three of Volume I) can now be investigated directly. This is the investigation which, as we know, occupies the major part of Volume I.

In Chapter One, Volume II, Marx *returns* to the process of circulation, or he comes back to the commodity. But now he can investigate the circulation of commodities directly as a circulation of *capital*. The formal determinations of simple circulation (commodity and money as means of circulation) are now posited as 'aspects', or forms of appearance, of the relations of production which initially they presupposed. Moreover, they are themselves posited as presupposed by capital, as forms essential to the process of realisation. In this spiral return to the point of departure the commodity is treated explicitly as a 'depository of capital' (*Results*, p. 975), as one of its 'forms of existence' within the process of circulation. 'The independence of circulation', the aspect in which the commodity initially presented itself to us, 'is here reduced to a mere semblance', that is, an illusory appearance (*Grundrisse*, p. 514).

The possibility of returning to the Sphere of Circulation and the necessity of now investigating it directly as a Circulation and, at first implicitly, a Reproduction of Capital signifies the conclusion of the first cycle of abstraction in *Capital*. However, as we have seen, this cycle of abstraction is itself only possible because Chapter One (Volume I) takes us from the individual commodity to value. As we shall see, *both* are points of departure within the process of thought, but they are nonetheless quite distinct moments of this process. It is now possible to see that Colletti's exposition simply confuses these specific moments. It confuses the individual commodity as *immediate appearance* of the process of capital with value or the commodity-form as the *essential ground* of the movement that can finally posit the commodity as a moment, a form of appearance, of its own process. And because of this confusion intrinsic to his analysis, Colletti is forced to ascribe to the *commodity-form* logical properties that characterise the commodity as such. It is the commodity-form, or value, that Colletti calls 'secondary feature', 'subordinate element', 'non-essential aspect' and so on. He thereby reduces the method of conceptual development (the dialectical development of the concept of capital) to an incomprehensible mystery.

Against Colletti's fabulations, it is important to stress that in the theory of value Marx saw the whole basis for the distinction between himself and the tradition of classical economy. As he told Engels, moreover, 'the matter is too decisive for the whole book' (*Selected Correspondence*, p. 228). Which means quite simply that a correct understanding of the chapters that follow, and therefore, of course, our very ability to be able to develop the theory of Marx further, depends on a correct understanding of Chapter One.[5] This is something that Lenin came over to seeing *after* reading the *Science of Logic*. Lenin's flexibility, however, his ability to reassess a problem, his burning restlessness, his capacity to swing from empiricism to Hegel, were only expressions of the fluid, practical mould of his thought. To be able to revise the foundations of your philosophical outlook within the space of three months, you must first be a person who *acts*, an *actor*. The demolition of the *Logic* is, however, Colletti's point of departure, and this proceeds not in a world of action, but within the unreal and immobilised world of the university.

Thus in its most simple and essential definition capital is a form of value where value itself is grasped as a form of social labour. From this it follows that when capital seeks to *overcome* or to *subordinate* the commodity-form of its own relations of production, to regulate the 'market' according to the combination of its individual wills (cf. Sohn-Rethel, 1975, p. 41 ff.), then it merely seeks to overcome or to subordinate *itself* as a form of value, or itself in its most essential definition. And this is impossible except as the *contradiction* which capital becomes.

The Double Structure of the Beginning

'If you compare the development from commodity to capital in

Marx with development from Being to Essence in Hegel, you will get quite a good parallel. . .' (Engels to Schmidt, 1.11.91).

In the previous section it was said that the commodity re-emerges as a 'form of *existence*' of capital at the start of Volume Two. We started with it, however, as capital in its immediate *being*. Translated into the terms of Hegel's *Logic*, this implies that the movement of Volume One contains a decisive logical step from being to existence which Hegel and, following him, Marx call the 'return into the ground'. The general principle of this retreat into the ground (into essence that *posits itself* as such),

'means in general nothing else but: what *is*, is not to be taken for a positive immediacy *(seiendes Unmittelbares)* but as something posited.' (*Science of Logic*, p. 446)

That is, being is not to be taken as immediate *in the sense of* unmediated or lacking all mediation (cf. Henrich, 1971, p. 95 ff.).

'Being is the immediate. Since knowledge has for its goal cognition of the true . . . it does not stop at the immediate and its determinations, but penetrates it on the supposition that at the back of this being there is something else, something other than being itself, that this background constitutes the truth of being.' (*Science of Logic*, p. 389. Translation modified in both passages.)

What is this hidden background? As we would expect, it is none other than essence. 'The truth of being is essence' (ibid.).

The terms in which Marx describes the transition from the individual commodity to capital are strikingly reminiscent of these and other passages of the *Logic*. Marx writes, Simple Circulation

'does not carry within itself the principle of self-renewal. The moments of the latter (production) are presupposed to it, not posited by it. Commodities constantly have to be thrown into it anew from the outside, like fuel into a fire. Otherwise it flickers out in indifference. . . Circulation, therefore, which appears as that which is immediately present on the surface of bourgeois society',

which appears as its 'immediate being',

'exists only insofar as it is constantly *mediated*. Looked at in itself, it is the mediation of presupposed extremes (i.e., the two commodities which begin and end the circuit). But it does not posit these extremes. Thus it has to be mediated not only in each of its moments, but as a whole of mediation, as a total process itself. Its immediate being is therefore pure semblance *(reiner Schein)*. It is the appearance of a process taking place behind it...' *(Grundrisse*, p. 255, translation modified slightly.)

Through our analysis of the simple commodity we arrive at the concept of value and thus at a basis for defining, dialectico-logically, the concept of capital. Now it is capital that produces commodities which form the substance and lifeblood of the process of circulation. Therefore,

'Circulation itself returns back into the activity which posits or produces exchange-values. *It returns into it as into its ground.*' (Ibid. Emphasis mine.)

The 'activity' which forms the 'ground' of the process of circulation and into which it returns (in the sense explained above) is capital in its specific determination as a process of production. The immediate result of this process is the commodity 'impregnated with surplus-value' *(Results*, p. 975). So it is possible to say, as Hegel does, that the general course of a dialectical enquiry advances as

'a retreat into the ground, into what is primary and true, on which depends and ... from which originates, that with which the beginning is made... The ground ... is that from which the first proceeds, that which at first appeared as an immediacy.' *(Science of Logic*, p. 71.)

The 'first', the commodity, proceeds from capital, whose own development posits it as a mediated immediacy, i.e. a 'moment' of its own process, hence something mediated. This enables us to say that Marx regarded *capital* as the ground of the movement of his investigation. However, it is through the analysis of the individual commodity that we *arrive at* this fundamental or ground category (capital). Therefore it is equally true to say that capital, the ground into which we retreat from circulation, from the individual commodity, is a *result*. And 'in this respect the first', the individual commodity, 'is *equally the ground*' *(Science of Logic*, p. 71, emphasis mine.).

This appears to jeopardise the whole argument, for it appears to ascribe to an immediate appearance (the individual commodity) the character and function of 'ground', that is, of a basis for the movement of the entire investigation. In fact, it is only this statement that finally enables us to reveal the true structure of every dialectical beginning.

About the beginning as such Hegel says at the end of the *Logic* that

'its content is an immediate but an immediate that has the significance and form of *abstract universality*.' (*Science of Logic*, p. 827)

Thus a dialectical beginning, such as Marx accomplished, contains two dimensions—a dimension of *immediacy* (of concreteness) and a dimension of *universality* (but the universal in its *abstract form*). As something universal, however, the latter *presupposes nothing*—except, Marx will say, the *historical process* through it has come about (which is why 'the dialectical form of presentation is only correct when it knows *its own limits*', GKP p. 945). To say it 'presupposes nothing' except a historical process which lies 'suspended' within it (cf. *Grundrisse*, p. 460 f.) is to say that the universal which forms the 'significance' of the immediate-concrete that stands at the point of departure is something 'absolute', or related only to itself, 'self-related' (*Science of Logic*, p. 70, p. 404, p. 829). *As such*, as this 'absolute' which relates only to itself, the universal 'counts as the *essence* of that immediate which forms the starting-point' (*Science of Logic*, p. 405, emphasis mine).

Now we know that *capital* is the *essence* of the individual commodity (of simple circulation), it is its 'ground' or its 'principle of self-renewal', and the commodity is only a 'moment' of its process. On the other hand, capital itself is only the developed and self-developing form *of value*, or capital in its own simple definition is *value*-in-process (*Grundrisse*, p. 536), *value* as the dominant subject, etc. So value is *likewise* the essence of the simple commodity, and the difference can then be put like this: as the merely *abstract, universal form of capital* (cf. *Grundrisse*, p, 776, *Capital*, I, p. 174, note), value can be called the 'abstract essence' of the simple commodity; the *posited* form of value, can be called its 'concrete essence'. Or, capital is only the essence of the simple commodity because *value is its own essence*, the essence of capital, for capital is a *form* of value. Finally, as the immediate aspect *of value*, which is its abstract essence, the commodity which forms the starting-point can also be called the ground of the entire movement.

In fact, there is a much clearer form in which this point can be made, as long as it is seen as a statement about the structure of the beginning. Namely, *the beginning is a movement between two points of departure*. (This is what ninety-nine percent of commentators fail to grasp). As the immediate appearance of the total process of capital (this can also be called *value as a totality reflected-into-itself* for all categories of capital are categories of value), the individual commodity forms the *analytic* point of departure. From this, however, we do not pass over directly to the concept of capital. By analysing the commodity, drawing out its determinations, we arrive at the concept of *value* as the abstract-reified form of social labour. This as the ground of all further conceptual determinations (money, capital) forms the *synthetic* point of departure of *Capital*. (The distinction is clearly understood and explicitly stated by Berger, 1974, p. 86.) The passage from one point to the other forms the structure of the beginning as such. In logical terms this movement is a transition from Immediacy to Mediation, or from Being to Essence. Analysis is simply a prelude, as Marx points out, even if a necessary one, to the process that he calls 'genetic presentation' (*genetische Darstellung*) (*Theories*, 3, p. 500). This process is one we have been concerned with through most of this essay. It is the logically continuous movement from the abstract to the concrete, the movement that Hegel calls 'the development of form', the movement that Marx describes as 'the principle entering into appearance', or as the development of the different forms through their inner genesis.

In the dialectical method of development the movement from abstract to concrete is not a straight-line process. One returns to the concrete at expanded levels of the total curve, reconstructing the surface of society by 'stages', as a structure of several dimensions (cf. Hochberger, 1974, p. 155 f., p. 166 f.). And this implies, finally, that in Marx's *Capital* we shall find a continuous 'oscillation between essence and appearance' (Zeleny, 1973, p. 164 ff.). Yet there is a point at which this movement, the very development of the concept of capital, breaks down in *Capital* as we have it today. There is a point at which the 'form of enquiry' is no longer reflected back to us in the dialectically perfected shape of a 'method of presentation'. To say this is only to say that Marx's *Capital* remains incomplete as a reproduction of the concrete in thought, What is remarkable here is not that Marx should have left the book incomplete but that close to four generations of Marxists should have done so. There are, of course, historical reasons why this is so, reasons related to the renovated expansion and qualitative consolidation of capitalism. But one of the most striking manifestations of the underlying crisis in the movement as a whole is the contemporary state of Western Marxism—the ecstatic leap from the uppermost floors of an imposing skyscraper of immobilised dogma to the granite pavements of confused eclecticism.

Footnotes

Wherever possible I have consulted the original of all passages cited from Marx's writings or from Hegel's Preface to the *Phenomenology*, or from his *Logic*. Thus where existing translations have been modified, it is, of course, only after consultation of the original German text (the *MEW* edition in Marx's case, and the twenty-volume Frankfurt edition in Hegel's).

1. Della Volpe, like Popper, was fundamentally concerned with the 'demarcation problem', the problem of establishing criteria in terms of which science might be distinguished from metaphysics, e.g. Marx from Hegel (for Della Volpe), or Einstein from Marx (for Popper). Like Popper, Della Volpe saw the hallmark of 'scientific method' in the subordination of our rational constructions to the test of 'experience'. Like Popper, Della Volpe argued that 'experience' could play this role only 'negatively', or as falsification (Della Volpe, 1969, p. 171 f.). Like Popper, finally, he came to see theories or laws as purely tentative, or conjectural or intrinsically 'corrigible' (Della Volpe, 1969, p. 184, p. 186, p. 201). Where, then, can we locate the difference between Marxism and a tradition like Positivism, say? In the fact that Positivism is characterised, for Della Volpe, by its 'worship of facts and repugnance towards hypothesis' (1969, p. 205)—an argument that might have carried conviction in the heyday of Logical Positivism, but certainly does not today.

   Perhaps it should be stated here that throughout this essay, a minimal presupposition is the critique of empiricism elaborated in some of the recent philosophy of science, notably, by Wartofsky 1967, Feyerabend 1970_1, Feyerabend 1970_2, and Koyre, 1968.

2. It is worth emphasising here that the reaction against Hegel in Western Marxism went *side by side* with the revival of a systematic, scholarly interest in Hegel and the 'logic of *Capital*' in post-Stalinist Eastern Europe. Notable representatives of this tendency, whose work has still to be translated into English, are E V Ilyenkov 1960, M Rozental 1957 and J Zeleny 1973 (originally 1962). This body of work and interpretation, together with that done by Rosdolsky 1968, Reichelt 1973, Backhaus 1975 and others *decisively refutes* the quite shallow nonsense which asserts that 'Hegel's influence on Marx was *largely terminological*' (Sowell, 1976, p. 54). When Marx refers to his 'flirtation' with Hegel's 'mode of expression' (*Capital*, I, p. 103), he is referring only to the *densely Hegelian* flavour and quality of the *1867 version* of Chapter One. Many of the explicit references to the *Logic* which this version contained, and which,

from the point of view of the *presentation* of the argument, were quite irrelevant, were subsequently eliminated by Marx in his re-working of the chapter. For example, the 1867 version contains this sentence: 'This form is rather difficult to analyse because it is simple. It is in a sense the cell form, *or, as Hegel would say, the 'in itself' of money.'* (cited Zeleny, 1973, p. 78). This was the kind of thing that Marx removed in his reworking.

3. The idea that Marx starts with a 'pre-capitalist' commodity is very widespread among those who read *Capital* without the faintest conception of its method. It is shared by de Brunhoff 1973, for she tells us that 'exchange value . . . is first conceived at the level of a commodity production which is *not specific to any particular mode of production*' (p. 424). This is probably the only *substantive*, non-obvious point made in the article, which is no accident, because de Brunhoff starts off by asserting that 'the articulation between com-modity and capital must be reviewed . . . *without using a Hegelian method*, which I *think*, following *Althusser's* demonstrations, is *profoundly alien* to Marx's procedure in *Capital*' (p. 422, emphases mine). For Althusser see note 5 below.

4. In this sense Zeleny (1973, chapter six) is right in arguing that the 'dialectical-logical derivation of the *money*-form of value' composes 'the *whole* of chapter one (not only the section on the individual forms of value)' (p. 91). While this is perfectly true in the specific sense that Marx's theory of value cannot be understood except as a theory of money, it is also the case that Marx's particular presen-tation, even in its revised form, tends to obscure this fact, so that it is not difficult to suppose, as Rubin (1975 p. 36) wrongly does, that we can actually discuss value without discussing money. For criti-cisms of Marx see Itoh 1976.

5. This is a point we should make even more strongly against Althusser, who, in attempting to divorce the 'theory of fetishism', the con-ception of value as a *reified* form of social labour, from the theory of value, as if these were separate aspects, simply endorses the crude positivism of Joan Robinson and others who find the 'metaphysics' of Chapter One irreconcilable with the naturally superior claims of good common-sense. Joining the camp of positivism, Althusser in-vitably *finds it quite impossible to understand Chapter One*, as he confesses, indirectly, to the French readers of Marx. In his character-istically sanctimonious tone, he writes,

'I therefore give the following advice: put the whole of Part One aside for the time being and begin your reading with Part Two. . . In my opinion, it is impossible to begin (even to begin) to

understand Part One until you have read and re-read the whole of
Volume I, starting with Part Two.' (Althusser, 1971, p. 79)

Of course, Althusser does not bother to explain to his readers, the
readers of *Capital, why* they should find it any easier to understand
Chapter One after reading the rest of the Volume. It seems as if Marx
wrote the bulk of the volume to throw light on its introductory
chapter, and not precisely the other way round! Or perhaps we are
dealing with one of those famous 'inversions'?

Bibliography

Althusser, Louis (1971) *Lenin and Philosophy and Other Essays*,
London, NLB.

Althusser, Louis (1969) *For Marx*, London, Allen Lane.

Backhaus, H-G (1975) 'Materialien zur Rekonstruktion der Marxschen
Werttheorie, 2', in *Gesellschaft. Beitrage zur Marxschen Theorie 3*,
Frankfurt, Suhrkamp.

Berger, J (1974) 'Der gesellschaftstheoretische Gehalt der Marxschen
Werttheorie', in G Breitenburger/G Schnitzler (edd.), *Marx und
Marxismus heute*, Hamburg.

de Brunhoff, S (1973) 'Marx as an a-Ricardian: value, money and price
at the beginning of *Capital*', *Economy and Society*, Vol. 2, no. 4,
p. 421 ff.

Colletti, Lucio (1973) *Marxism and Hegel*, London, NLB.

Dobb, M (1976) 'Marx's *Capital* and its place in economic thought', in
Howard and King, op. cit.

Feyerabend, P K $(1970)_1$ 'Classical empiricism', in R E Butts and J W
Davis (edd.), *The Methodological Heritage of Newton*, Toronto.

Feyerabend, P K $(1970)_2$ 'Against method', *Minnesota Studies in the
Philosophy of Science, Vol. 4*, Minneapolis.

Goldmann, Lucien (1959) *Recherches Dialectiques*, Paris, Gallimard.

Grossmann, Henryk (1970) *Das Akkumulations – und Zusammen-
bruchs – gesetz des kapitalistischen Systems*, Frankfurt.

Grossmann, Henryk (1971) *Aufsatze zur Krisentheorie*, Frankfurt.

Hegel, G W F (1966) *Preface de la Phenomenologie de l'Esprit*, translated Jean Hyppolite, Paris.

Hegel, G W F (1969) *Hegel's Science of Logic*, translated A V Miller,
London, George Allen & Unwin.

Hegel, G W F (1969) *Werke in zwanzig Banden. Bd. 5/6. Wissenschaft
der Logik I/II*, Frankfurt.

Hegel, G W F (1970) *Werke . . . Bd. 13. Vorlesungen uber die Asthetik
I*, Frankfurt (translated by T M Knox as *Aesthetics, Lectures on*

Fine Art, Oxford 1975).

Henrich, D (1971) 'Hegels Logik der Reflexion', *Hegel im Kontext*, p. 95 ff., Frankfurt.

Himmelmann, G (1974) *Arbeitswert, Mehrwert und Verteilung*, Opladen.

Howard, M and King, J (1976) *The Economics of Marx*, London.

Hochberger, H (1974) 'Probleme einer materialistischen Bestimmung des Staates', in *Gesellschaft 2*, Frankfurt.

Ilyenkov, E V (1960) *The Dialectic of Abstract and Concrete in Marx's Capital* (Russian. Italian translation, Milan 1961).

Ilyenkov, E V (1977) *Dialectical Logic*, translated H Campbell, Moscow.

Itoh, Makoto (1976) 'A study of Marx's theory of value', *Science and Society* XL, No. 3, p. 307 ff.

Koyre, Alexandre (1968) *Metaphysics and Measurement: Essays in Scientific Revolution*, London.

Lenin, V I (1972) *Collected Works, 38. Philosophical Notebooks*, Moscow.

Marx, Karl (1976) *Capital, Volume I*, translated B Fowkes, London, Penguin Books.

Marx, Karl (1959) *Capital, Volume III*, Moscow.

Marx, Karl (1976) *Results of the Immediate Process of Production* in *Capital, Volume I*, (Fowkes).

Marx, Karl (1969) *Theories of Surplus-Value. Part 1*, Moscow.

Marx, Karl (1968) *Theories of Surplus-Value. Part 2*, Moscow.

Marx, Karl (1971) *Theories of Surplus-Value. Part 3*, Moscow.

Marx, Karl (1970) *A Contribution to the Critique of Political Economy*, Moscow.

Marx, Karl (1973) *Grundrisse*, translated M Nicolaus, London.

Marx, Karl (n.d.) *Grundrisse der Kritik der politischen Okonomie (Rohentwurf) 1857/8* (GKP) Frankfurt.

Marx, Karl (1975) *Difference between the Democritean and Epicurean Philosophy of Nature*, in *Collected Works Volume I*, Moscow.

Marx, Karl and Engels F (n.d.) *Selected Correspondence*, Moscow.

Meek, R (1973) *Studies in the Labour Theory of Value*, London.

Nicolaus, M (1973) 'Foreword', *Grundrisse*, London.

Reichelt, H (1973) *Zur logischen Struktur des Kapitalbegriffs bei Karl Marx*, Frankfurt.

Rosdolsky, R (1968) *Zur Entstehungsgeschichte des Marxschen 'Kapital'*, Frankfurt (translated as *The Making of Marx's Capital*, London 1977).

Rozental, M (1957) *Die Dialektik in Marx' 'Kapital'*, Berlin.

Rubin, I I (1972) *Essays on Marx's Theory of Value*, Detroit.

Rubin, I I (1975) 'Abstrakt Arbeit und Wert im Marxschen System', in

Dialektik der Kategorien. Debatte in der UdSSR 1927-29, Berlin (translated in *Capital and Class*, No. 5, Summer 1978).

Sohn-Rethel, Alfred (1975) *Okonomie und Klassenstruktur des deutschen Faschismus*, Frankfurt, Suhrkamp.

Sowell, T (1976) 'Marx's *Capital* after one hundred years', in Howard and King, op. cit.

Sweezy, P (1976) 'The qualitative-value problem', in Howard and King, op. cit.

della Volpe, Galvano (1969) *Logica come scienza storica*, Rome, Editori Riuniti.

Wartofsky, M W (1967) 'Metaphysics as heuristic for science', *Boston Studies in the Philosophy of Science, Volume 3*, Dordrecht.

Zeleny, Jindrich (1973) *Die Wissenschaftslogic und 'Das Kapital'*, translated from Czech by P Bollhagen, Frankfurt.

WHY LABOUR IS THE STARTING POINT OF CAPITAL

Geoffrey Kay

Eugen von Bohm-Bawerk (1851-1914) is one of those nineteenth century intellectuals remembered more today as antagonists of Marxism than for the positive contributions they made to their own fields of study. It is true that Bohm-Bawerk's pioneering work on neo-classical economic theory, characterised contemptuously by Bukharin as the economic theory of a leisure class, ensures him a place in the history of economic thought alongside the other founders of that doctrine. But as a critic of Marx from an economic point of view he stands alone. According to Franz X Weiss, the editor of his collected works in the twenties, his book, *Karl Marx and the Close of his System,*[1] 'was rightly regarded as the best criticism of the Marxian theories of value and surplus value' (p. IX). Paul Sweezy endorsed this view in his introduction to the English edition of 1949. 'So far as the United States is concerned', wrote Sweezy, 'all the serious criticisms of Marxian economics ... recognise the authority if not the primacy of Bohm-Bawerk in this field; while the similarity of the anti-Marxist arguments in the average textbooks to those of Bohm-Bawerk is too striking not to be considered a coincidence' (pp. IX-X). The recent republication of Bohm-Bawerk's tract underlines this judgment: to this day it remains ahead in its field as the most coherent and systematic challenge to Marxism by any bourgeois economist.

From the time of its first publication in 1896, Bohm-Bawerk's critique has haunted Marxism, and response to it traces a theme in Marxist literature from the very first by Hilferding and Bukharin down to the present day. One reason for this is the close attention that Bohm-Bawerk pays to the text of *Capital* giving the reader the very definite impression that it is no simple ideological hatchet-job but a determined effort to wrestle with Marx on his own terrain. Another is that he touched a very sensitive area of Marxism when he raised the transformation problem as the Achilles heel of *Capital*. But most importantly, Bohm-Bawerk has haunted Marxism because his is a systematic positivist critique. It challenges not only the content of *Capital*, but also its method; and in this respect it engages with powerful tendencies within the Marxist movement itself. For the success of positivism as anti-Marxism is not confined to the development of social sciences whose content opposes Marxism directly – in this case neo-classical economics: if anything, its greater victory has been to penetrate Marxism itself and wage war as a fifth columnist. Bohm-Bawerk's polemic has played a most vital part in this counter-offensive and its republication today is no less a challenge to Marxism than it was some eighty years ago.

It was the publication of *Capital*, III in 1894 that spurred Bohm-Bawerk to pull his various attacks on Marx together. The chapters in this third volume dealing with the formation of the average rate of profit, the famous transformation problem, were, for Bohm-Bawerk, the 'Russian campaign' of Marxism. 'I cannot help myself,' he confesses, 'I see here no explanation and reconciliation of a contradiction but the bare contradiction itself. Marx's third volume contradicts the first. The theory of the average rate of profit and of the prices of production cannot be reconciled with the theory of value' (p. 30). Why? Because 'the "great law of value" which is "immanent in the exchange of commodities" . . . states and must state that commodities are exchanged according to the socially necessary labour time embodied within them' (p. 12). But although the third volume is the taking-off point of Bohm-Bawerk's critique and his title suggests that his main concern is with the 'close' or 'completion' of the Marxist 'system', the most significant section of his book deals with its 'opening'. 'A firmly rooted system' such as Marxism, he writes, 'can only be effectually overthrown by discovering with absolute precision the point in which the error made its way into this system. . .' (p. 64). And this point is right at the start of *Capital*, where Marx 'in the systematic proof of his fundamental doctrine exhibits a logic continuously and palpably wrong' (p. 80). Tracking down and then demonstrating this 'error in the Marxist system' is the actual more fruitful and instructive part of the criticism' (p. 65). It has another dimension. The critique of bourgeois economy runs seam-like through the whole of *Capital* but in the first few pages of *Capital* against which Bohm-Bawerk directs the main thrust of his attack, it forms the bedrock of the text. For in establishing his own theoretical ground, Marx simultaneously challenged the foundations of bourgeois economics. Whether Bohm-Bawerk was fully aware of the issues at stake, it is hard to say; even if he were not his instinct took him to the heart of the matter. 'The theory of value', he recognised, 'stands, as it were, in the centre of the entire doctrine of political economy'. And once a 'labour theory of value' is conceded, Marx's conclusions about surplus value, exploitation and the class struggle follow inexorably. 'In the middle part of the Marxian system', Bohm-Bawerk concedes, 'the logical development and connection present a really imposing closeness and intrinsic consistency' (p. 88). This is the first reason why it is so important for him to dismiss once and for all the 'hypothesis' on which it is based – the proposition advanced right at the beginning of *Capital* that the value of commodities is determined by the amount of (abstract) labour socially necessary for their production. The second is that no other theory of value, and particularly the various forms of neo-classical value theory, can claim legitimacy until Marxism has been thoroughly discredited. Thus when Bohm-Bawerk locks horns with the opening pages of *Capital* it is not merely Marxism that is thrown into the melting-pot but the whole of bourgeois economy.

THE 'ERROR' IN THE MARXIST SYSTEM

According to Bohm-Bawerk, Marx's method of discovering the nature of value is 'a purely logical proof' (p. 63). Starting with an 'old-fashioned' idea derived from Aristotle that the exchange of commodities is a quantitative relationship pre-supposing some property they share in common, 'Marx searches for the 'common factor' which is characteristic of exchange value in the following way: he passes in review the various properties possessed by objects made equal in exchange, and according to the method of exclusion, separates all those that cannot stand the test until at last only one property remains, that of being the product of labour. This therefore must be the sought-for common property' (p. 69). Although this method of 'purely negative proof' does not commend itself to Bohm-Bawerk, he accepts it as 'singular but not in itself objectionable' (pp. 68-9). The problem is the way Marx made use of it. And on this point Bohm-Bawerk launches a three-pronged attack. First, he says, Marx rigged the result by leaving certain things out of his 'logical sieve'. Second, letting this by, there are other common facts than labour that Marx has no right to ignore. And third, Marx's entire logic can be reversed and 'value in use could be substituted for labour' (p. 77). These three lines of attack stake out in the clearest possible way the terrain of fundamental theory on which Marxism and neo-classical economics confront each other. The remainder of this section deals with each in turn.

1. Marx's commodity is not coterminous with goods that exchange in the market. The 'gifts of nature', land, natural resources, trees, minerals and so on, exchange in the same way as commodities but unlike them they do not embody labour. Thus Bohm-Bawerk concludes: 'If Marx had not confined his research, at this decisive point, but had sought for the common factor in the exchangeable gifts of nature as well, it would

have become obvious that work cannot be the common factor' (p. 73). This is an ingenious gambit. It appears at one stroke to separate Marx's theory from the most obvious and easily verifiable features of reality, while at the same time opening the way for the alternative view that the real common factor of goods, natural as well as man-made, is their utility and scarcity. Furthermore it appears to expose Marx to another criticism that Bohm-Bawerk is quick to press home. Marx was fully aware that non-commodities exchange and their exclusion from the logical sieve can, therefore, be nothing more than a deliberate ommission. 'That Marx was truly and honestly convinced of the truth of his thesis I do not doubt', patronises Bohm-Bawerk, 'but the grounds of his conviction are not those which he gives in his system. They are in reality opinions rather than thought out conclusions' (p. 78). And later: 'he knew the result he wished to obtain, and so he twisted and manipulated the long-suffering ideas with admirable skill and subtlety until they yielded the desired result in a respectable syllogistic form' (p. 79). In the language of modern bourgeois theory, Marx's failure to take account of exchangeable goods not produced by labour is evidence of the *ideological* nature of his theory, the unacceptable subordination of positive economics to value judgement.

Let us get to the heart of the matter – the significance of the un-disputed fact that non-commodities such as the free gifts of nature exchange as though they were commodities. Trees grown in a virgin forest, for example, can exchange, that is have a price,[2] in much the same way as commodities that embody labour. But this exchangeability does not arise out of their natural properties. It is true, as Marx emphasised continually, that only those items that satisfy some human need will enter into human intercourse; but the nature of this intercourse is not determined by the physical and natural characteristics of the items as such: these make the item a use-value not an exchange value. For virgin trees to be exchanged requires that they not only satisfy some human need – construction material or fuel or whatever – but that they are private property. The natural properties of trees that make them suitable for building or burning merely tells us that some men will make use of them: it does not tell us that these users will also be *buyers*. This requires further specifications: the users of trees must be prevented from appropriating them directly; or, what is to say the same thing, the trees must be the property of some individual whose claim over them is recognised and substantiated socially. For the gifts of nature to enter the market alongside commodities requires the existence of the market and the system of property relations associated with it. The apparent plausibility of Bohm-Bawerk's criticism begins to melt away at this point. Consider land and its 'price', money-rent, which is the most important economic transaction involving gifts of nature. Historically the emergence of money-rent, the exchange of the use of land for money, followed the development of commodity production; that is to say, it happened only after a decisive proportion of agricultural production had taken the form of commodities.[3] But what is even more to the point here is that not only is rent historically subsequent to commodity production, but it is also dependent upon it; Ricardo demonstrated this in detail and we have here one of the few parts of classical political economy that was assimilated into neo-classical theory. The magnitude of rent does not determine the prices of commodities; on the contrary, it is determined by these prices. Thus in excluding non-commodities from his sieve Marx was pursuing a line perfectly in keeping not only with classical political economy but also with the school of thought which Bohm-Bawerk represents. This part of Bohm-Bawerk's criticism, so plausible at first sight, collapses completely when confronted with the theory of rent and the logic of Marx's position that we can only analyse the exchange of non-commodities once we have analysed commodities stands its ground with ease.

2. The second prong of Bohm-Bawerk's attack is not dissimilar. He quotes Marx to the effect that 'if the use value of commodities be disregarded there remains only one other property, that of being the products of labour.' And then adds: 'Is it so? I ask today as I asked twelve years ago: is there only one other property? Is not the property of being scarce in relation to demand also common to all exchangeable goods. Or that they are the subjects of supply and demand? Or that they are appropriated? Or that they are natural products?. . . Or is the property that they cause expense to their producers . . . common to exhangeable goods? . . . may not the principle of value reside in any one of these common properties as well as in the property of being the products of labour? For in support of this latter proposition Marx has not adduced a shred of positive evidence.' (p. 75). As this list could be extended indefinitely to include such things as being subject to the law of gravity, in orbit around the sun and so on Bohm-Bawerk surely did not intend that every item on it be taken equally seriously. Some anyway simply do not qualify. To say that all commodities are subject to supply and demand merely says that they are exhange values and therefore is no explanation. Others can be easily rendered consistent with the law of value. What is the expense suffered by producers other than labour? And leaving aside the idea of man's insatiability, for which as a general fact Bohm-Bawerk could not adduce a single shred of positive evidence that could not be countered by other equally positive evidence, is not labour the true scarce factor? The point is not worth pursuing further.

Marx' argument is not that commodity exchange arises on the basis of a common factor shared by all commodities. It is more substantial and straight-forward: that in exchange, labour is the common property that regulates the terms of trade. Bohm-Bawerk does not challenge this. He merely misrepresents Marx's argument as formalist – and this brings us to the crux of the matter.

3. The final thrust of Bohm-Bawerk's critique is a confrontation of his own theory with that of Marx in an attempt to show that if Marx had used his 'purely logical method of deduction' correctly he would have reached the conclusion that labour was not the basis of value. 'If Marx had chosen to reverse the order of the examination, the same reasoning that led to the exclusion of value in use would have excluded labour: and then the reasoning that resulted in the crowning of labour might have led him to declare the value in use to be the only property left, and therefore to be the sought-for common property, and value to be the cellular tissue of value in use' (p. 77). At best then, the 'negative' approach cannot dismiss use-value, so that Marx's method fails at one and the same time to establish the premises of its own theory upon an unambiguous base and provide a determinate criticism of the neo-classical alternative. At this point Bohm-Bawerk challenges the dialectical method head on.

We have seen that according to Bohm-Bawerk, Marx's method is 'a purely logical proof, a dialectic deduction from the very nature of exchange' (p. 68). The fact that these two expressions are not equivalent does not strike the Austrian. 'A dialectical deduction from the very nature of exchange' is not 'a purely logical proof': the one refers to a method which is enquiring into a particular phenomenon – i.e. exchange; the other is, as it says, purely logical, it has no particular object. If Marx's method had been of this latter kind it could be represented as follows: imagine a population P consisting of individuals each of which has two characteristics of properties, A and B. In every member of the population, these properties A and B, are present; though in specific forms that vary from one individual to the next. Thus the generic property A presents itself as a', a'' . . . while property B presents itself as b', b'' . . . And under conditions such as these, neither Marx nor anyone else could claim that property B is the only common property on the grounds it alone can exist in the general form B, while A can only exist in the specific forms a', a'' . . . For in a purely logical analysis there is no reason why one property should have different characteristics to another. Believing that Marx had in fact employed, and abused a logical method of this kind, Bohm-Bawerk claimed there is no reason why the particular types of labour that exist in commodities can be generalised as the common property of abstract labour, while particular use-value cannot be generalised in exactly the same way. He says this because he sees the problem as a logical one in which labour and utility are merely names given to symbols: the two are formal equivalents in a logical system, therefore they are real equivalents. No logical method can distinguish the one from the other — hence the need for some positive proof. This brings the differences between the two methods into sharp focus. In neo-classical thought, theory is a purely formalist activity with no real content, and its link with the historical process it attempts to confront must be through a leap into observations which are not and cannot be organically related to the theory. The dialectical method makes no such separation. Its theory is never purely formal, but always has a real content. It is, therefore, never separated from the concrete by an unbridgeable gulf. Thus when Marx claims that the specific concrete labour that creates commodities is reduced to abstract labour, while use-value can only exist in particular forms and is not generalised in the same way; he is making a proposition that has to do with the real nature of labour and use-value. The asymmetry between his analysis of labour on the one side and use-value on the other, is not due to a false application of a logic which should treat them as though they were the same: the asymmetry follows from the different natures of labour and use-value. In other words, it is the category under examination that determines the path and the movement of logic in the dialectical method. The methodology of *Capital*, therefore, and here, particularly its opening section, is inseparably linked to its content, since Marx like Hegel, did not make the separation between logic and category that is characteristic of the 'model-real world' separation that we find in the positivism of the social sciences. The issue at stake is the substantial one of discovering the basis of exchange in capitalist society, and Marx knew better than Bohm-Bawerk that this was not a task of pure logic.

The crux, then, of Bohm-Bawerk's criticism at this point is that the same reasoning that led to the exclusion of value in use could have excluded labour as the basis of value (p. 77). Clearly he pre-supposes a method in which logic stands, so to speak, outside the object of study, and the 'reasoning' he talks of exists solely in the mind and has no organic relation with the world outside. In other words, his formalist logic leads him to conclude that the abstraction from particular use-value to use-value in general is just as acceptable, in principle, as the abstraction from concrete to abstract labour; and that, therefore, on strictly logical grounds there is nothing to choose between the two 'models', one of which takes embodied labour as the common property of commodities and therefore the basis of value, and the other of which casts the function of commodities of satisfying needs in this role. At the centre of this argument lies the idea of general utility which Marx considered and dismissed in a few lines at the very start of *Capital*. 'The usefulness of a thing', he wrote, 'makes it a use-value. But this usefulness does not dangle in mid air. It is conditioned by the physical properties of the commodity and has no existence apart from the latter. It is therefore the physical body of the commodity itself, for instance, iron, corn, a diamond, which is the use-value or useful thing.' (*Capital*, I, p. 126). In other words, for Marx, utility means nothing except when it has a particular material form. As something in general, it has no existence and is therefore unreal.

Thus at the very start of *Capital*, and on a point crucial to the distinction between Marxist and bourgeois theory, we see the close affinity between the methods of Marx and Hegel. In Hegel's objective idealism, the link between the phenomenal world of existence and the reality that stands behind it is indissoluble: in fact, reality is embodied in existence and only becomes real in this way. Thus when Marx says that usefulness has no existence apart from the physical properties of the commodity, he is following Hegel quite closely. For if use-value in general can, by its nature, have no existence, it can also have no reality —except, that is, in the mind of the neo-classical economist. It has the same reality as a dream, for instance, and while a dream might tell us something about the mind of the dreamer it is hardly a reliable guide to the world he inhabits. (See, for instance, Weiskopf, 1949). Bohm-Bawerk does not understand this. He does not understand that Marx dismissed the idea of use-value in general not on logical grounds, but because it has no reality. For Marx it is precisely the fact that use-value can only exist in specific forms that provides the *reason* for exchange in its most basic form of one commodity for another: i.e. because use-value is specific, commodities differ from each other as use-values and this provides a reason for exchanging them. To insist with Bohm-Bawerk that use-value is not only the reason for exchange in this sense, but also its basis and its measure, posits among other things the category of general utility. But as such a category is incapable by its nature of achieving any form of existence, it is doomed to unreality, and any theory based upon it must be a contentless abstraction.

The obvious rejoinder to this is that the same method can be used to disqualify labour as the common property of commodities, and in a somewhat different context Bohm-Bawerk does in fact take this line.

'The plain truth is that . . . products embody *different kinds* of labour in *different amounts*, and every unprejudiced person will admit that this means a state of things exactly contrary to the conditions which Marx demands and must affirm, namely that they embody labour of the same amount and the same kind.' (p. 82)

It is only the qualitative aspect of labour that concerns us here, and Bohm-Bawerk is undoubtedly correct when he states that different commodities embody different kinds of labour. Labour as such must always take the form of concrete labour; it can only exist as this or that type of labour—tailoring or weaving. To posit abstract or general human labour is apparently, therefore, to advance an abstraction which has no more content than the category of general utility that Bohm-Bawerk's criticism implies. In short, because abstract labour can exist only as concrete labour, it is surely impossible to say that labour is the common property of commodities since different commodities are the products of different types of labour. The law of value, no less than the theory of utility, appears to collapse upon its own dialectical foundations.

It is certainly true that at times Marx's method of dealing with this problem is less than satisfactory. The position he appears to adopt at various points in his writings, that all the different types of labour undertaken in capitalist society are nothing more than specific forms of abstract or average labour is, methodologically speaking, no different from Bohm-Bawerk's contention that the multitude of use-values produced and consumed are particular expressions of general use-value. And as such it exposes itself to exactly the same type of criticism. If abstract labour exists only as concrete labour, if it can have no mode of existence apart from concrete labour in all its various forms; then how is it any different from general utility that can only exist as specific use-values? Thus when Marx claims that 'all human labour is an expenditure of human labour-power in a physiological sense and it is in this quality of being equal or abstract that it forms the value of commodities' (*Capital*, I, p. 137); Bohm-Bawerk could easily retort that all use-values are use-values in a psychological sense and that it is here that we can discover the secret of value. In which case, the method of the two theories is the same and Bohm-Bawerk's contention that the only way to choose between them is on the grounds of 'positive proof' apparently rests on firm ground.

Let us take the point further. In the *Critique of Political Economy* Marx writes as follows: 'This abstraction human labour in general exists in the form of average labour, which in any given society the average person can perform, productive expenditure of human muscles, nerves, brains etc.' (op. cit., p. 31). This road to abstract labour is more or less the same as that Bohm-Bawerk would follow to reach general utility and the method employed certainly approximates very closely to that which Bohm-Bawerk characterised as 'purely logical deduction.' Whatever else may be said about it, it is certainly not dialectical; for the abstraction it constructs is a purely mental category that has no existence in its own right. By analogy: to recognise cats and dogs as mammals—specific forms of a genus—may represent a step forward in the biological sciences insofar as we no longer see each species as totally separate and distinct; on the other hand, nobody has ever seen and examined a mammal as such. It is a purely classificatory category and as such has no existence. In the same way, if we constitute abstract labour as the common property of concrete labour—the expenditure of muscles, brains etc.—we are inventing a mental abstraction and not discovering the real abstraction that Marx was after. In analysing exchange value, Marx remarked that 'it cannot be anything other than the mode of expression, the 'form of appearance' of a content distinguishable from it.' (*Capital*, I, p. 127) The distinguishable content he was referring to here was, of course, value. Similarly we can talk of concrete labour being the form of appearance of a content distinguishable from it, here meaning abstract labour. But abstract labour defined simply as the common property of concrete labour is not distinguishable at all. It can no more be distinguished from concrete labour than the quality of being a mammal can be distinguished from the feline body of a cat or the canine one of the dog. It cannot be distinguished quite simply because there is nothing to distinguish, because it does not exist.

Moreover, as the few lines cited above show, this method of procedure leads inexorably towards a dehistoricisation of the categories. For if our abstractions are derived merely as common properties—i.e. from specific form to genus—not only can they have no form of existence at all, but equally they have the same status, the same possibility of non-existence and therefore existence, at all periods in history. As regards our immediate subject, labour: if abstract labour is merely the common property of concrete labour, then as concrete labour indisputably exists in every form of society, it must follow that abstract labour has the same universal presence. And if abstract labour is universally present then its product, value, cannot be far from the scene, even where we do not find the definite historical form of commodity production. Thus wherever we depart from dialecticism and employ a mode of abstraction that moves from specific form to genus, we inevitably lose the historical dimension which is such a vital element of Marx's theory.

The plain fact is that despite the odd remarks we might find in *Capital* and elsewhere in Marx's works to the contrary, abstract labour is not the common property of concrete labour, nor is concrete labour the mode of existence of abstract labour.[4] If we take Marx's analysis as a whole and do not focus our attention on individual passages this becomes abundantly clear.

There is no doubt that part of the difficulty in this case arises from the term 'abstract'; the alternative term that Marx sometimes employs, *social labour*, is preferable in that it is much less prone to ambiguity. While it can easily appear that abstract labour is somehow the interior essence of concrete labour, so that the two cannot exist together on the same plane so to speak, the terms 'individual' or 'specific' when substituted for 'concrete' labour on the one side and 'social' for 'abstract' labour on the other, do not present the same confusion. For in the first place, these terms do not impede us in understanding that any single piece of labour is, at one and the same time, individual in the sense that it is carried out by a particular worker, and social in the sense that it is an organic part of the labour of the whole society, and, moreover, derives a part of its significance from this fact. It is much easier to understand labour as being both individual and social at the same time than it is to understand its being both concrete and abstract simultaneously. And secondly, the terms offer us no temptation to believe that we are dealing with an abstraction to genus from specific forms. When we talk of the common property of individual labour that makes it social, we are not tempted to think in terms of the expenditure of muscles and brains etc., but of the fact that each individual labour shares the character of being part of the labour of society, no matter how different its particular content might be. Whereas the opposition, 'concrete-abstract' labour, can all too easily suggest a tendency for all the different forms of concrete labour to be reduced towards a common content; the opposition, 'individual-social' labour carries no such connotation. In this respect it does not confuse one of the essential features of Marx's theory, that it is variations in the content of individual labour rather than its homogeneity that constitute the real basis for commodity production and the emergence of abstract labour.

Consider an elementary act of exchange where one individual makes a coat and exchanges it for twenty yards of linen made by another individual. In the case of both individuals, the labour is specific and concrete; tailoring in the one case, and weaving in the other. But when they exchange their commodities in order to acquire a different use-value, each individual learns in the most practical way possible that through the expenditure of his own particular type of labour he can acquire the product of another particular type of labour. Through the process of exchange the tailor can by tailoring acquire the product of weaving. When exchange becomes general and all use-values enter the market as commodities, any one type of labour becomes the means to acquire the product of any other type of labour. As Marx puts it: 'one use-value is worth just as much as another provided only that it is present in the appropriate quantity.' (*Capital*, I, p. 127) Which means that any one type of labour, when embodied in a commodity, becomes the equivalent in a qualitative sense of every other type of labour that is also embodied in commodities no matter how different they may be. Thus it is not the disappearance of differences among all the various types of concrete labour that provides the form of existence of abstract or social labour; on the contrary it is these differences and their development that provide the necessity for such a form. As concrete labour becomes more varied, that is to say as the division of labour develops and with it commodity production, individual labour ceases to be exclusively individual and increasingly becomes an aspect of social labour. Or to look at it another way, labour remains specific, it is still this or that type of labour, but it does not and cannot operate in isolation. Under a situation of generalised commodity production, even when production is organised on an individual basis, labour is at once individual but also social, at once specific but an organic part of social labour, at once concrete but also abstract. Thus Bohm-Bawerk's criticism that the existence of different forms of labour, particularly skilled and unskilled labour, excludes the possibility of abstract labour, labour as the common factor, is completely superseded, since these differences far from being ignored by Marx or conjured away by some trick of dialectical logic, are posited as the very basis for the existence of abstract labour.

But one problem still remains: if concrete labour is not and cannot be the form of existence of abstract labour what then, is its form? For it must have one otherwise it can achieve no reality. Marx poses and resolves this question in section 3 of the first chapter of *Capital*, The Value-form or Exchange Value. Labour only becomes abstract once it is embodied in a commodity and constitutes the value of that commodity, so in searching for the form of existence of abstract labour we are merely looking for the value-form. Now in an elementary exchange that involves two commodities, the value of the one is expressed as a definite amount of the other. In Marx's example, where 20 yards of linen exchange for a coat, the coat becomes the form of existence of the linen: 'Use-value becomes the form of appearance of its opposite, value.' (*Capital*, I, p. 148) That is to say, when an individual exchanges his commodity for another, the labour he has put into his commodity is now represented directly, and actually, in the use-value of the commodity he acquires.[5] When a commodity represents the value of another, Marx calls it the *equivalent form of value*. In a situation of simple exchange, one commodity acts as the equivalent form of value of another; but when exchange becomes more systematic, a single and universal equivalent emerges — i.e. one commodity emerges to act as the form of value of all other commodities: *money*. In its role of universal equivalent, money shows not only that all commodities do in fact have a common property, it acts as this common property. As the medium of circulation, it is the means through which the particular individual concrete labour embodied in any one commodity can become transformed into any, and every, other type of labour. That is to say it is the medium through which concrete labour becomes abstract labour. In a word it is money that is the form of existence of abstract labour.

QUANTITY AND QUALITY

We can now pick up an important matter mentioned in passing at the start: Bohm-Bawerk's firmly held conviction that if the law of value means anything it is that the prices of commodities are proportionate to their values. For him there can be no solution to the transformation problem, for any systematic deviation of prices from (relative) values stands in flat contradiction to the theory of value which he finds in *Capital*, I. There are two aspects to this issue. The first concerns the quantitative relationship between value and price (of production), and here it can be shown with ease that Bohm-Bawerk defined the question too narrowly. He sees the magnitude of value as the sole determinant of price, whereas it is the magnitude of value in conjunction with its composition that in fact determines prices — and, this, of course, is perfectly consistent with the general proposition that the prices of commodities are determined by their values. Insofar as the problems raised here exist on the same plain of abstraction they are of little fundamental importance, and in this sense Joan Robinson was right to call the transformation problem 'merely an analytical puzzle which like all puzzles ceases to be of interest once it has been solved.' (Robinson and Eatwell, 1973, p. 30) The second aspect of Bohm-Bawerk's critique is much more than a puzzle as it comprises what is perhaps the most important point of separation and opposition of Marxism and bourgeois economics — the relationship between quantity and quality.

We have seen that the contentless abstraction is characteristic of the positivist method with the consequence that theory is separated from the historical process by an unbridgeable gulf. Its concepts cannot progress from the abstract to the concrete through a series of *specifications* and *mediations* because they contain nothing that can be specified or mediated. They must therefore attempt to grasp reality directly, *immediately*. So at the very moment that the theory of positivist science is organised around empty abstractions it prizes the operationality of its concepts. Thus Bohm-Bawerk simultaneously proposed a theory of value based upon the utterly intangible notion of generalised utility and advanced the immediate explanation of relative prices as the criterion by which a theory of value is to be judged: a theory must explain the magnitude of value at the same time as it explains its nature. In contradistinction to some modern streams of economic thought, Bohm-Bawerk did not think that 'the whole thing (i.e. value theory) analytically considered was a great fuss about nothing.' (Robinson, 1962, p. 41) He recognised that economic magnitudes could not be explained in terms of each other like a carefully constructed dome that floats of its own accord without any supports. He accepted the need for a theory of value but only in so far as it gave an immediate and direct explanation of relative prices. Thus when he turned to *Capital*, he took it for granted that the proposition that the value of a commodity is determined by the amount of labour socially necessary for its production meant that commodities would actually exchange for each other, in practice, in a ratio proportionate to their relative values. A cursory reader of the text who has already got a firm idea of value and price from neo-classical economics might find ample evidence to support this view, but in point of fact, it is absolutely inconsistent with Marx's method and entirely unnecessary to the elaboration of his theory.

If the idea that equivalent exchange was in some way or other an essential part of the theoretical structure of *Capital* was held only by economists such as Bohm-Bawerk, it could be cited simply as a misreading that arose from pre-conceived notions. But in fact the idea recurs continuously within the Marxist camp. In his reply to Bohm-Bawerk, Hilferding toyed with the idea, suggesting that 'under certain specific historical conditions exchange for corresponding values is indispensible.' By adding later that 'Marxist law of value is not cancelled by the data of the third volume but merely modified in a definite way' (p. 157), he gives the impression that the departure from equal exchange is a movement from a norm. In a contemporary contribution Morishima and Catephores deny the idea that conditions of equal exchange have existed historically: that is to say they deny the historical existence of a society of simple commodity production where equivalent exchange took place. But their adherence to the idea as an essential part of Marxist theory is so strong that it surfaces again immediately, only now as a heuristic device, a 'logical simulation': 'the model

of simple commodity production (which) is different from the capitalist production model only with respect to the ownership of the means
of production.' We are back in a positivist world and soon we learn that
not only is the idea of equal exchange merely an element of a model
but value itself is an 'analytical device'. Engels' rejection of Sombart's
'interpretation of the concept of value as only a logical tool' is not, so
it is suggested, fully consistent with the 'evidence on the total approach
of Marx to the question of value that we have tried to present here. . .'
It is interesting that Bohm-Bawerk, though for different reasons,
criticised Sombart on the same grounds as Engels. 'For my own part',
he wrote, 'I hold it (i.e. value as merely a tool of logic) to be wholly
irreconcilable with the letter and spirit of the Marxian teaching.'
(p. 103)

    These two contributions separated by seventy years testify the
on-going fascination of Marxists with the idea of equal exchange. They
also specify the only two grounds on which it can be treated: (1) as a
real process that existed under definite historical conditions; or (2) as a
model. But since the first ground is not historically valid and the second
requires a positivism which is utterly inconsistent with Marxism, only
one conclusion is possible – equal exchange plays no fundamental part
in Marxism. Marx at times might use the idea for simplicity, or exposition, but no substantial part of his theory is dependent upon it. This
can be demonstrated through the two most vital points of Marx's
theory: first, the establishment of value as a category; and second, the
theory of surplus value.

1. The logic Marx uses to track down value at the start of *Capital*, I
seems very definitely to imply an assumption of equal exchange. 'The
valid exchange values of a particular commodity,' he says, 'express
something equal.' He then gives as an example '1 quarter corn = x cwt.
iron. What does this equation signify?' he asks, 'It signifies a common
element of identical magnitude in two different things – in 1 quarter of
corn and x cwt. of iron.' (*Capital*, I, p. 127) Bohm-Bawerk clearly
believed that the dimension of 'equal quantities' was so essential to the
argument that he did not draw special attention to it when he cited the
passage (p. 10). But it is clearly remarks of this nature, several of which
can be found in the early sections of *Capital*, I, that give the impression
that Marx was for one reason or another, making substantial use of the
notion of equal exchange or simple commodity production. But in this
context, which is perhaps the most important, it can be seen that equal
exchange is not at all necessary. For the conclusion to which Marx is
working, that aside from being use-values 'commodities . . . have only
one common property left, that of being products of labour,' in no way

depends upon equal exchange. Suppose double the amount of labour-time is needed to harvest the corn than to smelt the iron, so that the corn has double the value of the iron. An exchange of these commodities still brings a given quantity of the one commodity face to face with a given quantity of another. What does this tell us? It tells us that in two different things, to paraphrase Marx, there exists something common to both, *though not necessarily in equal amounts*. In other words, the position advanced by Marx that the process of exchange reveals the most diverse use-values to share the common property of being the products of labour does not mean, nor does it depend upon, a quite different proposition that only commodities that contain the same amount of labour exchange with each other. Consider the exchange 1 quarter of corn = ¼ cwt. of iron. Here the iron is the equivalent form of value; that is to say its use-value not its value, represents the value of the corn. It is true that only a commodity that is itself a value can get into the position of being an equivalent, but once in this position it is its use-value that represents the value of the relative form. Thus on the side of the equivalent form there exists the possibility of a quantitative "incongruity" between the value the equivalent (use-value) represents, and its own value. This incongruity is an essential feature of Marx's analysis of money and in so far as it presupposes unequal exchange, then, to that extent, it is possible to go beyond arguing that not only does the law of value not rest upon equal exchange, but that in fact the reverse is true: *the law of value presupposes unequal exchange*.

The importance attached to equal exchange by Bohm-Bawerk is understandable. As Hilferding says, his 'mistake is that he confuses value with price, being led to this confusion by his own theory' (p. 156). Marx's position in the opening pages of *Capital*, I, that commodities are alike in that they are the products of labour, and that this only becomes apparent and real through the process of systematic exchange, is not a theory of prices as understood in neo-classical economics. It is no part of Marx's purpose at this stage of his work to provide a theory of the rates at which commodities exchange for each other; before this can be done it is necessary to discover the nature of the value- and price-forms. In other words, the opening chapters of *Capital*, I, are an enquiry into the *nature* of value, value as a *quality*; the progress from this to the quantitative aspect of the question moves through many mediations. But positivist thought, whether it presents itself in a neo-classical or even a Marxist guise, disregards this progress and leaps directly from quality to quantity. In its modern vulgar form it ignores quality altogether. Bohm-Bawerk's critique collapses on this point which is, one way or another, the most vulnerable of the whole neo-classical edifice.

2. The relationship between economic forms (quality) and their magnitudes (quantity) is just as vital in the theory of surplus value though generally speaking it has received less attention. Bohm-Bawerk deals with the matter only in passing for fairly obvious reasons. 'In the middle part of the Marxian system,' he writes, 'the logical development and connection present a really imposing closeness and logical consistency' (p. 88). This gives an important clue to the manner in which Bohm-Bawerk would have criticised the theory of surplus value had he thought it necessary. In the Marxian system, he would no doubt have argued, labour-power is a commodity which like other commodities exchanges at its value. But remove this false premise and the theory comes apart, for once the wage is no longer tied to the value of labour-power, not only does the rate of surplus value become totally indeterminate, but even its existence as an economic category is called into question. For surplus value is essentially a quantitative phenomenon. It is the difference between two magnitudes, the value produced by a given expenditure of labour-power, and the value of this labour power. Marx took it for granted that the difference between these two magnitudes was positive, but he knows that is not sufficient to prove his point. In order for capital to appropriate this difference as surplus value and profit, it is necessary for him to show that wages will be consistently less than the value labour-power produces, and this is possible only within the framework of his system by assuming what he never establishes positively – namely that wages equal the value of labour-power. 'In this case, as in many others, he manages to glide with admirable dialectical skill over the difficult points of his argument.' He introduces equal exchange but nor for what it is, the only and necessary support for his argument, but as a virtue, as though it were a difficulty for him to overcome. 'Our friend, (Moneybags) . . . must buy his commodities at their value (and) must sell them at their value,' he writes in *Capital*, I (p. 269). In *Value, Price and Profit* he sets himself the same difficult problem. 'To explain the general nature of profits you must start from the theorem that, on an average, commodities are *sold at their real values*, and *that profits are derived from selling them at their values* . . .If you cannot explain profit upon this supposition you cannot explain it at all.' (Marx, 1962, p. 424) Whichever way you look at it, Bohm-Bawerk might well have concluded the existence of surplus value as a consistently positive magnitude depends upon the equal exchange of the commodity labour-power. This is why the proposition that commodities exchange at their value is the pivot of the whole Marxist system. Drop it and you drop what Marx readily admits to be his most important category – surplus value and exploitation. *Hic Rhodus, hic salta.*

It is as well to acknowledge from the outset that the existence of surplus value as a category of capitalist political economy does involve and must involve a tendency for labour-power to exchange at its value. Marx would have been the last person to deny this. But for him the connection between the value of the wage and surplus value was quite the opposite of that attributed to him by the positivist. That is to say for Marx the tendency of the wage to equal the value of labour-power *follows* from the existence of surplus value as a category and vice versa. Demonstrating this point quickly is virtually impossible, as it involves nothing less than tracing the movement of his theory through the first six chapters of *Capital*, I, but we can note, at least, the vital point that he has already arrived at the concept of surplus value in *Chapter 4* well before he has turned to the buying and selling of labour-power in *Chapter 6*. Summarised in the most sketchy detail, the path of his logic passes the following points. In the systematic exchange of commodities, value finds for itself a form of social existence in the use-value or body of one commodity that becomes the universal equivalent—money. The money commodity starts life like any other commodity, but as its role of being universal equivalent becomes socially established, it separates itself off and becomes a commodity on its own. Its own particular use-value drops into the background and it exists more and more exclusively as the form of value of all other commodities. It is at this point, rather than through some artificial assumption of equal exchange, that we get the transformation of quality into quantity. As value, commodities are indistinguishable from one another except in respect to their size, and money, the value-form, confirms this is so far that sums differ from each other only as magnitudes. In the simple circulation of commodities, $C-M-C$, where money acts merely as a medium of exchange, this property is still latent or secondary. But when we move to the circulation of value, $M-C-M$, the transformation of money into capital, it becomes manifest and determinant. The reason for the circulation of value is surplus value, the exchange of one sum of money, M, for a larger sum, M^1. By the time labour-power comes on to the stage as a commodity, circulation as a whole is firmly subjected to this reason. It must, therefore, like any other commodity act as a medium of circulating value and subject itself to this reason. In the case of labour-power, however, this has special implications. We know that this is a special commodity in that its use-value is to produce all value, surplus value included. Thus if capital is to appropriate the surplus product of society, wages must lie below the value labour produces, i.e. the value of its use-value. At the same time, the purely quantitative nature of value means that the appropriation of surplus value is simultaneously the appropriation of maximum surplus value. Thus capital is driven by its own position not merely to force the wage down below the value produced by labour, but to the lowest possible level – namely the value of labour-power. In a word, the magnitude of the wage, and with it the rate of surplus value, follows from the nature of surplus value as an economic category. Nowhere can the subordination of economic magnitude to economic forms, of quantity to quality, be more vividly apparent.

The conclusion that follows from all this is that Bohm-Bawerk's critique does not have a single point of validity. The Marxist need not concede a single thing to him. But paradoxically, this is what makes his book so valuable, for refuting it, as we have tried to show, involves reaching down to the very fundamentals of Marxism. At the same time, *Karl Marx and the Close of his System* is indoubtedly the most substantive criticism that any bourgeois economist has ever levelled against *Capital*. It has inspired all other criticisms as Sweezy points out. But more than this, it lays neo-classical theory on the line. For in attempting to attack Marx on what was, if anything his strongest front, the opening of *Capital*, Bohm-Bawerk revealed the foundations of his own science, and revealed them to be faulty. The Russian retreat of Marxism turns into the Waterloo of neo-classicism, but sadly the latter has not been banished to obscurity. Its flourishing survival, though, is perhaps the least of problems in itself: more important for the working-class movement is the damaging effect its positivistic method has had upon Marxism from within. With the collapse of neo-classicism under the weight of its misconceptions and inconsistencies, this becomes even more important. Within the realm of economics Marxism can no longer be challenged frontally from a neo-classical perspective; it can however be emasculated from within. The republication of Bohm-Bawerk's book will be a timely and valuable addition to the literature only if it is read with this danger in mind.

Notes

1 The Sweezy edition of *Karl Marx and the Close of his System*, which includes the response by Hilferding, entitled 'Bohm-Bawerk's criticism of Marx', has recently been republished in Britain. All references in the text and notes of this chapter, which simply give a page number, refer to this publication.

2 For example, Marx writes: 'The price-form . . . (may) . . . harbour a qualitative contradiction, with the result that price ceases altogether to express value despite the fact that money is nothing but the price-form of commodities. Things which in and for themselves are not commodities, things such as conscience, honour, etc. . . can be offered for sale by their holders, and thus acquire the form of

commodities through their price. Hence a thing can, formally speaking, have a price without having a value. The expression of price is in this case imaginary. On the other hand, the imaginary price-form may also conceal a real value-relation, or one derived from it, as for instance the price of uncultivated land, which is without value because no human labour is objectified in it'. (*Capital*, I, p. 197)

3. In colonies and parts of the world where commodity production was imposed from outside, the process often happened in reverse. Thus in the Highlands of Scotland, for example, the imposition of money rent developed alongside and even preceded the emergence of commodity production and was widely used as an instrument to achieve this latter. (See Prebble, 1969). But this does not invalidate the general point in any way. For the use of money rent as a catalyst of commodity production in one part of the world depended upon the prior development of commodity production upon its own foundations in another.

4. The problem of concrete and abstract labour has become confused with another related question, that of the reduction of skilled to unskilled labour. This issue, which has surfaced again recently – see Rowthorne, 1974 and Kay, 1976 – finds its source, like so many other confusions in the work of Bohm-Bawerk (pp. 80-5). Part of the problem is terminological. In the *Critique of Political Economy*, for example, Marx talks of *simple* labour, where in context he clearly means abstract labour. The background meaning of 'simple', namely 'uniform' is clearly the one that Marx had in mind, and this lessens the purely terminological possibility of assimilating the notions of abstract and unskilled labour. Whatever ambiguities might arise from language, in theory at least, the relationship between skilled and unskilled labour is not that of concrete and abstract labour. The categories of skill can apply only to concrete labour and even if all concrete labour were unskilled in the sense that it could be performed without any special training or faculties, it would still assume different forms – machine minding and cleaning for example – and therefore would not be uniform like abstract labour. Insisting upon this, that concrete labour can never be the immediate form of abstract labour, does not mean that we dismiss the idea advanced by Marx in the *Grundrisse* (p. 297) that the process of capitalist development tends towards abstracting labour in the sense of reducing it to a formal activity emptied of content. Only this process of abstraction does not follow immediately from the category of abstract labour, but from the development of the capitalist mode of production as a whole. Braverman is actually sensitive to this issue

but he presents it in a facile fashion. (Braverman, 1974, p. 181-2)
5. 'The value of the (commodity) can be expressed only as an 'objectivity', a thing which is materially different from the (commodity) itself and yet common to the (commodity) and all other commodities'. (*Capital*, I, p. 142). 'Thus the commodity acquires a value-form different from its natural form.' (*Capital*, I, p. 143)

Bibliography

von Bohm-Bawerk, E (1975), *Karl Marx and the Close of his System*, Merlin Press, London. This edition, prepared by Paul Sweezy, also includes R Hilferding's reply, entitled 'Bohm-Bawerk's Criticism of Marx'.

Braverman, H (1974), *Labour and Monopoly Capital*, Monthly Review Press, London and New York.

Bukharin, N (1972), *The Economic Theory of the Leisure Class*, Monthly Review Press, London and New York.

Kay, G (1976), 'A Note on Abstract Labour', *Bulletin of the Conference of Socialist Economists*, March.

Marx, K (1976), *Capital*, I, Penguin Books, London.

Marx, K (1971), *A Contribution to the Critique of Political Economy*, Lawrence and Wishart, London.

Marx, K (1973), *Grundrisse*, Penguin Books, London.

Marx, K (1962), *Selected Works*, Volume I, Moscow.

Morishima, M and Catephores, G (1975), 'Is there an Historical Transformation Problem?' *Economic Journal*, June.

Prebble, J (1969), *The Highland Clearances*, Penguin, London.

Robinson, J (1962), *Economic Philosophy*, Penguin Books, London.

Robinson, J and Eatwell, J (1973), *An Introduction to Modern Economics*, McGraw Hill, London.

Rowthorn, B (1974), 'Skilled Labour in the Marxist System', *Bulletin of the Conference of Socialist Economists*, Spring.

Weisskopf, W A (1949), 'Psychological Aspects of Economic Thought', *Journal of Political Economy*, Volume LVII, No. 4, August.

DIALECTIC OF THE VALUE-FORM

C J Arthur

Marx admits that the development of the value-form is the most difficult part of his critique of political economy (*Capital*, I, p. 90). It is not surprising, therefore, that he continually reworked it. The difficulty in presenting the material in scientific form is indicated by Marx in a letter of 1866 to Kugelmann where he states that *A Contribution to the Critique of Political Economy* (1859) ought to be summarised at the beginning of *Capital*: 'not only for completeness, but because even good brains did not comprehend the thing completely correctly; therefore there must be something defective in the first presentation, particularly the analysis of the commodity'. Yet the problem emerged again with *Capital* (1867) itself. When the first proofs reached Marx he was staying with Kugelmann in Hanover and the latter convinced him that readers needed a supplementary, more didactic, exposition of the form of value, because they lacked dialectics. Marx therefore wrote a special Appendix for the First Volume, for—he explains to Engels—'the matter is too decisive for the whole book'. (*Selected Correspondence*, p. 189). For the second edition Marx rewrote the whole first chapter again—thus making any appendix redundant.

In the Postface to the Second Edition Marx recalls that he 'here and there in the chapter on the theory of value coquetted with the mode of expression peculiar to' Hegel (*Capital*, I, p. 102-3). This admission is expressed in the context of a discussion of dialectic—and the development of the value-form is one of the most clearly dialectical passages in *Capital*. I would argue that this section articulates the dialectical relationships of 'value', 'use-value', 'equivalent' and so on, in order to exhibit the concrete structure of commodity exchange and thus correct the one-sided abstractions, and analytical reductions, of the previous sections. It is true to say that the flirtation with Hegel is less evident with the second edition—following the strictures of Kugelmann and Engels, Marx no doubt wanted to give the philistine the least possible excuse for complaining of dialectical paradoxes—so, from the point of view of dialectics, the first edition, and especially its appendix, is of great interest, and we will cite it below.

The Necessity of the Value-Form

By the value-form Marx means the form of appearance of value. Value does not appear as such in the single individual commodity: 'We may twist and turn a single commodity as we wish; it remains impossible to grasp it as a thing possessing value' (*Capital*, I, p. 138). Only if a commodity enters into exchange relations with others does it acquire, in the exchange-value it has against these others, a form of appearance of its value.

Classical Political Economy ignored the problem of the value-form in favour of the analysis of the substance, and, even more, the magnitude, of value; in treating commodity relations in an ahistorical fashion, it was led to abstract from the specific forms involved and to concentrate on value as an essential attribute of the product of labour without recognition of the fact that there is a problem about the form of appearance of this content. If the necessity of a material form of appearance of value is not recognised then value theory becomes nothing but metaphysical essentialism founded in abstract thought; an abstraction – value – inheres in the commodity as such. Marx, however, is acutely aware of this:

> 'If we say that, as values, commodities are simply congealed quantities of human labour, our analysis reduces them, it is true, to the level of *abstract value*, but does not give them a form of value distinct from their natural forms.' (*Capital*, I, p. 141).

It is true that the natural form of a coat, for example, bears the imprint of the tailor's labour – one can see a lot of work has gone into it, so to speak. But this has little to do with value for such concrete useful labour is a necessity in all modes of production; it tells us nothing about the specific relations of production concerned. Only if the coat is produced *as a commodity* does its character as a product of labour that is equatable with all other kinds of labour, that is, taken in abstraction from its specificity as tailoring, give it value. It does not have this character immediately; it can only embody general social labour insofar as immediately private labour is realised as universal social labour, in and through the mediation of exchange, as an emerging result. (See Arthur, 1978).

'However', says Marx, 'it is not enough to express the specific character of the labour which goes to make up value. Human labour-power in its fluid state, or human labour, creates value, but is not itself value. It becomes value only in its coagulated state, in objective form'. (*Capital*, I, p. 142). But value can objectify itself concretely only through a form that neglects the specific character of a commodity, as a certain use-value shaped by particular kinds of labour, in favour of its commonality with other products of social labour. The value-form makes this possible insofar as another commodity is posited as representing the value of the first.

Just as in a balance the iron weights represent weight alone for the heavy object being weighed, quite independently of their specific character as iron, so the body of the value-equivalent represents value alone independently of its bodily form, and the concrete useful labour it contains represents only universal human labour in the abstract, from the standpoint of the commodity whose value is expressed in it; in this way the value of a commodity is realised *relative to another*.

Exchange is therefore a crucial presupposition of Marx's investigation; it is the process through which the value-form develops 'from its simplest, almost imperceptible outline to the dazzling money-form'. (*Capital*, I, p. 139)

Exchange and Equivalence

Marx assumes that commodity exchange is an exchange of equivalents. Before considering in detail Marx's analysis of the value-form in this light, we deal with two objections that have been raised to this assumption.

Let us first look at the objection raised by Bohm-Bawerk (1975, p. 68):

'Where equality and exact equilibrium obtains, no change is likely to occur to disturb the balance. When, therefore, in the case of exchange the matter terminates with a change of ownership of the commodities, it points rather to the existence of some inequality or preponderance which produces the alteration.'

This brilliant observation proves nothing except the profoundly undialectical character of the formalist thinking of the bourgeois critic. For Marx, however, it is precisely through the dialectical unity of use-value and value in the commodity that we understand the basis of the alteration in ownership, on the one hand, and the termination of the transaction resulting in the holding of an equivalent of the original commodity held, on the other. It is precisely the fact that commodities *differ* as use-values, but are *equivalent* as values that is the basis of capitalist exchange.

'For the owner, his commodity possesses no direct use-value.

Otherwise, he would not bring it to market. It has use-value for others; but for himself its only direct use-value is as a bearer of exchange-value, and consequently a means of exchange. He therefore makes up his mind to sell it in return for commodities whose use-value is of service to him. All commodities are non-use-values for their owners, and use-values for their non-owners. Consequently they must all change hands. But this changing of hands constitutes their exchange, and their exchange puts them in relation with each other as values and realises them as values. Hence commodities must be realised as values before they can be realised as use-values.' (*Capital*, I, p. 179).

One should note that a purely formal analysis of the relation of exchange cannot sustain the conclusion that exchange *must* involve exchange of *equivalents*. If Marx's initial presentation of the matter, in *Capital*, is taken to provide a purely *logical* argument from exchange, to equivalence, to the substance of this equivalence, then it does not work.

This has been seized on recently by the post-Althusserians:

'Marx conceives exchange as an *equation*, as being effected through the identity of the objects exchanged . . .But is is by no means inevitable that exchange be conceived as an equation. Exchange may be conceived as being *equivalent*, in the juridical sense, that is, that both parties to it agree to the equity of the terms of the exchange and receive what they were promised, *but not as an equation* (there not being any substantive identity between the things exchanged) . . .Exchange as equation and exchange proportionality as necessity are products of definite theoretical conditions, conditions which give certain questions pertinence. . . That these questions are theoretical rather than an inevitable part of the nature of things (and for which answers must be sought) is often forgotten. It is possible to argue that prices and exchange-values have no *general* functions or general determinants, and that there is in general no necessity for the proportions in which commodities exchange.' (Cutler et al., 1977, pp. 12-14)

It is true that scientific questions are not given in the nature of things, but, on the contrary, the nature of things is illuminated by posing, and answering, theoretical questions. What has to be justified is the research programme that embodies a certain theoretical problematic. The entire value-problematic should be junked, it is alleged, since there are no *general* determinants of exchange. One wonders what these authors would say about Newton's laws of motion; observing the convoluted trajectory of a leaf fluttering to the ground should he not have resigned immediately the search for *general* determinants of motion? In order to validate Marx's research programme one has to recognise straight away that its pertinence must be limited to exchange in the context of definite historically developed material conditions. Marx says that 'the law of value presupposes for its full development an industrial society in which production is carried on a large scale and free competition prevails, i.e. the modern capitalist society.' (*Contribution to the Critique of Political Economy*, p. 69). It follows that his theory of exchange depends not merely on the products of labour being exchanged, but being exchanged under these definite social conditions. Barter of surpluses occuring now and then between self-sufficient communities should be excluded. Likewise if two friends notice that one person has a spare bed while the other has surplus bookshelves they may not bother their heads further than to reassign these use-values; in such a case no qualitative identity or quantative necessity need be posited.

In capitalist economies, however, it is quite different. Here we are dealing with myriads of commodities at once autonomous and interchangeable (and in that sense identical). They are autonomous in that commodities are the product of many individual private production processes, linked only by the market; and identical in the sense that each commodity is interchangeable in definite, known proportions with thousands and thousands of other commodities whether or not it is actually exchanged with them. It is the fact that the interchangeability is independent of any one particular act of exchange, but is nevertheless the unplanned outcome of the sum total of autonomous acts of exchange, which posits capitalist exchange as exchange of equivalents. (See Elson, below.) It is not exchanges as individual acts which posits equivalence, but interchangeability—the fact that we know the exchange-value of one commodity in terms of many other commodities even though it has not actually exchanged with any of them.

In the remainder of this note we presuppose that the form of value expresses a relationship of equivalence and seek to show that formal, undialectical thinking cannot comprehend the analysis of the value-form because it divorces itself from the concrete relationships involved.

The Logic of the Value-Form

Marx proceeds from the simple form of value, to the expanded form, to the general form, to the money form. Schematically, the development can be summarised thus:

1. *Simple Form* $x = y$; in this relation the value of x is said to be given in relative form, while y is in the equivalent form.

2. *Expanded Form* $x = y$, and $x = z$, and $x = a$, and $x = n$ etc.

3. *General Form*

$$\left. \begin{array}{l} y = \\ z = \\ a = \\ b = \\ n = \end{array} \right\} x(\text{x is said to be in universal equivalent form})$$

4. *Money Form* As before—but x is an amount of gold or of whatever the historically evolved universal equivalent happens to be in a given society.

From the point of view of formal thinking nothing is going on here except the complication of a tautology—'a value is a value is a value'. (From a bourgeois point of view no empirical significance attaches to any of it until the money form is mentioned, which can be misrecognised as a reference to familiar phenomena—market prices. Marx, of course, is concerned to show, as against conventionalist theories of money, that it is rooted, in germ, in the simple exchange of values.) This is because, for the formalist, the development of the value-form is the mere elaboration of an abstraction, not the synthesis of the appearance of a real relation.

Stanley Moore (1963) for example, mistakes the development of the value-form as an analysis meant to buttress Marx's earlier derivation of value from exchange-value. He takes Marx to be employing the *principle of abstraction* throughout this section. He quotes Tarski on this principle as follows:

'Every relation which is at the same time reflexive, symmetrical, and transitive is thought of as some kind of equality. Instead of saying therefore that such a relation holds between two things, one can, in this sense, also say that these things are equal in such and such a respect, or—in a more precise mode of speech—that certain properties of the things are identical. Thus, instead of saying that two segments are congruent, or two people equally old, or two words synonomous, it may just as well be stated that the segments are equal in respect of their length, that the people have the same age, or that the meanings of the two words are identical.' (Tarski, 1946, section 30.)

In other words, according to Moore, Marx takes it that the relation between commodities in exchange is *reflexive, symmetrical and transitive*; and abstracts from this the conclusion that the commodities share an identical property: they have the same value.

According to the canons of formal thought, a relation of equality obtains if and only if it is reflexive, symmetrical and transitive.

1) A relation R is reflexive in the class K when for any x which is a member of K, xRx.

2) A relation R is symmetrical in the class K when for any x and y which are members of K, if xRy and yRx.

3) A relation is transitive in the class when for any x, y and z, which are members of K, if xRy and yRz, then xRz.

I refer to the formal properties of the equality relation (x = x; if x = y then y = x; if x = y, and y = x, then x = z) collectively as 'RST'.

We have already said that Marx takes exchange to be structured as equivalent exchange, but the importance of the *development of the value form* is precisely that certain contradictions, hidden in the analytical identity of values with each other, emerge insofar as value *appears materially* as exchange-value, its necessary form of appearance. I will show that Marx's analysis of the value-form, which he characterises as a relation of equivalence, violates RST, or at least that it draws attention to material characteristics of the exchange relation which cannot be expressed in RST forms of analysis. This is because what Marx is tracing in the development of the value-form is not the movement of abstractions but *the logic of the concrete*.

Lack of Reflexivity in the Simple Form of Value

In considering the simple expression of value, 'x = y', Marx argues that, although the relative and equivalent forms are clearly inseparable in it, there is, nonetheless a real polarity here in that these two forms are distributed among *different commodities*, and he goes on: 'I cannot, for example, express the value of linen in linen: 20 yards of linen = 20 yards of linen is not an expression of value.' (*Capital*, I, p. 140) (It simply expresses a definite quantity of an object of use, linen.) Here, then, he denies reflexivity insofar as 'x = x' is said not to be an expression of value. In relating x to itself we cannot do anything except say that it is identical to itself as a determinate body with naturally given properties (relevant to its *use-value* only). 'x = x' is not an expression of *value* because value is expressed only in a relation between different commodities and can be assigned to a particular commodity only through the value-form which expresses the value of one commodity *relative* to another. In 'x = y' *the equivalent* 'y' stands for the value of x.

To understand this better we must take a step back. Use-value and value are not merely different determinations of the commodity but may be *opposed* in that, when serving as a use-value, a commodity cannot also be a value, and, when treated as a value, its particular use is ignored; that is, it is either being *exchanged*, in which relation only value is important and abstraction is made from the particular use of each commodity, or it is being *consumed* and is no longer viewed as potentially exchangeable.

However, the matter is by no means so simple that we can rest content with this *antithesis* by assigning use-value to the sphere of consumption and value to the sphere of exchange; because when we say that we abstract from the particular use-values involved in exchanging commodities, it is nonetheless the case that what is exchanged, that is, actually handed over, are use-values which must be *treated as* values such that a commodity x takes as its value-equivalent the body of y. Marx says in the First Edition of *Capital*:

> 'We stand here at the jumping-off point of all difficulties which hinder the understanding of the *value-form*. It is relatively easy to distinguish the value of a commodity from its use-value, or the labour which forms the use-value from that same labour insofar as it is merely reckoned as the expenditure of human labour power in the commodity-value. If one considers commodity or labour in one form, then one fails to consider it in the other, and vice versa. These abstract opposites fall apart on their own and hence are easy to keep separate. It is different with the *value-form* which exists only in the relation of commodity to commodity. The use-value or commodity-body is here playing a new role. It is turning into the form of appearance of the commodity-*value*, thus of its own opposite. Similarly, the *concrete*, useful labour contained in the use-value turns into its own opposite, to the mere form of realisation of *abstract* human labour. Instead of falling apart, the opposing determinations of the commodity are reflected against one another. However incomprehensible this seems at first sight, it reveals itself on further consideration to be necessary. The commodity is right from the start a *dual* thing, use-value *and* value, product of useful labour *and* abstract coagulate of labour. In order to manifest itself as what it is, it must therefore *double* its form.' (*Value: Studies*, p. 21.)

Value and use-value enter on a dialectic here in that *value*, although opposed to *use-value* in Section 1 of chapter one, cannot, in fact, be separated from its other, because the exchange transaction consists, in actuality, of the handing over of *use-values*; hence in exchange the value relations have to be mediated in the use-values and the role they play in the exchange relation. A product on its own does not have value; hence a commodity cannot express its value in its *own* form, as naturally constituted (i.e. as a use-value); but the *double form* of the commodity (viz. value and use-value) can find expression in the dialectical relation of identity and difference whereby the material use-value y takes on the form of the equivalent of the value of x.

That is to say, the identity of a commodity as a value cannot be expressed through equating it with itself; such a relation to its own self grasps only what it is *immediately*, namely a use-value. To be a value is to have a status as a *social* object, which status has to be mediated, therefore, through its equation to another commodity, immediately *different* from it, yet (in virtue of their common origin in the universal labour of society) of *identical social substance*. A value is identical with itself only in this its other because the substance of value being essentially social 'it can only appear in the social relation between commodity and commodity' (*Capital*, I, p. 139) — it has to appear as exchange-value, that is, in *mediated form*.

We see then, that in a purely formal analysis 'abstract opposites fall apart' — a is a and b is b; we are looking at the thing either as a use-value *or* as a value. Marx on the other hand, is dealing here with the social existence of the commodity as the interpenetration of opposites which are 'reflected against one another' in the value-form in such a way that 'x = x' cannot express a value relation where 'x = y' can — such is *the logic of the concrete*.

Let us turn now to the question of symmetry.

Lack of Symmetry in the Simple Form of Value

While it is clear that the value expression 'y = x' may be derived from that of 'x = y' because this relation has the property of symmetry, Marx stresses the point that these expressions must be taken in a definite direction such that, in the one, x is in relative form, and, in the other, in equivalent form: these are therefore two *different* expressions of value.

> 'The relative form of the value of linen . . .' presupposes that some other commodity confronts it in the equivalent form. On the other hand, this other commodity, which figures as the equivalent, cannot simultaneously be in the relative form of value. It is not the latter commodity whose value is being expressed. It only provides the material in which the value of the first commodity is expressed. Of course, the expression 20 yards of linen = 1 coat . . . also includes its converse: 1 coat = 20 yards of linen . . . But in this case I must reverse the equation, in order to express

the value of the coat relatively; and, if I do that, the linen becomes the equivalent instead of the coat. The same commodity
cannot, therefore, simultaneously appear in both forms in the
same expression of values. These forms rather exclude each other
as polar opposites.' (*Capital*, I, p. 140)

One essential asymmetry between the commodities in relative
form and in equivalent form is that as an equivalent a commodity has
the status of *immediate exchangeability* insofar as it represents *the
value of that in the relative form*, whereas in the relative form a commodity exchanges with its equivalent only through the mediation constituted through this other commodity expressing *its* value *relative to
the first*. (To anticipate our exposition a little) this problem is more
obvious if the equivalent is taken to be the money-commodity in that
people tend to assume that, unlike the things that express their values
in it, money has by nature the special quality of immediate exchangeability. The hypostatisation involved in attributing such a property to
the natural form of a commodity was not transcended by those who
recognised that gold is not the only use-value that can play the role of
money. Only Marx traced the form of immediate exchangeability to its
most primitive root in the relationship established in the simplest
expression of value, such as 20 yards of linen = 1 coat. (See *Capital*, I,
p. 149-40.)

If we take an exchange, we can consider the matter form the
point of view of either party, but Marx insists that there are concretely
two such points of view; and this must not be overlooked if we are to
stay close to the concrete character of exchange, and avoid getting en-
trapped in formalisms which omit this vital character of commodity
dynamics.

From the point of view of the owner of x the commodity y
features merely as its value equivalent. Of course, at the same time,
from the point of view of the owner of y it is x that is *its* equivalent. As
Marx puts it in the Appendix to Chapter 1 of First Edition of *Capital*, I:

'Here *both*, linen and coat, are at the same time in relative value-
form and in equivalent form. But, nota bene, for *two different
persons* and in *two different expressions of value*, which simply
occur *at the same time*'. (*The Value Form*, p. 135.)

In the course of explaining this point, Marx makes an interesting reference to *the principle of abstraction* (see above p. 72): after stressing
again that symmetry in exchange actually involves us in *two* different
expressions of value at the same time because each commodity *in turn*

must be taken in relative and equivalent form, he admits that we can draw from either formula, 'x = y' or 'y = x', the conclusion that the values of x and y are identical or equivalent. He says:

'We can also express the formula 20 yards of linen = 1 coat ... in the following way: 20 yards of linen *and* 1 coat *are equivalents* or *both are values of equal magnitude*. Here we do not *express the value* of either of the two commodities in *the use-value of the other. Neither* of the two commodities is hence set up *in equivalent form. Equivalent* means here only *something equal in magnitude*, both things having been silently reduced in our heads to the abstraction *value*.' (*The Value Form*, p. 138.)

Nothing could be clearer: if one loses one's grip on the *concrete character* of exchange, and the dialectic of the moments value and use-value, by moving into the realm of *abstraction* then of course 'in *our heads*' everything collapses into a lifeless abstraction—value; and the analysis of the value-form may as well be ignored since all we can discover is the vast tautology 'x = y = x = y = x'. This formalism is, of course, emminently suitable for abstract analysis whereby value precisely becomes nothing more than a standard measure of all things. Moore himself in the paper we cited misses the point precisely in this fashion when he says that in Universal Equivalent Form 'worth is measured by its price in terms of some arbitrarily selected standard commodity, a *numeraire*.' (Moore, 1963, p. 80). Even those like Ricardo who understand that the search for a standard commodity is misplaced and that it is necessary to analyse the *substance* of value in terms of labour do not realise that one cannot just assume the substance of value and then see each commodity merely as a given magnitude, a given portion of the total value produced, for these products only become commodities with value insofar as in reality (and not 'in our heads') *exchange imposes this equivalence* on them through a material process of commensuration (not an ideal comparison) whereby the value of each is externalised in the use-value of the other. The other here is the material equivalent of the first. This irreducible fact about the process of exchange cannot be removed by invoking a formal principle of symmetry leading to a principle of abstraction which reduces each to the same lifeless identity.

Lack of Symmetry in the Universal Equivalent Form

This becomes clear in the general form of value where a universal equivalent expresses the value of all other commodities. As we have said, we need to avoid that formalism which characterises the universal equivalent as a mere *numeraire*; rather we should grasp it as the concrete exclusion of one commodity from the others, as the incarnation of their *social* being as values and as products of abstract human labour. We cannot speak about a standard commodity in a way which presupposes that we are concerned with a range of values until we have proved the material validity of the category value, and, since this — value — *attains phenomenal expression* only through the value-form, it follows that the universal equivalent is by no means a simple convenience of the scientific observer for ordering his data, it is a very concrete necessity for the unification in value of the products of labour — the labour embodied in this universal equivalent represents all human labour (taken as abstracted from its various concrete forms). We have a universal order self-differentiated through the universal equivalent which *unifies* commodities as *values*, thus overcoming their *separateness* as *use-values*.

The opposition between the relative and equivalent forms of value, implicit in the simple form of value, articulates itself concretely in the universal equivalent form:

'In *form 1* the two forms already exclude one another, but *only formally*. According to whether the same equation is read forwards or backwards, each of the two commodities in the extreme positions, like linen and coat, are similarly now in the relative value-form, now in the equivalent-form. At this point it still takes some effort to hold fast to the polar opposition . . .

In *form 3* the *world of commodities* possesses general social relative value-form only because and insofar as all the commodities belonging to it *are excluded* from the *equivalent-form* or *the form of immediate exchangeability*. Conversely, the commodity which is *in the general equivalent form* or figures as *general equivalent* is excluded from the *unified* and hence *general relative value-form of the world of commodities*.' (*The Value Form*, p. 148; compare *Capital*, I, p. 160-61.)

Here then, *symmetry* breaks down, as it does in the money form as well, of course. In the *money form* we have a definite commodity, evolved through historical practice, playing the role of universal equivalent (gold is an obvious example). If other commodities may be formally equated as values with the money commodity it is not the case in fact that each can play the role of money (that is, have the form of universal equivalent — of immediate exchangeability). Marx comments:

'Like the relative form of value in general, price expresses the value of a commodity (for instance a ton of iron) by asserting that a given quantity of the equivalent (for instance an ounce of gold) is directly exchangeable with iron. But it by no means asserts the converse, that iron is directly exchangeable with gold ... Though a commodity may, alongside its real shape (iron for instance), possess an ideal value-shape or an imagined gold-shape in the form of its price, it cannot simultaneously be both real iron and real gold.' (*Capital*, I, p. 197.)

Lack of Transitivity in the Money-Form

We see here, also, that *transitivity* breaks down in a money economy. Marx says that 'if the owner of the iron were to go to the owner of some other earthly commodity, and were to refer him to the price of iron as proof that it was already money' (*Capital*, I, p. 197-8)—he would get a dusty answer, for the owner of this other commodity is not prepared to accept iron even though the iron is worth an amount of gold which is of equivalent value to his own product and for which he would gladly exchange it. Let us say this other commodity is a pound of saffron, then, even if one ton of iron = an ounce of gold = a pound of saffron, it may still be the case that the owner of the saffron will not part with it for the iron, but only for gold, or for some necessity he needs for consumption. One may in imagination take iron to be the universal equivalent, and all the equations will be formally correct, but the exchanges corresponding to them will not occur unless iron is in actuality the universal equivalent, that is, the money commodity. Hegel says:

'When the universal is made into a mere form and co-ordinated with the particular, as if it were on the same level, it sinks into a particular itself. Even commonsense in everyday matters is above the absurdity of settling a universal *beside* the particulars. Would anyone, who wished for fruit, reject cherries, pears and grapes, on the ground that they were cherries, pears or grapes, and not fruit?' (Hegel, 1975, p. 19.)

True—yet in the market-place vendors will reject various other commodities in exchange for their own on the ground that they are not *money*, their externalised identity as values. Only the money-commodity (e.g. gold) has the *social form* of universal equivalent (which gives it *immediate exchangeability*) in addition to its *formal* status as a value identical with others. In other words money is *not* a '*mere* form' of the abstract universal: value; rather, it *concretely mediates* the identity of values with each other.

A final point to consider is that, whereas people might concede 1lb of iron does not give its worth in itself, with money (since it has the social form of immediate exchangeability) the illusion arises that —just as it is—it *is* value: 'the movement through which this process has been mediated vanishes in its own result, leaving no trace behind.' (*Capital*, I, p. 187.)

Marx, however, insists that:

'the equivalent form of a commodity does not imply that the magnitude of its value can be determined. Therefore, even if we know that gold is money, and consequently directly exchangeable with all other commodities, this still does not tell us how much 10lb of gold is worth, for instance. Money, like every other commodity, cannot express the magnitude of its value except relatively in other commodities.' (*Capital*, I, p. 186.)

Hence, even though the value of other commodities is given as a function of the money-commodity, the identity function is a non-starter. This is because value emerges from the dialectical relations of commodity exchange; it is not an abstract essence inhering in a product in a pseudo-natural fashion.

Bibliography

Arthur, C J, 'Marx's Concrete Universal – Labour' in *Inquiry* 1978.

Bohm-Bawerk, E V, *Karl Marx and the Close of his System* (Merlin Press, London, 1975).

Cutler, A, Hussain, A, Hindess, B, Hirst P Q, *Marx's 'Capital' and Capitalism Today*, Volume I, (Routledge, London, 1977).

Hegel, G W F *Hegel's Logic* trans. W Wallace (Oxford University Press, 3rd ed., 1975).

Marx, K *Contribution to the Critique of Political Economy* (trans. N I Stone, Chicago, 1904).

Marx, K, 'Chapter One: The Commodity' from the first edition of *Capital* – in *Value: Studies by Marx*, trans. A Dragstedt (New Park, London, 1976).

Marx, K, 'The Value Form' (Appendix to first edition of *Capital*), trans. M Roth and W Suchting in *Capital and Class* 4, Spring, 1978.

Marx, K *Capital* Volume I, (Penguin, Harmondsworth, Middx, 1976).

Marx, K, Letters to Kugelmann, 13 October 1866; and to Engels, 22 June, 1867; in *Selected Correspondence* (Moscow, 1965).

Moore, S, 'The Metaphysical Argument in Marx's Labour Theory of Value' in *Cahiers de l'institut de Science Economique appliquee*, Supplt. No. 140, Aout 1963.

Tarski, A *An Introduction to Modern Logic*, Second ed., New York, 1946.

MISREADING MARX'S THEORY OF VALUE: MARX'S MARGINAL NOTES ON WAGNER

Athar Hussain

Directions for use

This article bears the mark of the context in which it appeared. It was published in a review named 'Theoretical Practice' which ceased publication in 1973. The aim of the review was to develop Marxist theory on the assumption that the analyses of Althusser and his associates had removed the obstacles which stood in the way of its further development. This article takes as its point of departure what has been crucial to Althusser's analysis, namely, the assumption that there is a scientific problematic—rules and relation governing discourse—which underlies *Capital* and that problematic has been masked by layers of the ideological readings of *Capital*—both by Marxists and non-Marxists. It is this assumption which makes *Marx's Notes on Wagner* of special importance; what this article does is to gauge the correctness or incorrectness of various readings of the sections of *Capital* on value by Marx's own comments on a gross misreading of *Capital* (in particular Section 1 on commodities) by a conservative German economist, Wagner. But once this assumption is removed the arguments of the article become vulnerable. What the assumption of scientificity does is to suspend those questions which cast doubt on the basic concepts of *Capital*, e.g. value, laws of tendency, etc. Now what we need to take into account is that the barrier to the development of Marxist theory is not simply the misreadings of *Capital*—of which there are many—but more importantly the concepts of *Capital* themselves.

* * *

Marx's Marginal Notes on Wagner's *Lehrbuch der politischen Okonomie* constitute one of his last texts. In his introduction to the French paperback edition of *Capital*, Althusser singles out this text for special mention:

> 'It reveals irrefutably the direction in which Marx's thoughts tended: no longer the shadow of a trace of Feuerbachian humanist or Hegelian influence.' (Althusser, 1971, p. 99.)

Thus, for Althusser, these Notes are important because they specify the epistemological break that detaches science from ideology.

In these Notes, Marx demonstrates that Wagner's reading of *Capital* takes the form of the suppression of conceptual distinctions and the transformation of concepts into free words, free in the sense that they can be replaced by other words. This transformation, like the rest of Wagner's *Lehrbuch*, is an effect of a specific problematic, the problematic of Philosophical Anthropology. The theoretical importance of this text derives from the fact that the problematic of Philosophical Anthropology is not confined to Wagner's *Lehrbuch* but, as will be demonstrated in this introduction, also governs more recent works, including those of certain revisionist economists. In these Notes, Marx not only read Wagner, but also reflects on his own problematic, which thus also makes these Notes nothing less than a reflection of the problematic governing *Capital*. This is the theoretical justification for Althusser's comment that these Notes reveal irrefutably the direction in which Marx's thoughts tended.

Wagner's discussion of *Capital* centres around the question of the theory of value. Before coming on to the specific effects of his ideological transformation of Marx's discourse, we should make one very general point. Wagner's comment that Marx's theory of value is *'the cornerstone of his socialist system'* assigns a teleology to the 'theory of value' and thereby denies its autonomy as scientific practice, autonomy in the sense of being governed by the laws specific to that practice. Marx's retort: *'As I have never set up a "socialist system" this is a fantasy of Wagner, Schaffle and tutti quanti'*, is his affirmation of the autonomy of 'historical materialism'. It is not subjugated to any ideology, not even to a revolutionary ideology. In the Preface to *A Contribution to the Critique of Political Economy*, Marx affirmed this autonomy of scientific practice in the following words:

'At the entrance to science, as at the entrance to hell, the demand must be made,

Qui si convien lasciare ogni sospetto;

ogni vilta convien che qui sia morta.'[1] (Op. cit., p. 23.)

Wagner, and as we shall see, he is not the only one, regards labour as the 'common social substance of exchange-value.' Marx points out that exchange-value is the necessary mode of expression (*Darstellungsweise*) of value, and the concept of value is different from the notion of exchange-value, which is invested in the commercial practice of the exchange of commodities. The difference between the two is the difference between 'what is represented' and the 'mode of representation of what is represented'. Marx goes on to specify the order of the discourse in *Capital*:

> 'The progress of our investigation will bring us back to exchange-
> value as the necessary mode of expression or phenomenal form of
> value, which, *however*, we have for the present to consider in-
> dependently of this form.' (*Capital*, I, p. 46, emphasis added.)

The 'order of the discourse', as Marx points out in the *1857 Introduction*,[2] is distinct from the order of concrete historical events. This
difference is a corollary of the fact that discursive practice is a process
in thought and the thought-object is different from the real object. This
particular difference reveals the error in the historicist reading of
Capital according to which the discussion of the concept of value precedes the analysis of the determination of prices of production (i.e.,
exchange-values denominated in terms of money which in general diverge from values), because prices in the initial stage of capitalism are
equal to values while in the later stages they are equal to prices of production.[3] The statement by Marx quoted above is based on a theo-
retically specified relation between value and exchange-value and
cannot be construed to specify the order of concrete historical events.

The statement that exchange-value is 'the necessary mode of expression or phenomenal form of value' is crucial to the specification of
the difference between Marx and the classical economists. Exchange-
value is the necessary mode of expression of value only under a specific
mode of production, i.e., one characterised by generalised commodity
production. The theoretical connection between value, exchange-value
and generalised commodity production is as follows: the generalised
commodity production specifies the 'social space', i.e. the capitalist
mode of production, in which value is represented in the form of exchange-value (see Ranciere, 1971). Throughout the first chapter of
Capital I, the terms 'value-form' and 'exchange-value' are used inter-
changeably, while the term 'natural form' is used to denote 'use-value'.
Wagner overlooks the theoretical connection between the concepts of
'value', 'exchange-value' and 'commodities'. Marx therefore has to re-
mind him that 'for me' (in the first chapter of *Capital* I), 'Neither
"value" nor "exchange-value" are subjects but commodities.'

Nearly all critiques of *Capital* by bourgeois economists from
Bohm-Bawerk to Joan Robinson[4] have been based on the assumption
that the first chapter of *Capital* is devoted to the quantitative determination of exchange-value. This particular assumption enables these
critics to replace the question asked in the text by another question:
what determines the exchange-value of commodities? Marx comments
on the effects of the problematic governing bourgeois political

economy:

> 'The few economists, among whom is S Bailey, who have occu-
> pied themselves with the analysis of form of value' (exchange-
> value) 'have been unable to arrive at any result, first, because they
> confuse the form of value with value itself; and second, because,
> under the coarse influence of the practical bourgeois they ex-
> clusively give their attention to the quantitative aspect of the
> question.' (*Capital*, I, p. 56n.)

The coarse influence of the practical bourgeois that Marx is referring to is the object invested in the commercial practice of exchange,
i.e., the quantitative magnitude of exchange-value. Marx points out in
these Notes that 'apart from this, as every promoter, swindler etc.
knows, there is certainly a formation of exchange-value in present day
commerce, which has nothing to do with the formation of value.'

The difference between Marx and Ricardo, which Wagner overlooks, is specified by Marx in *Capital*, I, when he writes:

> 'It is one of the chief failings of classical economy that it has
> never succeeded, by means of its analysis of commodities, and, in
> particular, of their value, in discovering that form under which
> value becomes exchange-value. Even Adam Smith and Ricardo,
> the best representatives of the school, treat the form of value as a
> thing of no importance, as having no connection with the in-
> herent nature of commodities. The reason for this is not solely
> because their attention is entirely absorbed in the analysis of the
> magnitude of value. It lies deeper. The value-form of the product
> of labour is not only the most abstract, but is also the most uni-
> versal form taken by the product in bourgeois production, and
> stamps that production as a particular species of social pro-
> duction, and thereby gives it its special historical character. If
> then we treat this mode of production as one eternally fixed by
> nature for every society, we necessarily overlook that which is
> the differentia specifica of the value-form, and consequently of
> the commodity form and capital form, etc. (*Capital*, I, p. 85n.)

Ricardo asked the question, what determines the magnitude of
value, and provided the answer to it, the value of a commodity is equal
to the labour embodied in it. Marx asks a different question, what is the
social structure (referred to as 'that form' in the above quotation) in
which the value of goods is represented in the form of exchange value?
Of course, the statement in the text quoted above is slightly ambiguous, for value does not *become* exchange-value, but is *represented* in

exchange-value, but this ambiguity is easily removed by referring to other passages from these Notes. Neither Ricardo nor any other bourgeois economist, classical or non-classical, asked the second question. Marx goes on to account for the absence of the second question in the following terms:

> 'If then we treat this mode of production as one eternally fixed by nature for every society, we necessarily overlook that which is the differentia specifica of the value-form'. (*Capital*, I, p. 85n.)

What does the statement beginning 'treat this mode of production' (the capitalist mode of production) refer to? Obviously not to the simple fact known from historical chronicles that capitalism has not always existed. In fact, Adam Smith gave a detailed account of the changes in the organisation of production in his discussion of the division of labour. The oversight of Ricardo et al. cannot be corrected by a simple injection of 'time perspective' or by providing that ambiguous 'historical angle' to which Dobb refers.[5] The oversight of Ricardo et al. is the oversight of their problematic; the 'treatment of this mode of production as one eternally fixed by nature' is a metaphoric (and hence ambiguous) reference to the problematic governing the discourse of Adam Smith and Ricardo. The main characteristic of that problematic is that it is directly or indirectly determined by the commercial and economic practices specific to the capitalist mode of production. The main effects of that determination, which are specified throughout *Capital*, are as follows:

(i) exclusive concentration on the quantitative magnitude of exchange-value;

(ii) the equation of 'surplus labour' with profit — a category which is specific to the capitalist mode of production;

(iii) the failure to distinguish between the value of labour and the value of labour-power.

The reason why Ricardo and bourgeois political economy do not ask the second question can be discovered by determining the theoretical requirements for answering it. The specification of the social structure in which exchange-value is the 'mode of expression of value' requires the concept of the 'mode of production' and the concepts required to specify the pertinent difference of a particular 'mode of production' *vis-a-vis* others. Marx's counter-question, i.e., the second question above, signifies the change of problematic. The object of the science of history is no longer conceived as a process with a subject, but as a process without a subject. This second question is a question of a specific problematic and it is also a 'non-question' of the problematic governing Ricardo's discourse; the absence of the question is the symptom of the problematic. It is this concept of a process without a subject that Marx owes to Hegel. Althusser points out that in Chapter one of *Capital* I, Ricardo provides the Generality I, the object of the theoretical labour, while Hegel's 'process without a subject' is used as Generality II, i.e., the means of transformation, to produce Generality III, i.e., historical knowledge.

I have given no demonstration of the assertion that Ricardo's problematic is that of a process with a subject. This demonstration would have to be based on a wider question which I cannot answer here: Is an ideological discourse necessarily governed by the problematic of a process with a subject? Ricardo's exclusive concern with the first question has the necessary consequence, as Marx points out in these Notes, that he can find no connection between his theory of value and the nature of money. Ricardo does not see that money need not be a commodity for generalised commodity production and money (including paper money) as a universal equivalent to be the effects of one and the same social structure, i.e., the capitalist mode of production. Ricardo confined his discussion of money to specie and regarded the value of coin as being equal to the value of the labour embodied in it. In this instance at least, two distinct features of the mode of production are reduced to expressions of labour, the activity of a subject, whereas for Marx the value form and the money form are distinct effects of the mode of generalised commodity production.

Wagner derives exchange-value and use-value from the concept of value. The so-called concept of value is derived by Wagner from 'Man's' natural drive to evaluate (*schatzen*) things of the external world *qua* goods, i.e., use-values. Wagner goes on to specify the mode of his derivation: 'One starts from the need and the economic nature of man, reaches the concept of the good, and links this to the concept of value.' Marx characterises this mode of derivation as follows: 'Now one can, assuming one feels the "natural drive" of a professor, derive the concept of value in general as follows: endow "the things of the external world" with the attribute "goods" and also "endow them with value" by name.' Marx goes on to point out that, 'But insofar as "attributing value" to the things of the external world is here only another form of words for the expression, endowing them with the attribute "goods", the "goods" themselves are absolutely not attributed "value" as a determination different from their "being goods" as Wagner would like to pretend.'

In other words, Wagner has set himself the task of excluding "use-value" from science. He manages this by a play on words. He derives the term value from the notion of goods, i.e., use-values, and then substitutes the term value for use-value. Wagner's reading transforms the two distinct concepts of the scientific discourse of *Capital* – value and use-value – into two words that are interchangeable with each other. What is the means of this transformation (or alternatively, what is the problematic that governs Wagner's reading of *Capital*)? Marx specifies it as follows:

> 'What lies in the murky background to the bombastic phrases is simply the immortal discovery that in all conditions man must eat, drink, etc. (one can go no further: clothe himself, have knives and forks or beds and housing, for this is not the case in all conditions); in short, that he must in all conditions either find external things for the satisfaction of his needs pre-existing in nature and take possession of them, or make them for himself from what does pre-exist in nature; in this his actual procedure he thus constatnly relates in fact to certain external things as "use-values", i.e., he constantly treats them as objects for his use; hence use-value is for Rodbertus a "logical" concept; therefore since man must also breathe, 'breath' is a "logical" concept, but for heaven's sake not a "physiological" one'.

In fact, Wagner's problematic is nothing but the problematic of Philosophical Anthropology, i.e. the Feuerbachian-humanist problematic of the early Marx. The characteristic features of this problematic can be schematically enumerated as follows:

> (i) History is a process with the subject 'Man'.
> (ii) The subject 'Man', his species-being in the terminology of Feuerbach and the early Marx, is endowed with certain attributes, e.g. he consumes, produces, creates, etc. These attributes, alternatively referred to as the predicates of the subject, constitute the essence of Man. The relation of the subject to its essence can vary within the problematic of Philosophical Anthropology between idealism of the essence and empiricism of the subject on the one hand, and idealism of the subject and empiricism of the essence on the other.
> (iii) The banal notion of alienation signifies the relation between the subject, the essence and the alien object.

Alienation signifies the embodiment of the essence into the alien object and the reversal of the relationship between subject and objects, subject and predicates. The following are the immediate effects of the problematic in economic theory:

(i) Consumption is always the consumption by the species-being 'Man' and not consumption by the supports (Trager) of the relations of production.

(ii) Production is always a relation between Man and nature and not a relation between communal labour (or collective labour) and nature.

The problematic of Philosophical Anthropology, as I have already pointed out, is not, however, restricted to Wagner's *Lehrbuch*. Wagner emphasises the anthropology of consumption, while others focus on the anthropology of production (the *homo faber* etc.); but in either case, the same subject 'Man' appears under a different mask determined by the variant of the problematic. This same problematic even appears in Maurice Dobb's introduction to the new English translation of *A Contribution to the Critique of Political Economy*, where it is particularly pernicious because of the trade-mark under which it is marketed—i.e., as an introduction to Marx by a Marxist economist. Dobb specifies Marx's problematic as follows:

'It is sometimes said that, whereas for Hegel the dialectic as a principle and structural pattern of development started from abstract Being as Mind or "Spirit", for Marx the dialectic of development started from Nature, and from Man as initially an integral part of Nature. But while part of Nature and subject to the determination of its laws, Man as a conscious being was at the same time capable of struggling with and against Nature—of subordinating it and ultimately transforming it for his own purposes.' (Dobb, 1971, p. 7.)

Further specific effects of the problematic of Philosophical Anthropology need to be pointed out. In the beginning of these Notes, Marx points out that 'Wagner does not distinguish between the concrete character of each kind of labour and the expenditure of labour power common to all these concrete kinds of labour.' If production is treated as the generic activity of 'Man' to satisfy his 'generic needs', then the determinate historical conditions in which labour, i.e., specific kinds of labour, is performed become invisible. The distinction between concrete labour and abstract social labour rests on the following two constituents of the conceptualisation of the process of production:

(i) production is always production of a specific good;

(ii) production qua production always takes place under determinate historical conditions.

These two aspects of the process of production are aptly specified in the *1857 Introduction*:

> 'Just as there is no production in general' (production always takes place under determinate historical conditions), 'so also there is no general production' (production is always a production of specific products). (Op. cit., p. 196-7.)

The concept of concrete labour refers to the fact (a fact which is not an empirical given but a construct of the general theory of modes of production) that labour is employed in the production of a specific product, while the concept of abstract social labour refers to the fact that labour is performed under specific historical conditions (or as Marx puts it in these Notes, 'the process of making a thing has a social character').

The distinction between abstract social labour and concrete labour is the unseen of the problematic of Philosophical Anthropology, since that problematic, by putting 'Man' in perpetual communion with Nature, suppresses the theoretical preconditions for specifying the determinate historical conditions in which production takes place. Faced with the patent presence of the verbal distinction in *Capital*, more careful readers than Wagner within this same anthropological problematic reduce it to a relation of 'alienation': labour power being a commodity in the capitalist mode of production, the concrete labour of human beings is 'fetishised' in the labour market into the alien form of abstract social labour. But this interpolation of 'reified' forms between 'Man' and Nature does not alter the misrecognition of the place of the relation between abstract social labour and concrete labours in the theory of the mode of production expounded in *Capital*.[6]

The problematic of Philosophical Anthropology also enables Wagner to import universal ethical standards into his discourse. On the basis of such standards ('Thou shalt not steal', etc.), Wagner equates the extraction of surplus-value under the capitalist mode of production with robbery. Such importations of ethical standards into political economy are not confined to Wagner. Joan Robinson, in *An Essay on Marxian Economics*, writes:

> 'Marx's method of treating profit as unpaid labour and the whole apparatus of constant and variable capital and the rate of

exploitation keep insistently before the mind of the reader a picture of the capitalist process as a system of piracy, preying upon the very life of the workers. His terminology derives its force from the moral indignation with which it is saturated.' (Op. cit., p. 22.)

Wagner is an apologist for capitalism, Joan Robinson a critic of it, but their respective readings of the concepts of variable and constant capital and the mode of extraction of surplus value in the capitalist mode of production are exactly the same. In these Notes, Marx makes the following comment on Wagner's reading:

'Now in my presentation profit on capital is in fact also not "only a deduction or 'theft' from the labourer". On the contrary, I represent the capitalist as the necessary functionary of capitalist production, and indicate at length that he does not only "deduct" or "rob" but enforces the production of surplus-value and thus first helps to create what is to be deducted; I further indicate in detail that even if in commodity exchange only *equivalents* are exchanged, the capitalist — as soon as he has paid the labourer the real value of his labour power — quite rightfully, i.e., by the right corresponding to this mode of production, obtains surplus-value.'

Note that what is at issue in Marx's comment is not the 'inhuman' effects of the extraction of surplus-value, i.e., of exploitation under the capitalist mode of production (e.g., the lengthening of the working day, disregard for the physical safety of the workers, etc.), but the right of expropriation corresponding to the capitalist mode of production, a right which receives superstructural representation in legal property rights.

While specifying and criticising Wagner's anthropological problematic, Marx also reveals the problematic governing *Capital* itself. Numerous comments interspersed throughout these Notes are unmistakable symptoms of Marx's problematic. To cite a few examples:

'According to Herr Wagner, use-value and exchange-value should be derived *d'abord* from the concept of value, not as with me from a concrete entity the commodity (*konkretum der Ware*).' (As we shall soon see, this '*konkretum der Ware*' is not the simple empirical presence of the commodity but the historical condition of existence of commodities.) 'Man, if this means the category "Man", then in general he has no needs.'

'Hence our *vir obscurus*, who has not even noticed that my analytic method, which does not start from man but from the economically given period of society, has nothing in common with the German professorial concept-linking method.'

'The labour process, as purposeful activity for the provision of use-values etc. "is equally common to all its" (human life's) "forms of society" and "independent of each of the same". Firstly the individual does not confront the word "use-value", but concrete use-values, and which of these "confront" (*gegenuberstehen*) him (for these people everything "stands" (*steht*), everything pertains to status (*Stand*)), depends completely on the stage of the social process of production, and hence always corresponds to "a social organisation".'

These last three quotations irrefutably point to a complete break with all the variants of Philosophical Anthropology. 'Man in general has no needs', implies the break with the anthropology of consumption; there are no 'generic needs' of the 'species-being' Man. Needs of concrete individuals are always needs in a determinate historical totality. Further on Marx points out that 'an individual's need for the title of Professor or Privy Counsellor, or for a decoration, is possible only in a quite specific "social organisation".'

However, these Notes do not merely give a symptomatic indication of the theoretical terrain of *Capital*; they go on to specify the order of the discourse and the theoretical function of specific concepts. The starting-point of economic discourse is indicated in a descriptive form at the beginning of *Capital*:

'The wealth of those societies in which the capitalist mode of production prevails presents itself as "an immense accumulation of commodities," its unit being a single commodity. Our investigation must therefore begin with the analysis of a commodity.' (*Capital*, I, p. 43.)

The Notes on Wagner, however, specify the beginning of economic discourse in the following terms: 'What I start from is the simplest social form in which the labour product is represented in contemporary society, and this is the "commodity".' The descriptive formulation of *Capital* has been replaced by a formulation based on the fundamental concepts of the general theory of modes of production. To elaborate: the labour-product, i.e., the end-product of economic practice, is represented in a 'social form' because, as I have pointed out above there is no 'production in general' and production always takes place under determinate historical conditions. The representation of the labour-product in a social form is the effect of the determinate historical conditions in which production takes place. The term 'contemporary society' here does not signify society in its immediate 'actuality' but the abstract concept of the existing society or social formation. Elsewhere in these Notes, Marx specifies this:

> 'If one is concerned with analysing the commodity – the simplest concrete entity – all the considerations that have nothing to do with the immediate object of analysis have to be put aside.'

Thus the 'konkretum der Ware' referred to above denotes the determinate historical conditions in which the labour product is represented as a commodity. Marx's statement in these Notes (*De prime abord* I do not start from "concepts" and hence do not start from the "concept of value" '), does not counterpose thought constructs or 'concepts' to 'real facts', but counterposes the 'concepts' specific to the problematic of Philosophical Anthropology to the concepts of 'Historical Materialism'. Marx does not start from the concept of 'value', because he had discarded the problematic of Philosophical Anthropology. He starts from the 'concepts' that underlie the statement: 'What I start from is the simplest social form in which the labour-product is represented in contemporary society.'

Later in the same passage, Marx specifies that while analysing the commodity in the form in which it appears he finds that it is on the one hand a 'use-value' and on the other hand a bearer of 'exchange-value'. Marx is not content with the dual representation of the commodity, but goes on to specify that exchange-value is only a 'phenomenal form' (*Erscheinungsform*), an independent mode of representation (*selbstandige Darstellungsweise*) of value. As I pointed out above, it is only under a specific mode of production that exchange is the mode of production of 'value'. Hence Marx's statement that exchange-value is a historical 'concept', i.e., the concept 'pertinent to' a specific mode of production. The specification of the relation between exchange-value and value leads Marx to modify his representation of the commodity: 'I say specifically. . .

> "When, at the beginning of this chapter, we said, in common parlance, that a commodity is both a use-value and an exchange-value, we were, accurately speaking, wrong. A commodity is a use-value or object of utility, and a 'value'".'

The commodity is represented as a two-fold thing because the mode of representation of value is distinct from the natural form of the commodity, i.e., the form qua use-value. It should be pointed out that the mode of representation of value (exchange-value) is distinct from value. Hence some of the ambiguous sentences in *Capital* which bourgeois commentators on Marx rely so heavily on have to be modified accordingly, for example, the following sentence from Chapter 3 of Volume I which is quoted by Robinson: 'Price is the money-name of the labour realised in a commodity.' (*Capital*, I, p. 103.)[7]

The 'value' of a commodity, as Marx points out in these Notes, expresses in a historically developed form something which also exists in every other historical form of society, but in different forms, namely the social character of labour, insofar as the latter exists as the expenditure of 'social' labour power. The substance of value, which, claims Marx in these Notes, Rodbertus, like Ricardo, does not understand, is the 'common character of the labour process'. What is it that gives the labour process a 'common character'? It is the 'relation' between production and consumption, and the concept of that 'relation' in Marx is the 'mode of distribution' of the labour product. If the 'mode of distribution' (which can take different forms, depending on the mode of production) is such that the producer of a good and the consumer of that good are not identical (*identitas indiscernibilium*), then the labour employed in the production of goods has the common character referred to above. In the illustration Marx cites in these Notes, the primitive community is described as the common organism of the labour powers of its members because of the combination of the mode of production with a mode of distribution such that the producer and the consumer of a good are not identical. The capitalist mode of production has a mode of distribution specific to it which is distribution by means of the exchange of equivalents. A substantial part of the much mis-read section of Chapter 1 on 'The Fetishism of Commodities' is concerned with the elaboration of the mode of distribution of commodities, but the discussion there is conducted in terms of 'inter-personal' relations, terms which provide ample scope for the misrecognition of the object of analysis. The Notes on Wagner, however, are completely free of the misleading formulations of the substance of value to be found in Chapter 1 of *Capital*. To give an example, the substance of value is specified in *Capital* as follows:

'Betrachten wir nun das Residuum der Arbeitsprodukte. Es ist nichts von ihnen ubriggeblieben als dieselbe gespenstige Gegenstandlichkeit, eine blosse Gallerte unterschiedloser menschlicher Arbeit, d.h. der Verausgabung menschlicher Arbeitskraft ohne

Rucksicht auf die Form ihrer Verausgabung.' (*Das Kapital* in Marx-Engels, *Werke*, Bd. 23, p. 53.) ('Let us now consider the residue of the labour-product. Nothing remains but this phantomnlike objectivity, a mere gelatinous mass of indistinguishable labour, i.e. of human labour power expended regardless of the form of its expenditure.' (Compare with *Capital*, I, p. 46.)

The substance of value is abstract social labour—abstract because it is labour power expended regardless of the form of its expenditure, social because of the common character of the labour process in the sense referred to above. As Marx argues in *Capital*,

'Magnitude of value expresses a relation of social production, it expresses the connection that necessarily exists between a certain article and the portion of the total labour-time of society required to produce it.' (Op. cit., Vol I, p. 104.)

The value of a good (not necessarily of a commodity, since the concept of value is not specific to the capitalist mode of production) represents the expenditure of social labour power because the labour-process has the 'common character' we have discussed. The law of value is thus the law of the distribution of the social labour force into different branches of production. In other words, the law of value specifies the relation between abstract social labour and concrete labour; Marx defines concrete labour on the basis of the branch of production in which the labour is employed. He defines the law of value in *Capital* in the following terms:

'The different spheres of production, it is true, constantly tend to an equilibrium: for, on the one hand, while each producer of a commodity is bound to produce a use-value, to satisfy a particular social want, and while the extent of these wants differ quantitatively, still there exists an inner relation which settles their proportion into a regular system, and that system is one of spontaneous growth; and, on the other hand, the law of value of commodities ultimately determines how much of its disposable working time society can expend on each particular class of commodities'. (Vol. I, p. 336.)

The distribution of the social labour force into the various branches of production in the capitalist mode of production is determined by the following:

(i) the mode of consumption specific to the mode of production;

(ii) the rate of exploitation, i.e., the necessary and surplus portions of social labour time;

(iii) the forces of production, which determine the composition of the means of production in each branch of production – the 'inner relation which settles their proportion into a regular system' referred to by Marx is the detailed matrix of the production of commodities by means of the commodities of Department I, i.e., those that constitute constant capital, and labour;

(iv) and the form of reproduction.

Each of these factors determines the distribution of the social labour force between Departments I and II, and between the branches of production constituting those Departments. The law of value expresses the 'over-determination' of the distribution of the labour force into different branches of production, assuming that labour is paid the full value of its labour power (Marx sees this assumption as a scientifically necessarily procedure, as he remarks in these Notes, whereas Schaffle saw it as 'generous' and others, e.g. Samuelson and Joan Robinson, have believed that Marx subscribed to the so-called 'theory of immiseration'). The factors listed above in a general form determine the distribution of the social labour force in the capitalist mode of production and are specific to that mode. Hence Marx's exclamation in these Notes, 'What a dreadful thing for the "social state"' (i.e., the future socialist society which Schaffle kindly constructed for Marx), 'to violate the *laws of value* of the capitalist (bourgeois) state.'

Thus it comes as no surprise that Marx affirms in these Notes that 'price formation makes absolutely no difference to the determination of value.' The connection between the law of value and the formation of prices can be formulated as follows. In Volume III, the 'prices of production', i.e. the set of prices that equalise the rate of profit in all branches of production, assuming a given rate of exploitation, are determined on the assumption that the social labour force is distributed such that each branch of production produces no more nor less than the amount demanded of the goods in question, *qua* means of production or consumption. 'Prices of production' are thus determined by the 'rate of exploitation' and the forces of production, which, as we have seen, define the 'matrix' of the production of the commodities. 'Prices of production' cannot be realised if there is an imbalance between branches of production, i.e. any branch of production producing more or less than the amount demanded of that particular good. The precondition for the realisation of 'prices of production' obtain if and only if the social labour force is distributed in such a way that there is a balance between different branches of production. The relation of interdependence between the distribution of the social labour-force into different branches of production and the quantitative composition of those branches of production is clear once it is taken into account that each product is the product of a series of concrete labours.

Hence there is no inconsistency between the analyses of Volumes I and III of *Capital*, despite the allegations of Bohm-Bawerk and *tutti quanti*. As these Notes make clear, the analyses of Volume I are based on abstract labour, labour as the expenditure of labour power irrespectively of the useful way in which it is expended. In consequence the analysis of the process of production in Volume I does not refer to any specific branch of production, despite all the concrete illustrations. The problem of the determination of prices, as a theoretical problem, arises only when a distinction is made between different branches of production. This is the justification for the assumption that price is equal to value, an assumption which is removed in Volume III, where the determination of prices is posed as a theoretical problem. This assumption and its subsequent removal do not represent any contradiction but instead 'the order of presentation' of the discourse of *Capital*.

In the Notes on Wagner, Marx suggests the answer to the following important question: Why is value represented in a 'social form' distinct from the natural form of the labour product, i.e., its form *qua* use-value? *Qua* product of social labour one good is indistinguishable from another, the distinction between goods being based on their respective attributes *qua* means of consumption or production, or in short *qua* their use-values. As Marx points out:

'If he (Rodbertus) had further investigated value, he would have found further that in it the thing, the "use-value", counts as a mere *objectification* of human labour, as an expenditure of equal human labour power, and hence that this content is represented as an objective character of the thing, as a (character) which is materially fitting for itself, although this objectivity does not appear in its natural form (but this makes a special value-form necessary).'

Marx had already answered this question by his use of illustrations in Chapter 1 of *Capital* I.

'In the production of the coat, human labour power, in the shape of tailoring, must have been actually expended. Human labour is therefore accumulated in it. In this aspect the coat is a depository, but though worn to a thread, it does not let this fact show through.') (p. 58.)

The independent value-form or, in other words, the representation (*Darstellung*) of value is not specific to the capitalist mode of production; it is the necessary effect of the 'common character of the labour process'. The specification of the mode of representation (*Darstellungsweise*) proper to each different mode of production (including the socialist mode of production) remains an unfinished theoretical task for historical materialism.

I hope that, notwithstanding the sketchiness of some of these arguments, of which I am well aware, I have succeeded in demonstrating the theoretical importance of the Notes on Wagner. The specific points of importance can be listed schematically as follows:

(i) an irrefutable proof of the epistemological break with all variants of Philosophical Anthropology;

(ii) an unmistakeable absence of Hegelian modes of expression in discussing the concept of value (this last point is of particular importance, for in *Capital* itself, as Marx wrote in his Afterword to the Second German Edition (1873), 'I . . . openly avowed myself to be the pupil of that mighty thinker (Hegel) and even here and there, in the chapter on the theory of value, *coquetted* with the modes of expression peculiar to him');

(iii) valuable indications as to the 'order of discourse' in *Capital*; and

(iv) a specification of the theoretical function of the concept of 'value' and of the nature of the relation between 'the formation of value' and 'the formation of prices'.

Notes

1. The verse can be translated as follows:
   'Here must all distrust be abandoned, all cowardice must here be dead'. (Dante Alighieri, *The Divine Comedy*, Inferno, III, 14-15.)
2. 'It would be inexpedient and wrong therefore to present the economic categories successively in the order in which they have played the dominant role in history. On the contrary, the relation of succession is determined by their mutual relations in modern bourgeois society and this is quite the reverse of what appears to be natural to them or in accordance with the sequence of historical

development.' (*1857 Introduction*, in *A Contribution* . . . , op. cit., p. 213). Note that the emphasis is on the presentation of economic categories in the sequence determined by the mutual relation of those categories in modern bourgeois society. The discussion of value precedes the analysis of the formation of exchange-values or prices of production because of the theoretical relation postulated. Exchange-value is a mode of representation (*Darstellungsweise*) of value. Analysis of the 'order of the discourse' might seem trite or pedantic. So-called 'history of ideas' fails to ask questions about the order of discourse because it implicitly or explicitly subscribes to the empiricist theory of knowledge, according to which the distinction between the order of the discourse and the order of concrete events is not a pertinent one. But once the thought object is distinguished from the real object, this distinction between 'the two sequences' becomes a crucial one.

3. This interpretation was unfortunately lent weight by a remark of Engels in the *Supplement to Capital Volume III*, that 'the Marxian law of value holds generally . . . for the whole period of simple commodity production, that is, up to the time when the latter suffers a modification through the appearance of the capitalist form of production' (Vol. III, p. 876). For a more detailed critique of this passage, and of historicist interpretations which rely on it, see Ranciere, 1965. By historicist here, I mean those whose discourse is governed by the problematic of a 'process with a subject'.

The main effects of a historicist problematic are as follows:

(1) History, regardless of its specific forms, is always governed by the same organising principle. For example, history is the history of the struggle of 'Man' with nature, or the history of 'challenges' and responses. (ii) Given the presence of a single organising principle, the historicist problematic suppresses the concepts of the pertinent distinction between one social formation and another, as a necessary effect. The absence of these concepts of pertinent difference in the historicist discourse is represented in the equivalence of 'historical' and 'physical' time. (iii) The historicist problematic is always blended with either empiricism or idealism. The political effects of the historicist problematic take the form of 'reductionism', e.g. economism or ultra-left adventurism. There are many different variants of historicism.

4. Eugen von Bohm-Bawerk was an Austrian economist of the marginalist school. His book *Karl Marx and the Close of his System* (1896) is based on the alleged contradiction between the analyses of Volumes I and III (see below). Most bourgeois commentators still regard Bohm-Bawerk's critique as a definitive refutation of Marx.

See Eugen von Bohm-Bawerk: *Karl Marx and the Close of his System* (ed. P M Sweezy), Augustus M Kelly, New York 1966 — this translation includes Hilferding's reply to the critique. For Joan Robinson, see her book *An Essay on Marxian Economics*, Macmillan, London 1967.

5. In his introduction to *A Contribution* . . . , Dobb writes, 'The historical perspective from which he (Marx) surveyed the emergent "bourgeois" (capitalist) society of his day at once sets the distinctive focus and emphasis of his economic theory as well as its boundaries (both focus and boundaries which differentiate it sharply from the increasingly narrowed theories of "market equilibria" that were to characterise accepted economic theory at the end of the century and in the present century)' (op. cit., p. 6).

6. I am forced here to link with Adolph Wagner the name of as serious a Marxist scholar and theoretician as Lucio Colletti: 'In the production of commodities, . . . where social labour is presented as *equal* or *abstract* labour, the latter is not merely calculated irrespective of the individual and concrete labours, but also acquires a distinct existence independent of them. . . This *abstraction* of labour from the concrete labouring subject, this acquisition of its independence from man, culminates in the form of the modern wage labour . . . etc.' (Colletti, 1970).

7. Ibid., p. 14. Joan Robinson reads in *Capital* what she wants to read rather than what is there to be read. On the page following the one from which this quotation is taken, Marx goes on: 'Magnitude of value expresses a relation of social production, it expresses the connection that necessarily exists between a certain article and the portion of the total labour-time of society required to produce it . . . The possibility, therefore, of quantitative incongruity between price and magnitude of value, or the deviation of the former from the latter, is inherent in the price-form itself' (p. 102). Robinson never asks how on earth the sentence 'price is the money name of the labour realised in a commodity' implies that price is determined by the magnitude of value. (It should be pointed out that these quotations — the one cited by Joan Robinson and the two cited in this footnote — appear in two different paragraphs in the English edition, but in a single one in the German edition: i.e. they constitute part of the same argument. See *Das Kapital* in Marx-Engels: *Werke*, Bd. 23, pp. 116-7.)

Bibliography

Althusser, L, 'Preface to *Capital* Volume One', in *Lenin and Philosophy and Other Essays*, New Left Books, London, 1971.

von Bohm-Bawerk, E *Karl Marx and the Close of his System* (ed. P Sweezy), Augustus Kelly, New York, 1966.

Colletti, L *Ideologia e Societa*, Laterza, Bari, 1970.

Dobb, M, 'Introduction', to *A Contribution to the Critique of Political Economy*, Lawrence and Wishart, London, 1971.

Marx, K, *A Contribution to the Critique of Political Economy*, Lawrence and Wishart, London, 1971.

Marx, K *1857 Introduction*, in *A Contribution* . . . , op. cit.

Marx, K *Capital*, Lawrence and Wishart, London, 1974.

Marx, K *Das Kapital*, in Marx-Engels, *Werke*, Bd. 23.

Marx, K, 'Marginal Notes on Adolph Wagner's "Lehrbuch der politischen Okonomie" ', translated in *Theoretical Practice*, No. 5, Spring 1972, pp. 40-64.

Ranciere, J, 'The Concept of Critique and the Critique of Political Economy', *Theoretical Practice*, No. 2, April 1971, p. 37-47.

Robinson, J *An Essay on Marxian Economics*, Macmillan, London 1967.

MARX'S THEORY OF MARKET VALUE

Makoto Itoh
in collaboration with Nobuharu Yokokawa

The Problems in Marx's Theory of Market-Value

After transforming values of commodities into prices of production (*Capital*, III, chapter 9), Marx goes on to discuss market-value in Chapter 10, under the heading: 'Equalisation of the General Rate of Profit Through Competition. Market Prices and Market-Values. Surplus Profit'. Let us first examine the major contents of this complex chapter. It starts off with a review of the logical relation between values and prices of production. According to Marx's transformation procedure,

> 'In the case of capitals of average, or approximately average, composition, the price of production is ... the same or almost the same as the value, and the profit the same as the surplus-value produced by them. All other capitals, of whatever composition, tend toward this average under pressure of competition.' (*Capital*, III, p. 174.)

Therefore

> 'the sum of the profit ... must equal the sum of the surplus value, and the sum of the price of production ... equal the sum of its value'. (*Capital*, III, p. 173.)

Then Marx suggests:

> 'The really difficult question is this: how is this equalisation of profit into a general rate of profit brought about, since it is obviously a result rather than a point of departure?' (*Capital*, III, p. 174.)

Marx seems to answer this question near the end of this chapter, observing that it is capitalist competition which equalises different rates of profit in value terms into a general rate through redistribution of capital. We read:

'If the commodities are sold at their values, then, as we have shown, very different rates of profit arise in the various spheres of production, depending on the different organic composition of the masses of capital invested in them. But capital withdraws from a sphere with a low rate of profit and invades others, which yield a higher profit. Through this incessant outflow and influx, or, briefly, through its distribution among the various spheres, which depends on how the rate of profit falls here and rises there, it creates such a ratio of supply to demand that the average profit in the various spheres of production becomes the same, and values are, therefore, converted into prices of production'. (*Capital*, III, p. 195.)

Should we understand from this exposition that the allocation of dead and living labour regulated by capital will be changed when values are converted into prices of production? If the equilibrium ratio of supply and demand of each commodity under value relations differs from that under prices of production, can we still regard the former as an actual framework for the analysis of capitalist economy, not as a mere imaginary assumption without any actuality? These problems throw us back to a more fundamental point, i.e. how to prove the real relevance of the equal exchange of abstract labour embodied in commodities. Marx refers to this point just after his question about the formation of a general rate of profit, by asking

'how does this exchange of commodity at their real values come about?' (*Capital*, III, p. 175.)

To answer this, Marx presents a model of exchange by simple commodity producers where

'the labourers themselves are in possession of their respective means of production and exchange their commodities with one another'. (*Capital*, III, p. 175.)

and he proceeds to make a famous statement that

'the exchange of commodities at their values, or approximately at their values, thus requires a much lower stage than their exchange at their prices of production, which requires a definite level of capitalist development.' (*Capital*, III, p. 177.)

Engels in the 'Supplement to Capital, Volume III', and then Rudolf

Hilferding in his anti-critique of Bohm-Bawerk (See Sweezy (ed.), 1949), extended this view and asserted a historical-logical transformation theory from values into prices of production. However, the historical-logical transformation theory could not be a final solution. First, simple commodity producers cannot dominate a whole society, unlike capitalist producers, and as a result their exchange relations are not necessarily regulated by *socially* necessary labour expenditures. Secondly, Marx's *Capital* from Part III, Volume I onwards, clearly analyses capitalist production, and not a pre-capitalist economy, on the basis of the law of value. Marx's treatment of cost prices in his theory of prices of production also remained incomplete just as Bortkiewicz pointed out. (See Sweezy (ed.), 1949).

In order to overcome these transformation problems, I believe that it is essential to clarify and to utilise Marx's original distinction of the forms and the substance of value. We have to observe the prices of production as a developed form of value, and study how they are determined by the dimensionally different quantity of abstract labour time embodied in commodities, as the social substance of value. The role of prices of production in mediating the social distribution of the labour amounts also has to be clarified. This perspective has been elaborated elsewhere (Itoh, 1976), and will not be repeated here. For our topic is not transformation problems as such. But as we shall see later, it is important to review Marx's theory of market-value in this context, considering its logical relation with the proper theory of prices of production.

After reconsidering the case of the exchange of commodities at their real values, Marx then moves on to investigate how the unique market-value is determined in the case where the individual values of the same kind of commodities are unequal because of the differences in their conditions of production. This investigation of market-value occupies the major portion of this chapter. Marx's attempt to formulate a theory of market-value, however, was not fully completed. In particular, he seems to leave us with two contradictory theories.

One of them defines market-value as determined by the conditions of production. For instance, Marx says in this context:

'On the one hand, market-value is to be viewed as the average value of commodities produced in a single sphere, and, on the other, as the individual value of the commodities produced under average conditions of their respective sphere and forming the bulk of the products of that sphere.' (*Capital*, III, p. 178.)

In this definition the market-value is regarded as the average of different individual values of commodities produced under different conditions of production, or as the individual value of commodities produced under average and dominant conditions of production. This can be called the 'technical average' theory of market-value. Strictly speaking, the average and the dominant (or most common) conditions of production do not always have the equality which it assumes. In this theory, the situation of demand and supply in the market does not play any role in determining the level of market-value, though it causes fluctuations in market prices around the centre of gravity of market-value.

In contrast, Marx's second theory gives demand an important role in determining the market-value. Marx says for example:

'. . . if the demand is so great that it does not contract when the price is regulated by the value of commodities produced under the least favourable conditions, then these determine the market-value. This is not possible unless demand is greater than usual, or if supply drops below the usual level . . . if the mass of the produced commodities exceeds the quantity disposed of at average market-values, the commodities produced under the most favourable conditions regulate the market-value'. (*Capital*, III, p. 179.)

In this context,

'it is one of the extremes which determines the market value' (*Capital*, III, p. 185).

not the technical average condition of production. We can call this the demand and supply theory of market-value.

Throughout chapter 10 of *Capital*, III, Marx repeatedly states these two different theories. In which direction should we complete Marx's theory of market-value? Or can we unify Marx's intentions expressed in the two theories? Finally, how should we reconcile the theory of market-value with the theory of prices of production? We shall investigate these points by reviewing Japanese debates on this issue.[1] We hope that our investigation will clarify an important aspect of Marx's value theory, and also give an essential theoretical foundation for the theory of ground rent which has just begun to attract the attention of western Marxists.

The Technical Average Theory of Market-Value

If the ratio of demand to supply determines the level of market-value, it may obscure the determination of value by the quantity of abstract labour embodied in the production of the commodity, and it may resemble the marginalist demand and supply theory of price. In order to avoid such a position, the majority of Marxists have traditionally preferred Marx's first definition of market-value, and interpreted the market-value as determined by the average labour time technically necessary to produce a given commodity. This type of interpretation is presented for instance by Itsuro Sakisaka and Masahiko Yokoyama in Japanese debates. According to this technical average theory of market-value, changes in the relation between demand and supply can bring about only deviations of market prices from market-values, so long as the conditions of production remain unchanged. For us, this interpretation raises the question of whether Marx simply made a mistake in presenting the second theory of market-value. Or whether we can make consistent Marx's two theories of market-value? Various attempts have been made to answer these questions. Yokoyama (1955) gives one of the most orthodox interpretations (drawing on Rosenberg (1962-64)). According to Yokoyama, Marx's second type of explanation really concerns a case where the market-value is changed by a shift in the ruling technical conditions (op. cit., p. 147). It is only consistent with the first type of explanation where the increased social demand is satisfied overwhelmingly by the increased supply of commodities produced under the least favourable conditions so that the commodity produced under this condition now forms the bulk of the production of the commodity; or, conversely, where over production excludes commodities produced under worse conditions so that the most favourable conditions become those under which the bulk of the commodity is produced. (op. cit., p. 147-9). This is an attempt to give a consistent interpretation to Marx's second theory of market-value from the viewpoint of the technical average theory. This cannot provide a substantial integration of Marx's different views. First, the least or the most favourable condition of production cannot be a single regulator of market value in the technical average theory, in so far as other conditions do still exist. Secondly, this assertion is easily criticised as an arbitrary interpretation, because Marx himself does not refer to the alteration of the proportional weight of the worse or the better conditions of production in his second version of the theory.

In order to make the explanation entirely consistent with the determination of market-value by the technical average of conditions of production, Fumimaru Yamamoto (1962) came up with the ingenious suggestion that the words 'market-values' in Marx's second theory must all be misprints of 'market prices'. If this were true, there is no 'second theory' and Marx's position is simply reduced to the proposition that the alteration of the relation between demand and supply affects only the market prices but not market-values. However, Yamamoto could give no bibliographical evidence for his misprints theory, and perhaps not surprisingly he could obtain no followers for this interpretation.

Yuichi Ohshima (1974) attempts to be less one-sided. He thinks that Marx's first theory should be regarded as the general theory of market-value, whereas the second theory should not be abandoned but located as a special theory to analyse such cases as monopolistic pricing, some aspects of industrial cycles and the logic of differential rent. However, even in this interpretation, the general and the special theories are not integrated. They are just separated into the different cases. And the technical average theory is regarded as the general theory of market-value without taking the role of the market into consideration. In this way, the importance of the considerations discussed in the second version of the theory is still neglected.

Uno's Theory of Market-Value

The first and the second versions of the theory of market-value originally coexisted without any clear inner relation in Marx's own texts. In the first version, Marx defined market-value entirely on the basis of the static combination of conditions of production, without considering the fluctuaticn of demand and supply in the market. Whereas in the second, Marx seemed to claim that changes in the ratios between demand and supply immediately determined the regulative condition of production for market-value; As a result, in this version the fluctuation of market-values was not easily distinguishable from that of market prices.[2] Attempts to merely add together the two theories, or to maintain the first theory as it stands are both more or less unsatisfactory. We have to try to develop the theory in the direction for which Marx was searching in his dual notion of market-value.

The notion of *market*-value should not be a merely static and technical definition of value, but it should be related to the dynamic of the market. At the same time, market-value must be presented as the regulator of market prices through the fluctuations of the market. A complete notion of market-value must satisfy these requirements. From such a point of view, Kozo Uno attempted a more substantial reconstruction of Marx's dual theory, by suggesting the notion of market-value as 'social value determined through the mediation of market'. (Uno, 1950-52, Vol. 2, p. 90.) To quote Uno further,

> 'The market-value as the gravitating centre of market price is determined on the basis of an equilibrium of demand and supply. This means that the supply of a commodity increases in relation

to the demand for it when the market price raises above the
centre, and decreases in the reverse case. Thus, the determination
of the market-value of a commodity depends upon the condition
of production under which the supply of the commodity is
adjusted.to the fluctuating demand'. (Uno, 1964, p. 159.)

In this view, the motion of demand and supply in the market, observed
in Marx's second theory of market-value, is not related to the fluctuations of market price alone. On the contrary, through the fluctuations
of the market price, the commodity economy reveals anarchically
under what conditions of production the necessary amount of commodities for the social demand is supplied, showing the level of market-
value as the centre of the gravitation of market price. In general, there
is no reason to suppose that the regulative condition of production will
be one of the extremes, 'on the margin'. Of course, the market-value
itself also changes when the regulative condition of production changes.
However, such a shift of market-value cannot be directly deduced from
observing conditions of production in commodity economy, but must
be sought out through the anarchical fluctuations of market price. We
see here how the commodity economy actually makes the social value
apparent via the motion of market competition while various individual
values exist corresponding to the different conditions of production.[3]
At the same time, the theory of market-value shows the adjustment
mechanism of the distribution of socially necessary labour to each
sphere of commodity production: the regulative (or standard) condition of production in each sphere is revealed through the motion of
market prices. Uno's theory of market-value makes clear these important aspects of value theory as an extension of Marx's dual theory of
market-value.

Let us proceed further, to the next problem, namely: what are
included in the differences of condition of production which should be
discussed here in the theory of market-value? Three sorts of differences
in production conditions are conceivable. The first is differences in
condition of production which appear in the process of technical
improvements of the method of production. Secondly, differences in
the scale of capital may result in differences in the cost and the conditions of production of the commodity, even on the same technical
basis. The third sort relates to the different and restricted natural conditions represented by land.

Clearly, the first sort of difference of production conditions contains substantially the same problem which is discussed in the theory of
temporary extra surplus-value in the first volume of *Capital*, (p. 300-
302). This sort of difference appears and disappears from time to time

in the process of technical progress. Hence Uno sometimes suggested that this sort of difference should be regarded as a special case in the theory of market-value. Opposing the orthodox technical average theory of market-value, Uno asserted that differences in natural conditions of production (i.e. land) are directly related to the general theory of market-value. He located the theory of differential rent as an extended development, and not as a revision, of the theory of market-value.

But if technical differences in method of production are strictly regarded as a special case, then, does not Uno's theory of market-value come to depend too much upon persisting differences in conditions of production such as the scale of capital or the grade of land? In our opinion, Uno's notion of market-value shows rather the general formal determination of social value via the market, which is broadly common to *all* three sorts of differences in production conditions. In this reformulation, the mere average of individual values does not define market value. However, we think that the variant on the 'technical average' theory which defines market value as regulated by the technically dominant or most common condition of production is still substantially relevant to this reformulated theory in the first two cases. For the production condition under which the supply of the commodity is adjusted to the fluctuating demand ordinarily appears as the dominant and most common condition, in the case where it relates either to the technical conditions or to the scale of capital. In contrast, in the case of the restricted natural conditions of production in land, the marginal worst condition which is necessary to satisfy the social demand becomes the regulator of market-value. Therefore, the theory of competition among capitals requires here a specific theory of ground rent, which shows the specific social substance of differential rent.

In order to clarify further the nature of the social substance of value in these different cases, we have to investigate the substance of the extra surplus-value due to uneven technical progress and the substance of the extra profit which is converted into differential rent. The technical average theory interpreted the extra surplus-value acquired by capitalists with superior conditions of production as substantially a transfer of value from the other capitalists in the same sphere operating under production conditions worse than average. However, this interpretation is obviously inapplicable to the case of differential rent, where the worst marginal land regulates the market-value, so that all the commodities produced on better land have a higher market-value than their individual values. In this case, the balance between the market-value and the individual value does not seem to be mutually cancelled by the transfer of the substance of value within the same sphere of production. Hence Marx called this balance which is converted to differential rent 'a false social value'. (*Capital*, III, p. 661). It is a difficult problem for the technical average type of market-value theory to explain the social source of this 'false social value'. But before discussing this problem further we shall investigate the logical relation between the theory of prices of production and that of market-value.

Prices of Production and Market-Value

The critical question here is whether to pose the determination of market-value as something quite separate from the determination of price of production. The technical-average theory of market-value makes such a separation because it does not take the role of the anarchic market process into account in the determination of market-value. But in our view there are not two separate mechanisms. Rather there is a single process of competition in which both intra- and inter-sectoral competition play a role and which determines what Marx called 'market prices of production'. (*Capital*, III, p. 198). It seems to us clear, both from the title and the structure of Chapter 10, *Capital*, III, that Marx did intend to relate market-value to price of production.

Uno's theory of market-value helps to clarify this point. According to Uno, the representative condition of production, which determines market-value, is only defined through an anarchic process of intra-sectoral market competition. The pin-pointing of this representative condition of production is necessary for inter-sectoral competition between capitals. Only with reference to such a standard in each sector can profit rates across sectors be compared, and re-allocations of capital tending to equalise those rates take place. At the same time, intra-sectoral competition would be extremely limited and weak without inter-sectoral competition, and thus the latter is a necessary aspect of the definition of market-values.

The theory of prices of production is in a sense more basic than the theory of market-value in developing the law of value as the capitalist law of social reproduction. Nevertheless, the theory of the formation of prices of production through capitalist competition cannot be complete in so far as it lacks a theory of the formation of market-value by competition in each sector. Hence, the theory of market-value should be discussed later than the theory of prices of production, and should be regarded as an integral extension of the theory of prices of production. In this respect, I would like to agree with the suggestion raised by Tsuyoshi Sakurai (1968) and more definitely proposed by Koichiro Suzuki (1962-64) that intra-sectoral capitalist competition should not be discussed as a matter of market-value but as a matter of market price of production from the beginning.

Needless to say, even with an integrated theory of prices of production and market prices of production, we see that capitalist competition to equalise the rate of profit across industrial sectors does not eliminate but necessarily brings about the extra profit to capitalists with better conditions of production than the standard, and therefore representative, conditions in each sector. We can now observe the substance of value obtained in the form of such surplus profit from a new angle. In contrast to the case of the technical average theory of market-value, we need not limit the substantial source of extra profit gained by individual capitals using improved methods of production to the surplus labour extracted in the *same* sector of industry. The substance of this extra profit can be the transfer of surplus labour extracted in other industrial sectors, just as the substance of some portion of average profit, in the formation of market prices of production consists of transfers of surplus labour from other sectors. At the same time, such a source of extra profit becomes logically conceivable even in the case where capital of worse than the standard condition of production does not exist, and therefore where there is no countervailing transfer of the substance of value within the *same* industrial sector. This is also true of the substance of the extra profit which is converted into the differential rent. Marx called such a portion of value 'false social value' or 'what society overpays for agricultural products in its capacity as consumer'. (*Capital*, III, p. 661). This cannot mean in principle a creation of the substance of value by capitalist competition, nor a deduction from the substance of value of labour power. Therefore, the substance of the differential rent should be regarded as the transfer of a part of social surplus labour to land owners through capitalist competition to determine the market price of production of agricultural products.[4]

We must certainly clarify the different historical meaning and function of the two kinds of extra profit discussed above. The former, which must be investigated also as the matter of temporary extra surplus value, presented in the first volume of *Capital*, serves as an incentive to improve methods of production and thus to generate the social production of relative surplus value. As Uno suggests, it may contain the socially necessary labour cost of improving production methods, a cost which is common to more or less all forms of society, and certainly to a socialist society. In contrast, the extra profit which is converted to the differential rent does not have this positive role in increasing productivity, nor does it have a common basis in other forms of society. In that sense, differential rent is simply eliminated under socialism, where the total labour embodied in agricultural products is directly estimated by the actual number of labour hours. The above arguments help to dispel the notions that when labour is combined with improved production methods, it creates temporary extra surplus value as *intensified* labour; or that 'false social value' in agriculture is *created* in the process of capitalist competition. By integrating the theory of price of production and the theory of market value into a theory of market price of production, and by distinguishing the form and substance of the latter, we can come to a better understanding of the way the capitalist economy works.

Notes

*The authors would like to thank Sue Himmelweit and Diane Elson for their assistance in clarifying the text and turning it into readable English.

1. It is already known from the English edition of Isaak I Rubin's book, *Essay on Marx's Theory of Value*, that there was a controversy between Marxian economists about the concept of socially necessary labour in the 1920s in Germany and the USSR. The two versions of the theory of socially necessary labour were summarised by Rubin as follows:

   'An "economic" concept of necessary labour is that the value of a commodity depends not on the productivity of labour (which expresses that quantity of labour necessary for the production of a commodity under given average technical conditions), but also on the social needs or demand. Opponents of this conception ("technical" version) object that changes in demand which are not accompanied by changes in productivity of labour and in production technique bring about only temporary deviations of market prices from market-values, but not long-run, permanent changes in average prices, i.e., they do not bring about changes in value itself. (Rubin, 1973, p. 185.)

2. Roman Rosdolsky (1977, p. 92), for example, represents a position which is contrary to the orthodox technical average theory, and follows Marx's demand and supply theory of market-value just as it stands. He asserts that market-value is identical with market price within the range of individual values between those of the best and the worst condition of production in the same industry.

3. Though the redefinition of market-value in this way may seem close to Marshallian Marginal theory, it is not in its essence. Unlike the marginalist, we do not take demand for a subjective, individualistic

and independent factor which determines the equilibrium price. The fluctuations of demand are to be observed in our view, on the one hand, as a reflection of the anarchical motion of commodity production, and on the other, as the intermediary mechanism revealing the level of social value, which is basically determined from behind by the standard condition of production. In our view, the neo-Ricardians one-sidedly emphasize the technical conditions of production as the determinant of prices, ignoring the role of market competition. The so-called 'indeterminancy of social value' when a commodity is produced under different technical methods with the same cost, which figures in the recent neo-Sraffian critique of Marx, seems at least partly to come from the neglect of such a dynamic role of market competition in revealing the regulative condition of production.

Moreover, our theory of market-value is not a mere formal theory of price like those of the Marginalists or the neo-Ricardians, but also a theory which reveals the relations of labour quantities as the substance of values. Thus, our theory aims at the elucidation of the historically specific form in which, in the (capitalist) commodity economy, differences in labour-time necessary to produce the same sort of good, which arise from differences in production conditions, are related to one another.

4 As Robin Murray (1978) suggests, the surplus labour which is transferred from capitalists to land owners can be within the total surplus labour extracted in the agricultural sector, in so far as the organic composition of capital in agriculture is sufficiently lower than the social average. Such a restrictive condition is not, however, essential for the Marxian principle of differential rent in our view.

Bibliography

Itoh, M (1976), 'A Study of Marx's Theory of Value', *Science and Society*, 40-43, Fall.

Marx, K (1959), *Capital*, III, *The Process of Capitalist Production as a Whole*, Lawrence and Wishart, London.

Murray, R (1978), 'Value and Theory of Rent', Part I, *Capital and Class*, No. 3.

Ohshima, Y (1974), *Kakaku to Shihon no Riron* (*Theory of Price and Capital*) Chapter 7: Shijyo-Kakaku to Shijyo-Kachi (Market Price of Production and Market-Value), Mirai-sha, Tokyo.

Rosdolsky, R (1977), *The Making of Marx's Capital*, translated by Pete Burgess, Pluto Press, London.

Rozenberg, R I (1962-64), *Comment on K Marx's Capital*, Moscow 1961, Japanese edition, 5 vols, translated by T Soejima and M Udaka, Aoki-shoten, Tokyo.

Rubin, I I (1973), *Essay on Marx's Theory of Value*, Black Rose Books Ltd., Montreal.

Sakisaka, I (1962), *Marx Keizaigaku no Kihonmondai (The Fundamental Problems in Marxian Economics)*, Part III, Chapter 3: Shijyo Kachiron to Sotaiteki-Jyoyo-Kachiron (The Theory of Market-Value and the Theory of Relative Surplus Value), Iwanami-shoten, Tokyo.

Sakurai, T (1968), *Seisan Kakaku no Riron (Theories of Price of Production)*, University of Tokyo Press, Tokyo.

Suzuki, K ed. (1962-64), *Keizaigaku Genriron*, 2 Vols *(Principles of Political Economy)*, University of Tokyo Press, Tokyo.

Sweezy, P ed. (1949) *Karl Marx and the Close of His System* by Eugen von Bohm-Bawerk and *Bohm-Bawerk's Criticism of Marx* by Rudolf Hilferding, Kelley, New York.

Uno, K (1950-2), *Keizai Genron*, 2 vols, *(Principles of Economics)*, Iwanami-shoten, Tokyo.

Uno, K (1964), *Keizai Genron (Priciples of Economics)*, Iwanami-shoten, Tokyo. (We consulted Tomohiko Sekine's translation of this work which is ready for publication in English.)

Yamamoto, F (1962), *Kachiron Kenkyu (Studies on the Theory of Value)*, Chapter 4: Dai 3-kan dai 10-sho ni okeru "Fumeiryo na Kasho" no Kentou (Studies on the "Ambiguous Parts" of Chapter 10 in the Third Volume), Aoki-shoten, Tokyo.

Yokoyama, M (1955), *Keizaigaku no Kiban (Foundations of Economomics)*, Part III: *Marx Kachi-Kakaku-Ron no Kihon Mondai (Fundamental Problems in Marx's Theory of Value and Price)*, University of Tokyo Press, Tokyo.

THE VALUE THEORY OF LABOUR

Diane Elson

WHAT IS MARX'S THEORY OF VALUE A THEORY OF?

1. The theory of value: a proof of exploitation?

Let us first consider the interpretation which is very widespread on the left, particularly among activists, that Marx's theory of value constitutes a proof of exploitation. A good example of this position in CSE debates is that put forward by Armstrong, Glyn and Harrison. Their dogged defence of value rests on the belief that only by employing the category of value can the existence of capitalist exploitation be demonstrated and that to demonstrate this is the point of Marx's value theory:

> Any concept of surplus labour which is not derived from the position that labour is the source of *all* value is utterly trivial. (Armstrong, Glyn and Harrison, 1978, p. 21.)

Marx does not, however, seem to have shared this view:

> Since the exchange-value of commodities is indeed nothing but a mutual relation between various kinds of labour of individuals regarded as equal and universal labour, i.e. nothing but a material expression of a specific social form of labour, it is a tautology to say that labour is the *only* source of exchange-value, and accordingly of wealth in so far as this consists of exchange-value . . .It would be wrong to say that labour which produces use-values is the *only* source of the wealth produced by it, that is of material wealth. (*A Contribution to the Critique of Political Economy*[1], p. 35-36.)

> Capital did not invent surplus labour. Wherever a part of society possess the monopoly of the means of production, the worker, free or unfree, must add to the labour-time necessary for his own maintenance an extra quantity of labour-time in order to produce the means of subsistence for the owner of the means of production. (*Capital*, I, p. 344.)

Moreover to regard Marx's theory of value as a proof of exploitation tends to dehistoricise value, to make value synonymous with labour-time, and to make redundant Marx's distinction between surplus labour and surplus value. To know whether or not there is exploitation, we must examine the ownership and control of the means of production, and the process whereby the length of the working day is fixed. (See Rowthorn, 1974.) Marx's concern was with the particular *form* that exploitation took in capitalism (see *Capital*, I, p. 325), for in capitalism surplus labour could not be appropriated simply in the form of the immediate product of labour. It was necessary for that product to be sold and translated into *money*. As Dobb comments:

> The problem for Marx was not to prove the existence of surplus value and exploitation by means of a theory of value; it was, indeed to *reconcile* the existence of surplus value with the reign of market competition and of exchange of value equivalents. (Dobb, 1971. p. 12.)

The view that Marx's theory of value is intended as a proof of exploitation does, however, have the merit of seeing that theory as a *political* intervention. The problem is that it poses that politics in a way that is closer to the 'natural right' politics of 'Ricardian socialism' or German Social Democracy, than to the politics of Marx. (See for instance Marx's 'Critique of the Gotha programme', Marx-Engels, *Selected Works*, Vol.3; also, Dobb, 1973, p. 137-141.) Because of this it has no satisfactory answer to the claim that exploitation in capitalism can perfectly well be understood in terms of the appropriation of *surplus product*, with no need to bring in value at all. (See for instance Hodgson, 1976; Steedman, 1977.) But in rejecting this interpretation of Marx's value theory we must be careful not to de-politicise that theory. The politics of the theory is a question we shall return to at the end of this paper.

2. The theory of value: an explanation of prices?

This approach may be found separately or combined with the one we have just considered. It is the interpretation offered by most Marxist economists in the Anglo-Saxon world, that Marx's theory of value is an explanation of equilibrium or 'natural' prices in a capitalist economy.. As such it is one of a number of theories of equilibrium price, so that, for instance, in Dobb's *Theories of Value and Distribution*, Marx's theory of value can be examined alongside the theories of Smith, Ricardo, Mill, Jevons, Walras and Marshall, as if it were a theory with the same kind of object. Indeed the main distinction made by Dobb is

> 'between theories that approach the determination of prices, or the relations of exchange, through and by means of conditions of

production (costs, input-coefficients and the like) and those that approach it primarily from the side of demand.' (Dobb, 1973, p. 31.)

For Dobb the great divide is between Smith, Ricardo and Marx who are in the first category, and the others, who are in the second. A similar interpretation is offered by Meek:

'there is surely little doubt that he (Marx) wanted his theory of value ... to do another and more familiar job as well – the same job which theories of value had always been employed to do in economics, that is, to determine prices.' (Meek, 1977, p. 124.)

Of course, it is recognised, within this interpretation, that there are differences between Marx and other economists, even between Marx and Ricardo.

'Marx's theory of value was something *more* than a theory of value as generally conceived: it had the function not only of explaining exchange-value or prices in a quantitative sense, but of exhibiting the historico-social basis in the labour process of an exchange – or commodity – society with labour power itself become a commodity.' (Dobb, 1971, p. 11.)

The way of noting these differences that has become most popular is the distinction between the quantitative-value problem and the qualitative-value problem, introduced by Sweezy. The former is the problem of explaining the quantitative exchange-relation between commodities; the latter is the problem of explaining the social relations which underlie the commodity form. For Sweezy,

'The great originality of Marx's value theory lies in its recognition of these two elements of the problem and in its attempt to deal with them simultaneously within a single conceptual framework.' (Sweezy, 1962, p. 25.)

Or as Meek put it,

'The qualitative aspect of the solution was directed to the question: why do commodities possess price at all? The quantitative aspect was directed to the question: why do commodities possess the particular prices which they do?' (Meek, 1967, p. 10.)

It is clear that the object of Marx's theory of value is taken, in this tradition, to be the process of exchange or circulation.

'. . . the study of commodities is therefore the study of the economic relations of exchange.' (Sweezy, 1962, p. 23.)

Marx is interpreted as explaining this process in terms of a separate, more fundamental process, production. Dobb, for instance, writing an Introduction to Marx's *A Contribution to the Critique of Political Economy*, suggests that Marx's interest,

'is now centred on explaining exchange in *terms of production* . . . Exchange relations or market 'appearances' could only be understood . . . if they were seen as the expression of these more fundamental relations at the basis of society.' (Dobb, 1971, p. 9-10.)

According to Sweezy,

'Commodities exchange against each other on the market in certain definite proportions; they also absorb a certain definite quantity (measured in time units) of society's total available labour force. What is the relation between these two facts? As a first approximation Marx assumes that there is an exact correspondence between exchange ratios and labour-time ratios, or, in other words, that commodities which require an equal time to produce will exchange on a one-to-one basis. This is the simplest formula and hence a good starting point. Deviations which occur in practice can be dealt with in subsequent approximations to reality.' (Sweezy, 1962, p. 42.)

It has generally been suggested that this 'first approximation' is maintained throughout the first two volumes of *Capital*, and relinquished in Volume III, where the category of prices of production is introduced and 'values are transformed into prices.' The adequacy of Marx's 'solution' to the 'transformation problem', and the merits of various alternative solutions have until recently been the chief point of debate in this tradition of interpretation. (No attempt will be made here to review the lengthy literature. For references, see Fine and Harris, 1976.)

In what sense is it held that the labour-time required to produce commodities 'explains' or 'determines' their prices (either as a 'first approximation' or through some 'transformation')? I think two related arguments are deployed in the writings in this tradition. The 'first approximation' of prices to the labour-time required for production is supported by an argument that derives from Adam Smith's example of the principle of equalisation of advantage in a 'deer and beaver' economy. (See, for instance, Sweezy, 1962, p. 45-46.) Suppose we consider two commondities ('deer' and 'beaver'), one of which ('deer') takes one hour to produce, the other of which ('beaver') takes two hours; and suppose that on the market one deer exchanges for one beaver. The argument is that each producer will compare the time it takes him to produce the commodity (in this case by hunting) with its market price, expressed in terms of the other commodity. It is clear that you can get more beavers by producing deer and exchanging than for beaver, than by directly producing beaver. Therefore producers will tend to allocate their time to producing deer rather than beaver. This will increase the supply of deer, reduce the supply of beaver. Other things being equal, this will reduce the market price of deer and increase the market price of beaver. The movement of labour-time from beaver to deer will continue until the market price of deer in terms of beaver is equal to the relative amounts of labour required to produce the two commodities, i.e. until two deer exchange for one beaver. At this point the transfer of labour-time will stop, and the system will be in equilibrium, with prices equal to labour-time ratios.

A more complex argument is deployed to indicate how labour-time determines prices through a 'transformation.' Here labour-time and price of production are related through an equilibrium 'model' of dependent and independent variables. As Meek put it:

'In their basic models, all three economists (i.e. Ricardo, Marx and Sraffa) in effect envisage a set of technological and sociological conditions in which a net product or surplus is produced (over and above the subsistence of the worker, which is usually conceived to be determined by physiological and social conditions.) The magnitude of this net product or surplus is assumed to be given independently of prices, and to limit and determine the aggregate level of the profits (and other non-wage incomes) which are paid out of it. The main thing which the models are designed to show is that under the postulated conditions of production the process of distribution of the surplus will result in the simultaneous formation of a determinate average rate of profit and a determinate set of prices for all commodities.' (Meek, 1977, p. 160.)

The magnitude of the net product is measured in terms of the labour time socially required for its production.

The feature of both arguments which it is important to note is that they pose the socially-necessary labour-time embodied in commodities as something quite separate, discretely distinct from, and independent of, price. It is given solely in the process of production, whereas price is given solely in the process of circulation. The two processes are themselves discretely distinct, although they are of course linked. And it is in production that 'the key causal factor', 'the relatively independent 'determining constant'' is to be found. (See Meek, 1967, p. 95; Meek, 1977, p. 151.) It follows that we can, in principle, calculate values (i.e. socially-necessary labour-time embodied in commodities) quite independently of prices, and deduce equilibrium prices from those values. The last possibility is often regarded as the indispensable guarantee of the scientific status of Marx's value theory, of its distance from a metaphysical juggling of concepts. (Although, as writers in this tradition generally admit, in practice such a calculation would be impossible to make.)

The reading of Marx as a builder of economic models has been carried to its logical extreme in the recent work of some professional economists, perhaps most notably in the work of Morishima, in which,

'the classical labour theory of value is rigorously mathematised in a familiar form parallel to Leontief's inter-sectoral price-cost equations. The hidden assumptions are all revealed and, by the use of the mathematics of the input-output analysis, the comparative statical laws concerning the behaviour of the relative values of commodities (in terms of a standard commodity arbitrarily chosen) are proved. There is a duality between physical outputs and values of commodities, which is similar to the duality between physical outputs and competitive prices. It is seen that the labour theory of value may be compatible with the utility theory of consumers demand or any of its improved variations.' (Morishima, 1973, p. 5.)

All politics is ruthlessly excised in the interests of making Marx a respectable proto-mathematical economist.[2]

'(values) are determined only by technological coefficients . . . they are independent of the market, the class-structure of society, taxes and so on.' (Morishima, 1973, p. 15.)

More important in CSE debates has been the development within this general line of interpretation of an approach which excises not politics as such, but value. Arguing from the same premises as the Sweezy-Meek-Dobb tradition, it has come to the conclusion that,

'the project of providing a materialist account of capitalist societies is dependent on Marx's value magnitude analysis *only* in the negative sense that continued adherence to the latter is a major fetter on the development of the former.' (Steedman, 1977, p. 207; See also Hodgson and Steedman, 1975; Hodgson, 1976; Steedman, 1975a, 1975b.)

The quantity of socially-necessary labour-time embodied in a commodity has been found to be at best redundant to, at most incapable of, the determination of its equilibrium price. The so-called 'Neo-Ricardians' pose instead, as independent variables, the socially-necessary conditions of production and the real wage paid to workers, specified in terms of physical quantities of particular commodities. Unlike Morishima, Steedman does not take such quantities as purely technological: they are assumed to be determined socially and historically and reflect the 'balance of forces' between workers and capitalists in the work place.

There is no doubt that within its own terms this critique of the theory of value, as an explanation of equilibrium prices in terms of labour quantities, is quite correct. Attempts to preserve the traditional Anglo-Saxon version of the theory of value tend to dissolve into positions even more 'Ricardian' than that of the 'Neo-Ricardians' (a point made by Himmelweit and Mohun, 1978). This paper makes no attempt to rescue this traditional 'labour theory of value'. Instead it argues for a quite different reading of Marx's theory of value, in relation to which it is the Sraffa-based critique which is redundant, rather than value.

In some respects even more iconoclastic than the Neo-Ricardians is the work of Cutler, Hindess, Hirst and Hussain. Prefaced by a picture of Christ cleansing the temple, they claim:

> 'It is possible to argue that prices and exchange-values have no *general* functions or general determinants . . . Such a change of pertinence of problems would put us not only outside of the Marxist theory of value but also conventional economic theory.' (Cutler et al., 1977, p. 14.)

and declare:

> 'In this book we will challenge the notion that 'value' is such a general determinant' (op. cit., p. 19.)

I too will challenge the notion that value is such a general determinant, in the sense that Cutler et al. understand this, i.e. as a single 'origin' or 'cause' of prices and profits. But my challenge will be directed to the very notion that Marx's theory of value poses value as the origin or cause of anything. Among other things, I shall argue that Marx's concept of a determinant is quite different from those of authors considered in this section.

3. An abstract labour theory of value?

It is, of course, by no means original to question whether the 'labour theory of value' discussed in the last section is to be found in the works of Marx, (see for instance Pilling, 1972; Banaji, 1976). In recent CSE debates much stress has been placed on abstract labour as a means of differentiating Marx's theory of value from the interpretations so far discussed which are held to apply to Ricardo rather than to Marx. Marx certainly claims that his theory of value differs from that of Ricardo in the attention he pays to the form of labour, and the distinction he introduces between abstract labour and concrete labour. (See for instance, *Theories of Surplus Value*, Part 2, p. 164, 172.) In *Capital* we are told that the author,

> 'was the first to point out and examine critically this two-fold nature of labour contained in commodities . . . this point is crucial to an understanding of political economy.' (*Capital*, I, p. 132.)

This point is taken up by Himmelweit and Mohun, 1978, who base their reply to Steedman, 1977, on

> 'a distinction between Ricardian embodied-labour theory of value and a Marxian theory of value based on the category of abstract labour. While the former is intended immediately to be a theory of price, the latter is only so after several mediations.' (op. cit., p. 94.)

They suggest that if we bear this distinction in mind, we shall find that the allegations of redundancy and incoherence, while they apply to Ricardo's theory of value, cannot be sustained for that of Marx.

Their argument is not altogether convincing for two reasons. The first is that Steedman claims to have treated labour as abstract labour and to direct his critique precisely at an abstract labour theory of value (see Steedman, 1977, p. 19), and Himmelweit and Mohun nowhere explicitly confront this claim. Clearly much depends on how the concept of abstract labour is understood. Sweezy, for instance, sees in the concept of abstract labour not an alternative to the concepts of Ricardo and Smith, but a further development and clarification of their work. (Sweezy, 1962, p. 31.) Marx himself did not tend to use 'embodied labour' and 'abstract labour' as if they were opposites, stating for instance that,

> 'The body of the commodity, which serves as the equivalent,

always figures as the embodiment of abstract human labour.'
(*Capital*, I, p. 150.)

The second reason is that their argument becomes circular: they derive
the concept of abstract labour from the commodity form, and then
wish to use the concept of abstract labour to explain the commodity
form (op. cit., p. 73).

In my view the distinction between abstract and concrete labour
is an important differentiation between Marx's and Ricardo's theories,
but it is not the only differentiation. More fundamental are differences
in the object of the theory and the method of analysis. The clarification of these is required before the meaning and significance of the
concept of abstract labour becomes apparent.

4. Labour as the object of Marx's theory of value

My argument will be, not that Marx's value theory of price is
more complex than Ricardo's, but that the object of Marx's theory of
value is not price at all. This does not mean that Marx was not
concerned with price, nor its relation to the magnitude of value, but
that the phenomena of exchange are not the object of the theory.
(Again this is not a completely new thought, see Hussain, this volume,
p. 84.) My argument is that the *object* of Marx's theory of value was
labour. It is not a matter of seeking an explanation of why prices are
what they are and finding it in labour. But rather of seeking an inder-
standing of why labour takes the forms it does, and what the political
consequences are.

We can see Marx focusing on this question in his first intensive
study of Adam Smith ('Economic and Philosophical Manuscripts' in
Early Writings, esp. p. 287-9). *The German Ideology* is a sustained
argument for the centrality of this question:

'As individuals express their life, so they are. What they are,
therefore, coincides with their production, both with *what* they
produce and with *how* they produce.' (Op. cit., p. 42.)

And in *Capital*, Marx notes the critical question that separates the direction of his analysis from that of political economy as:

'why this content has assumed that particular form, that is to say
why labour is expressed in value, and why the measurement of
labour by its duration is expressed in the magnitude of the value
of the product. These formulas, which bear the unmistakable
stamp of belonging to a social formation in which the process of

production has mastery over man, instead of the opposite, appear to the political economists' bourgeois consciousness to be as much a self evident and nature-imposed necessity as productive labour itself.' (*Capital*, I, p. 174-5.)

Here Marx is signalling, not an 'addition of historical perspective' to political economy, but a difference in the object of the theory, (see also Hussain, this volume, p. 86). It is because labour is the object of the theory that Marx begins his analysis with produced commodities, as being 'the simplest social form in which the labour product is represented in contemporary society.' (*Marginal Notes on Wagner*, p. 50); and not, as Bohm-Bawerk claimed, to rig the terms of the explanation of prices (see also Kay, this volume, p. 48-50).

5. A possible misconception: the social distribution of labour

The question of why labour takes the forms it does is not simply a *distributional* question. Here the famous letter to Kugelmann in July 1868 can be very misleading, for Marx writes:

'the mass of products corresponding to the different needs require different and quantitatively determined masses of the total labour of society. That this necessity of distributing social labour in definite proportions cannot be done away with by the *particular form* of social production, but can only change the *form it assumes*, is self evident. No natural laws can be done away with. What can change in changing historical circumstances, is the *form* in which these laws operate.' (*Selected Correspondence*, p. 251.)

Taken by itself, this letter can lend support to the view that the object of the theory is simply the way in which individuals are distributed and linked together in a pre-given structure of tasks. This view is held by a wide spectrum of writers from the 'Hegelian' I. I. Rubin to the 'anti-Hegelian' Althusser.

For Rubin the theory of value is about the regulation of production in a commodity economy, where 'no one consciously supports or regulates the distribution of social labour among the various industrial branches to correspond with the given state of productive forces.' (Rubin, 1973, p. 77.) From the beginning of his book, Rubin makes it quite clear that the productive forces which constitute the various industrial branches are autonomous products of a material-technical process (Rubin, 1973, p. 1-3). What for him is social is merely the network of links between people in this pre-given structure:

'It is also incorrect to view Marx's theory as an analysis of *relations between labour and things*, things which are the products of labour. The relation of labour to things refers to a given concrete form of labour and a given concrete thing. This is a technical relation which is not, in itself, the subject of the theory of value. The subject matter of the theory of value is the *interrelations of various forms of labour* in the process of their distribution, which is established through the relation of exchange among things, i.e. products of labour.' (Rubin, 1973, p. 67).

But it is the pre-given structure which has ultimate causal significance:

'We can observe that social production relations among people are causally dependent on the material conditions of production and on the distribution of the technical means of production among the different social groups . . . From the point of view of the theory of historical materialism, this is a general sociological law which holds for all social formations.' (Rubin, 1973, p. 29.)

Clearly there are many differences between Rubin's reading of Marx and that of Althusser, but the latter also invokes the letter to Kugelmann, and writes:

'Marx's labour theory of value . . . is intelligible, but only as a special case of a theory which Marx and Engels called the 'law of value' or the law of the distribution of the available labour power between the various branches of production . . .' (Althusser, 1977, p. 87.)

or,

'the distribution of men into social classes exercising functions in the production process'. (Althusser, 1975, p. 167.)

These 'functions in the production process' are determined by the material and technical conditions of production.

'The labour process therefore implies an expenditure of the labour-power of men who, using defined instruments of labour according to adequate (technical) rules, transform the *object* of labour (either a natural material or an already worked material or raw material) into a useful product. . . the labour process as a

material mechanism is dominated by the physical laws of nature
and technology.' (Althusser, 1975, p. 170-1.)

While it is true that such a thesis is 'a denial of every 'humanist' conception of human labour as pure creativity', it is not a denial of, (indeed it
positively encourages) a *technicist* reading of Marx, with potentially
disastrous political implications.

What is more immediately important for our consideration of
Marx's theory of value is that the technicist reading of the theory, as
having as its object the process of distribution of individuals to pre-
given places or functions in the production process, tends to lead to a
re-introduction of the labour theory of value, albeit in more complex
form with reciprocal causality. Not only is labour-time seen as the
determinant of exchange-value; exchange-value is also seen as the determinant of labour-time. That is, exchange-values are in equilibrium equal
to socially necessary labour-time embodied in commodities; and the distribution of total labour-time between different commodities is regulated by the difference between market price and relative labour-time
requirements of different commodities. Rubin in fact presents an exposition of the way in which this works which is practically the same as
that of Sweezy. (See Rubin, 1973, chapters 8, 9 and 10; Sweezy,
1962, chapters II and III.)

> 'In a simple commodity economy, the exchange of 10 hours of
> labour in one branch of production, for example shoe-making, for
> the product of 8 hours labour in another branch, for example
> clothing production, necessarily leads (if the shoe-maker and
> clothes-maker are equally qualified) to different advantages of
> production in the two branches, and to the transfer of labour
> from shoe-making to clothing production.' (Rubin, 1973, p. 103.)

The difference is that while Sweezy explicitly acknowledges the pro-
venance of this type of argument in *The Wealth of Nations*, Rubin
claims that he has not repeated 'the mistakes of Adam Smith'. (Rubin,
1973, p. 167.) He claims to differ from Smith in showing that the
'equalisation of advantage' is enforced by an objective social process
which compels individuals to behave in this way. But this argument is
invalid. There is no social pressure on a simple commodity producer
who uses his own or his family's labour (but not hired labour) to compare the different rewards of an hour of labour in different branches of
production. (See Banaji, 1977, p. 32 for discussion in the case of
peasant agriculture.) It is only capitalists who are *forced* to account for
all labour-time spent in production because they are in competition

with other capitalists in the labour market (and all other markets). But capitalists make their calculations in *money* terms, not by a direct comparison of labour-time with market price, because it is not their own labour-time that they are accounting for.

There is some difference between Rubin's position and Sweezy's position, insofar as the former does not pose value as a category of the production process, whereas the latter does. But this simply means that in Rubin it is the relation between value and exchange-value which is obscured, while in Sweezy (and Meek, Dobb etc.) it is the relation between value and labour-time. What all four authors have in common is a tendency to reduce the categories of the analysis from the three found in Marx's writings (labour-time, value and exchange-value) to two. Rubin identifies value with

'that average level around which market prices fluctuate and with which prices would coincide if *social labour* were proportionately distributed among the various branches of production'. (Rubin, 1973, p. 64);

and thus poses it simply as a category of circulation, and has no systematic distinction between exchange value and value.

Sweezy, Dobb, Meek (and the tradition they represent) identify value with labour-time; for example,

'Marx began by defining the 'value' of a commodity as the total quantity of labour which was normally required from first to last to produce it.' (Meek, 1977, p. 95);

and thus pose it simply as a category of production.

Rubin also shares the view that production is a discretely distinct process in which are to be found the 'independent variables' which are of ultimate causal significance.

'. . . the moving force which transforms the entire system of value originates in the material-technical process of production. The increase of productivity of labour is expressed in a decrease in the quantity of concrete labour which is factually used up in production, on the average. As a result of this (because of the dual character of labour as concrete and abstract), the quantity of this labour, which is considered 'social' or 'abstract', i.e. as a share of the total, homogeneous labour of the society, decreases. The increase of productivity of labour changes the quantity of abstract labour necessary for production. It causes a change in

> the value of the products of labour. A change in the value of
> products in turn affects the distribution of social labour among
> the various branches of production. *Productivity of labour –
> abstract labour – value – distribution of social labour*: this is the
> scheme of a commodity economy.' (Rubin, 1973, p. 66.)

Thus Rubin is still on the terrain of the labour theory of value. The
object of the theory is still located in the process of circulation – it has
simply been widened to include the circulation of labour time as well
as of the products of labour.

6. The indeterminateness of human labour

But if Marx's theory of value does not have as its object the circulation (or distribution) of labour so as to fill the slots in a pre-given
structure of production, what is its object? One way of trying to explain would be to say that it is about the determination of the structure
of production *as well as* the distribution of labour in that structure. But
that is still far too mechanical, too structural a metaphor. In a vivid
passage in the *Grundrisse*, Marx describes labour thus:

> 'Labour is the living, form-giving fire; it is the transitoriness of
> things, their temporality, as their formation by living time.' (Op.
> cit., p. 361.)

It is a fluidity, a potential, which in any society has to be socially
'fixed' or objectified in the production of particular goods, by
particular people in particular ways. Human beings are not pre-
programmed biologically to perform particular tasks. Unlike ants or
bees, there is a potentially vast range in the tasks that any human being
can undertake. As Braverman puts it,

> 'Freed from the rigid paths dictated in animals by instinct, human
> labour becomes indeterminate.' (Braverman, 1974, p. 51).

This fluidity of labour is not simply an attribute of growing industrial
economies: human labour is fluid, requiring determination, in all states
of society. But it is true that only with industrialisation does the fluidity of labour become immediately *apparent*, because the jobs that
individuals do are obviously *not* completely determined by 'tradition',
religion, family ties etc.,[3] and individuals do quite frequently change the
job they do. As Marx put it:

> '. . . We can see at a glance that in our capitalist society a given

portion of labour is supplied alternatively in the form of tailoring and in the form of weaving, in accordance with changes in the direction of the demand for labour. This change in the form of labour may well not take place without friction, but it must take place.' (*Capital*, I, p. 134.)

Arthur, 1978, recognises that 'in a developed industrial economy social labour, as a productive force, has a fluidity in its forms of appearance' (op. cit. p. 89); but because he fails to distinguish between essence and forms of appearance, he limits this fluidity, this requirement for determination, to capitalist economies. The fact that the essential indeterminateness of human labour is not immediately *apparent* in pre-capitalist societies does not mean that it does not exist.

So the fundamental question about human labour in all societies is, how is it determined? To speak of 'determination' here does not, of course, mean the denial of *any* choice on the part of individuals about their work. Rather it is to point to the fact that individuals can't just choose *anything*, are unable to re-invent the world from scratch, but must choose from among alternatives presented to them.[4] As several authors pointed out, Marx's concept of determination is not 'deterministic'. (See for instance, Ollman, 1976, p. 17; Thompson 1978, p. 241-242.) Although Marx stresses that determination can never be simply an exercise of individual wills, he also stresses that it is not independent of and completely exterior to the actions of individuals:

'The social structure and the state are continually evolving out of the life process of definite individuals.' (*German Ideology*, p. 46.)

But

'of individuals, not as they may appear in their own or other people's imagination, but as they *really* are; i.e. as they operate, produce materially, and hence as they work under definite material limits, pre-suppositions and conditions independent of their will'. (*German Ideology*, p. 47.)

Distribution of social labour is not an adequate metaphor for this process of determination, because such distribution always begins from some pre-given, fixed, determinate structure, which is placed outside the process of social determination. What is required is a conceptualisation of a process of social determination that proceeds from the indeterminate to the determinate; from the potential to the actual;

from the formless to the formed. *Capital* is an attempt to provide just that. It uses a method of investigation which is peculiarly Marx's own, a method which he claimed had not previously been applied to economic subjects (Preface to French Edition, *Capital*, I, p. 104), and which has not been much applied since. I think that it is in large part the difficulties of understanding this method which have lead to mis-readings of Marx's theory of value. The next section considers this method in some detail, and contrasts it with the method of 'the labour theory of value' as traditionally understood.

Capital is, of course, the culmination of work on the social deter-mination of labour that began many years before, and went through various phases. I shall not be discussing the formation of the theory of value presented in *Capital*. I merely note that many of Marx's earlier texts are extremely ambiguous, probably because in investigating the social form that labour takes, Marx *began* from the problematic of political economy. Part of his transformation of this problematic was carried out by reading into the texts of political economy concerns which were those of Marx, rather than of Ricardo, Smith etc., in par-ticular the concern to locate the substance of value. (See Aumeeruddy and Tortajada, this volume, p. 11-12.) In some texts we may find ele-ments of both a 'labour theory of value' and a 'value theory of labour'. There are symptoms of this even in *Critique of Political Economy*, published in 1859, eight years before the first volume of *Capital*. In this text there is no clear distinction between value and exchange-value, between the inner relation and its form of appearance, a distinction which plays an important role in the argument of *Capital*, and which one can see being developed in the commentaries of *Theories of Surplus Value*, particularly in the critique of Bailey in Part 3. Accordingly, this paper will focus on the theory of value as it appears in *Capital*, supple-menting this where necessary with clarifications deriving from *Theories of Surplus Value*; and, in a few cases relating to money, from *Critique of Political Economy*.

MISPLACED CONCRETENESS AND MARX'S METHOD OF ABSTRACTION

1. Rationalist Concepts of Determination

All of the readings of Marx's value theory so far discussed have in common a misplaced concreteness, in that they understand that theory as a relation between certain already determined, 'given', independent variables located in the process of production, and certain to-be-determined, dependent variables located in the process of circulation. I think this is because it does not occur to the authors we have been considering that there is any other way of understanding the relation of determination. When questions about determination are raised it is usually only to discuss the choice of independent and dependent variables, or whether there *are* any *general* determinants. (See for instance Meek, 1977, p. 151-2; Steedman, 1977, p. 25; Cutler, et al. 1977, p. 19). It is simply taken for granted that any theory requires separable determining factors, discretely distinct from what they are supposed to determine. (See Georgescu-Roegen, 1966, p. 42; Ollman, 1976, discusses this in relation to interpretations of Marx's concept of mode of production, p. 5-11.) Althusser's 'structural causality' does not break with that view; it merely puts the independent variables one stage back, behind the 'structure'. Economic phenomena are

> '*determined by a (regional) structure* of the mode of production, itself determined by *the (global) structure* of the mode of production.' (Althusser, 1975, p. 185),

but the mode of production itself is constructed of a combination of 'determinate pre-existing elements' which are 'labour power, direct labourers, masters who are not direct labourers, object of production, instruments of production, etc.' (Althusser, 1975, p. 176.)

The abandonment of Althusser's concepts by Cutler et al. does not break with that view either. They dissolve Althusser's self-reproducing 'structures', but only to go back to the 'determinate pre-existing elements' that lie behind them, the 'conditions of existence'. (See for instance Cutler et al., 1977, p. 218-219). Their main distinction is simply to be more agnostic than most other writers in this framework in their choice of independent variables. (See Ohlin Wright, 1979, for a useful classification of different approaches to the 'labour theory of value' in terms of their choice and grouping of variables.)

This approach poses the relation of determination as an effect of some already given, discretely distinct elements or factors on some other, quite separate, element or factors, whose general form is given, but whose position within a possible range is not, using what Georgescu-Roegen calls 'arithmomorphic concepts'. Essentially a *rationalist* method, it assumes that the phenomena of the material world are like the symbols of arithmetic and formal logic, separate and self-bounded and relate to each other in the same way.[5] This is not Marx's method: his theory of value is not constructed on rationalist lines.

2. Determination in Marx's theory of value: the relation between labour-time, value and exchange-value

Ollman has pointed out that Marx's concept of the mode of

production in the *Preface to A Contribution to the Critique of Political Economy* is not one of independent variables determining dependent variables. He argues that some of the expressions used to categorise that which determines,

> 'appear to include in their meanings part of the reality which Marx says they 'determine'. Thus, property relations as a system of legal claims came under the heading of superstructure, but they are also a component of the relations of production which 'determine' this superstructure'. (Ollman, 1976, p. 7.)

We can see something similar in the first chapter of *Capital* I. The first reference to 'determination' is:

> 'It might seem that if the value of a commodity is determined by the quantity of labour expended to produce it, it would be more valuable the more unskilful and lazy the worker who produced it.' (*Capital* I, p. 129.)

Marx goes on to explain why this is not so, and concludes:

> 'What exclusively determines the magnitude of value of any article is therefore the amount of labour socially necessary, or the labour-time socially necessary for its production.' (*Capital* I, p. 129.)

There is a tendency to misread value as 'exchange-value' or 'price', and to mistake this for a statement of a relation between a dependent and an independent variable —a 'labour theory of value', in short. But just prior to this passage Marx has specifically distinguished value from exchange-value, and stated that for the moment it is value and not exchange-value which is under consideration. Does that mean that Marx is simply giving us a *definition* of the category value in the above quoted passages, is using 'determine' in the sense of 'logically define'? No, because value is not the *same* as a quantity of socially necessary labour-time: it is an objectification or materialisation of a certain aspect of that labour-time, its aspect of being simply an expenditure of human labour power in general, i.e. abstract labour. This is a rather peculiar kind of objectification. As Marx says

> 'Not an atom of matter enters into the objectivity of commodities as values; in this it is the direct opposite of the coarsely sensuous objectivity of commodities as physical objects.' (*Capital*,

I, p. 138.)

Considered simply as physical objects, commodities are objectifications of concrete not abstract labour. The peculiarity of the objectification of abstract labour is in fact signalled by Marx in the reference to 'phantomlike objectivity' in this well known passage:

'Let us look at the residue of the products of labour. There is nothing left of them in each case but the same phantomlike objectivity; they are merely congealed quantities of homogeneous human labour. i.e. of human labour power expended without regard to the form of its expenditure. All these things now tell us is that human labour, i.e. of human labour power expended without regard to the form of its expenditure. All these things now tell us is that human labour-power has been expended to produce them, human labour is accumulated in them. As crystals of this social substance, which is common to them all, they are values — commodity values.' (*Capital*, I, p. 128).

We should note the chemical metaphors — 'congealed', 'crystals' — which occur repeatedly in Chapter 1, Vol. I. For they indicate something of the character of Marx's concept of determination. The quantity of socially necessary labour-time does not determine the magnitude of value in the logical or mathematical sense of an independent variable determining a dependent variable, (or in the sense of defining the meaning of the term 'magnitude of value'), but in the sense that the quantity of a chemical substance in its fluid form determines the magnitude of its crystalline or jellied form. There is a continuity as well as a difference between what determines and what is determined.

But perhaps we have been looking in the wrong direction: what about the relation between value and exchange-value? If value is an objectification of a quantity of socially necessary abstract labour-time and exchange-value is the quantity of one commodity which is exchanged for a given quantity of another, surely these are our two separate variables, the one determining the other? Marx writes of exchange-value as 'the necessary mode of expression, or form of appearance, of value' (*Capital*, I, p. 128), but perhaps we could interpret that as meaning that exchange-values are discretely distinct from but *correspond* to or *approximate* to values, (as Steedman, 1977, implies in his appendix). After all, Marx writes that the measure of the magnitude of value is labour-time, whereas the magnitude of exchange-value is measured in terms of a quantity of some commodity, or most generally, in terms of money, which would seem to suggest that the two are quite independent.

However, it is extremely difficult to maintain that interpretation if we take into account the much-neglected third section of chapter 1,

'The Value-Form or Exchange Value'. Here Marx suggests that, divorced from its expression as exchange-value, value is simply an abstraction, without practical reality. It cannot stand on its own: it is not a category designating a reality which is independent of exchange-value, but a reality which is manifested through exchange-value. (See Kay, this volume, p. 57-8, and Arthur, ditto, p. 68.)

'If we say that, as values, commodities are simply congealed quantities of human labour, our analysis reduces them it is true, to the level of abstract value, but does not give them a form of value, distinct from their natural form.' (*Capital*, I, p. 141.)

If a product of labour is a value this must be reflected in some attribute of the product of labour which is immediately apparent, although not immediately recognisable as a reflection of value.[6] The simplest form of this reflection is when another commodity stands in a relation of equivalence to the first commodity, and serves as the material in which its value is expressed, as the embodiment of abstract labour. But this is a very limited expression of value, since it only expresses the equivalence of the first commodity with one other commodity. For an adequate expression of value, the first commodity must be able to express its value in terms of a universal equivalent, a commodity directly exchangeable with all other commodities, a commodity whose use value is its interchangeability. As the process of exchange develops one commodity is set apart from the others and comes to play this role, or, as Marx puts it, 'Money necessarily crystallises out of the process of exchange.' (*Capital*, I, p. 181.)

Marx thus locates the 'form of value' in the price of a commodity. For Marx, the price of a commodity is not the result of some process quite independent of (discretely distinct from) the formation of its value (the objectification in it of abstract labour). Rather,

'the money-form is merely the reflection thrown upon a single commodity by the relations between all other commodities'. (*Capital*, I, p. 184.)

This does not mean that money must always be commodity money (i.e. gold); nor that because price is a value-form, price and value are identical.

Marx explicitly recognised that 'money can, in certain functions, be replaced by mere symbols of itself'. (*Capital*, I, p. 185), and points out that,

'In its form of existence as coin, gold becomes completely divorced from the substance of its value. Relatively valueless objects, therefore, such as paper notes, can serve as coins in place of gold. This purely symbolic character of the currency is still somewhat disguised in the case of metal tokens. In paper money it stands out plainly.' (*Capital*, I, p. 244.)

What he is arguing against is the view that money can be completely autonomous, 'a convenient technical device which has been introduced into the sphere of exchange from the outside'. (*Critique of Political Economy*, p. 57); the product of a convention rather than of a 'blind' social process. He maintains that there are limits to the extent that paper money can supersede commodity money, in effect rejecting a bifurcation of economic relations into the 'money' and the 'real'. In maintaining that there must be an 'intrinsic connection between money and labour which posits exchange value' (*Critique of Political Economy*, p. 57), Marx is denying that value and price are two completely separate variables.

This does not, however, mean that Marx sees value and price as *identical*. Marx expressly criticised Bailey for making this reduction (see *Theories of Surplus Value*, Part 3, p. 147). There is for Marx both a continuity and a difference between value and price, irrespective of whether price is denominated in gold or in paper.

To summarise: in the argument of *Capital*, labour-time, value, and exchange-value (price) are not three discretely distinct variables, nor are they identical with one another. There is a continuity as well as a difference between all three. The relation between them (in any combination) is *not* posed in terms of an independent variable determining a dependent variable.

3. The measure of value: labour-time and money

One implication of the above argument is that the analysis of *Capital* is not predicated on the possibility of calculating values directly in terms of labour-time, quite independently of price, calculated in terms of money (or some numeraire); whereas, as we have already noted, this possibility is central to many readings of the 'labour theory of value' variety. Misconceptions are encouraged here by the fact that in *Capital*, Marx does not deal with this point explicitly at any length, simply referring us in a footnote to the *Critique of Political Economy* (see *Capital*, I, p. 188). Turning to the latter, we find this point discussed in the context of a consideration of Gray's labour-money scheme.[7] Gray proposed that a national bank should find out the labour-time expended in the production of various commodities; and in exchange for his commodity the producer would receive an official certificate of its value, consisting of a receipt for as much labour-time as his commodity contained. Marx objects to this on the grounds that it assumes

> 'that commodities could be directly compared with one another as products of social labour. But they are only comparable as the things they are. Commodities are the direct products of isolated independent individual kinds of labour, and through their alienation in the course of individual exchange they must prove that they are general social labour, in other words, on the basis of commodity production, labour becomes social labour only as a result of the universal alienation of individual kinds of labour. But as Gray presupposes that the labour-time contained in commodities is *immediately social* labour-time, he presupposes that it is communal labour-time of directly associated individuals'. (*Critique of Political Economy*, p. 85.)

In other words, the labour-time that can be directly measured in capitalist economies in terms of hours, quite independent of price, is the particular labour-time of particular individuals: labour-time in its private and concrete aspect. This is not the aspect objectified as value, which is its social and abstract aspect. As Marx put it in an earlier passage in *Critique of Political Economy*:

> 'Social labour-time exists in these commodities in a latent state, so to speak, and becomes evident only in the course of their exchange. The point of departure is not the labour of individuals considered as social labour, but on the contrary the particular kinds of labour of private individuals . . . Universal social labour is consequently not a ready-made pre-requisite but an emerging result.' (Op. cit., p. 45.)

The social necessity of labour in a capitalist economy cannot be determined independent of the price-form: hence values cannot be calculated or observed independently of prices.

But in that case what are we to make of Marx's repeated statements that labour-time is the measure of value? It is not surprising that this leads to misunderstandings, because in *Capital* Marx does not highlight the conceptual distinction which he makes between an 'immanent' or 'intrinsic' measure, and an 'external' measure, which is the mode of appearance of the 'immanent' measure. This distinction is implicit in the example of the measurement of weight (*Capital*, I, p. 148-9), and briefly stated at the beginning of the chapter on Money. Viz:

> 'Money as the measure of value is the necessary form of appear-
> ance of the measure of value which is immanent in commodities,
> namely labour-time.' (*Capital*, I, p. 188.)

It is only in the critique of Bailey (in *Theories of Surplus Value*,
Part 3, p. 124-159) that this distinction is explicitly discussed. The
'immanent' measure refers to the characteristics of something that
allow it to be measurable as pure quantity; the 'external measure
refers to the medium in which the measurements of this quantity are
actually made, the scale used, etc. The concept of 'immanent' measure
does not mean that the 'external' measure is 'given' by the object being
measured. There is room for convention in the choice of a particular
medium of measurement, calibration of scale of measurement, etc. It
is not, therefore, a matter of counter-posing a realist to a formalist
theory of measurement (as Cutler et al., 1977, suggest p. 15). Rather it
is a matter of insisting that there are both realist and formalist aspects
to cardinal measurability (i.e. measurability as absolute quantity, not
simply as bigger or smaller). Things that are cardinally measurable can
be added or subtracted to one another, not merely ranked in order of
size, (ranking is ordinal measurability).

A useful discussion of this issue is to be found in Georgescu-
Roegen, who emphasises that:

> 'Cardinal measurability, therefore, is not a measure just like any
> other, but it reflects a particular physical property of a category
> of things.' (Op. cit., p. 49.)

Only things with certain real properties can be cardinally measured.
This is the point that Marx is making with his concept of 'immanent'
measure, and that he makes in the example, in *Capital*, I, of the
measure of weight (p. 148-9). The external measure of weight is
quantities of iron (and there is of course a conventional choice to be
made about whether to calibrate them in ounces or grammes, or
whether, indeed, to use iron, rather than, say, steel). But unless both
the iron and whatever it is being used to weigh (in Marx's example, a
sugar loaf) both have weight, iron cannot express the weight of the
sugar loaf. Weight is the 'immanent' measure. But it can only be
actually measured in terms of a comparison between two objects, both
of which have weight and one of which is the 'external' measure, whose
weight is pre-supposed.

Thus when Marx says that labour-time is the measure of value, he means that the value of a commodity is measurable as pure quantity because it is an objectification of abstract labour, i.e. of 'indifferent' labour-time, hours of which can be added to or subtracted from one another. As such, as an objectification of pure duration of labour, it has cardinal measurability. This would not be the case if the commodity were simply a product of labour, an objectification of labour in its concrete aspect. For concrete labour is not cardinally measurable as pure time. Hours spent on tailoring and hours spent on weaving are qualitatively different: they can no more be added or subtracted to one another than apples can be added to or subtracted from pears. We can rank concrete labour in terms of hours spent in each task, just as we can rank apples and pears, and say which we have more of. But we can't measure the total quantity of labour in terms of hours, for we have no reason for supposing that one hour of weaving contains as much labour as one hour of tailoring, since they are qualitatively different.

Thus far from entailing that the *medium* of measurement of value must be labour-time, the argument that labour-time is the (immanent) measure of value entails that labour-time *cannot* be the medium of measurement. For we cannot, in the actual labour-time we can observe, separate the abstract from the concrete aspect. The only way that labour-time can be posed as the medium of measurement is by making the arbitrary assumption that there is no qualitative difference between different kinds of labour, an assumption that Marx precisely refuses to make with his insistence on the importance of the form of labour.

It is surprising that Cutler et al., 1977, who emphasise their critique of the supposed function of labour-time as a social standard of measurement in *Capital*, do not refer to Marx's distinction between 'immanent' and 'external' measure. Had they done so, they might have realised that it is *money*, and not labour-time, which functions as the social standard of measurement, in Marx's *Capital*, as in capitalist society itself. The reason that labour-time is stressed as the measure of value, is to argue that money in itself does not make the products of labour commensurable. They are only commensurable insofar as they are objectifications of the abstract aspect of labour.

None of these confusions are new. Unfortunately the following comment that Marx made on Boisguillebert[8] remains of relevance today:

'Boisguillebert's work proves that it is possible to regard labour-time as the measure of the value of commodities, while confusing the labour which is materialised in the exchange value of commodities and measured in time units with the direct physical activity of individuals.' (*Critique of Political Economy*, p. 55.)

One implication of this discussion of the measure of value which we should note is that the value-magnitude equations which Marx uses in *Capital*, do not refer to directly observable labour-time magnitudes (the direct physical activity of individuals), but are a way of indicating the intrinsic character, or substance, of the directly observable money magnitudes. Marx generally introduces these equations in their general form e.g. the value of a commodity $= (C + V) + S$; and then gives a specific example. These specific examples are always couched in money terms, *never* in terms of hours of labour-time. For example, the value of a commodity $= (£410 \text{ constant} + £90 \text{ variable}) + £90$ surplus (cf. *Capital*, I, p. 320). This does not mean that Marx is identifying values and prices; rather that he is indicating the inner value character of monetary magnitudes. The reason why Marx does not simply work at the level of money is that he wants to uncover social relations, such as the rate of surplus-value, which do not directly appear in money form.

Perhaps we can summarise this argument by saying that what Marx proposes is that in a capitalist economy (labour)-time becomes money in a more than purely metaphorical sense. Labour-time and money are not posed as discretely distinct variables which have to be brought into correspondence. Rather the relation between them is posed as one of both continuity and difference. Significantly the metaphors used to characterise this relation are not mechanical ('articulation'), nor mathematical/logical ('correspondence', 'approximation') but chemical and biological terms ('crystallisation', 'incarnation', 'embodiment', 'metabolism', 'metamorphosis'). The idea they carry is that of 'change of form'.

4. The analysis of form determination: the method of historical materialism.

Some may feel we have proved too much. They will suggest that in demonstrating that Marx's value theory has been misread, we have also demonstrated that it is incoherent; that it must fail to provide a proper explanation of labour, or prices, or anything else, because it does not pose determinants completely independent of what is determined. Surely, it will be said, this must inevitably make the argument 'circular'. This would be the case if Marx were seeking to provide explanations *ab initio*, were seeking to explain the 'origins' of phenomena in factors external to them; to set out their necessary and sufficient conditions of existence in terms of combinations of other factors, in the manner of an economic or sociological model. *But this was not Marx's project.*

Marx saw the determination of social forms as an historical process; a process eventuating through time in which every precipitated form becomes in turn dissolved, changes into a new form, a process whose dynamic is internal to it, which has no external 'cause', existing outside of history, of which it is an effect. This entails a view of the world as a qualitatively changing continuum, not an assembly of discretely distinct forms (see Ollman, 1976, especially Chapters 2 and 3). There is no methodological preface to *Capital* which systematically expounds this view, but there are indications of it in the Postface to the Second Edition of *Capital*, I, where we are told that Marx's main concern with phenomena is

'the law of their variation, of their development, i.e. of their transition from one form into another, from one series of connections into a different one.' (Op. cit., p. 100.)

and that,

'economic life offers us a phenomenon analogous to the history of evolution in other branches of biology'. (Op. cit., p. 101.)

This view of the determination of social forms is expounded more systematically by Engels in *Anti-Duhring*, an exposition read in manuscript by Marx and issued with his knowledge (see *Anti-Duhring*, p. 14). In it Engels writes that

'Political economy is therefore essentially a *historical* science. It deals with material that is historical, that is, constantly changing. (Op. cit. p. 204.)

This view of form determination as an historical process is not simply a matter of noting that the social forms of a particular epoch have not always existed (see Banaji, 1976, p. 37-8). It is a matter of analysing them as determinate and yet transient: as the Marxist historian Edward Thompson puts it,

'In investigating history we are not flicking through a series of 'stills', each of which shows us a moment of social time transfixed into a single eternal pose: for each of these stills is not only a moment of being but also a moment of becoming . . . Any historical moment is both the result of prior process and an index towards the direction of its future flow.' (Thompson, 1978, p. 239.)

The method of analysis appropriate for analysing historical process is not the mathematico-logical method of specifying independent and dependent variables, and their relation. Such a method can only identify static structures, and is forced to pose a qualitative change as a sudden discontinuity, a quantum leap between structures; and not as a process, a qualitatively changing continuum. (See Georgescu-Roegen, 1966, p. 29-41 for a useful discussion of this issue.) The point is that to analyse historical process we need 'a different kind of logic, appropriate to phenomena which are always in movement'. (Thompson, 1978, p. 230.)

But what kind of logic? Trying to explain the determination of a form by describing the succession of previous forms will not do. This only tells us what came after what; not how forms are crystallised and might re-dissolve. And in any case, where are we to start such a sequence, and how can we avoid posing the starting point as an 'origin', itself outside the historical process? Marx rejects this approach as early as 1844; in the *Economic and Philosophical Manuscripts* we find:

> 'We must avoid repeating the mistake of the political economist who bases his explanations on some imaginary primordial condition. Such a primordial condition explains nothing.' (*Early Writings*, p. 323.)

Such a sequential approach also finds it difficult to avoid posing the earlier forms as inevitably leading to the later, a problem discussed by Marx in the *1857 Introduction*; this discussion concludes:

> 'It would therefore be unfeasible and wrong to let the economic categories follow one another in the same sequence as that in which they were historically decisive. Their sequence is determined, rather, by their relation to one another in modern bourgeois society, which is precisely the opposite of that which seems to be their natural order or which corresponds to historical development. The point is not the historic position of the economic relations in the succession of different forms of society . . .Rather, their order within modern bourgeois society.' (Op. cit., p. 107-8.)

This is an elaboration of the conclusion of 1844:

> 'We shall start out from a *present day* economic fact.' (*Early Writings*, p. 323).

In other words, we start from the form that we want to understand, and we do not go backwards in time; rather we consider how to treat it as the precipitate of an on-going process without detaching it from that process.

Marx's solution was not to go *outside* the form looking for factors to explain it, but to go *inside* the form, to probe beneath its immediately apparent appearance. (See Banaji, this volume, pp. 17-21 for a detailed discussion of this point.) Going inside the form is achieved by treating it as the temporary precipitate of opposed *potentia*; what Thompson calls a moment of becoming, a moment of co-existent opposed possibilities, 'double-edged and double-tongued' (Thompson, 1978, p. 305-6). But these opposed *potentia* are not discretely distinct building blocks; rather they are different aspects of the continuum of forms in process, they share a continuity as well as a difference. It is in this sense that Marx treats determinate forms as embodiments of contradiction. In the same way elliptical motion can be treated as the resultant of two opposing *potentia*: a tendency of one body to continually move away from another, and an opposing tendency to move towards it. (Cf. *Capital*, I, p. 198.)

These different, counter-posed aspects are often referred to by Marx as 'determinants' or 'determinations' (just as the opposed movements whose resultant is the ellipse are referred to as 'determinants'). But that does not mean that the form is produced or caused by the 'determination' or 'determinants' acting in some autonomous way. For instance, Marx writes that the case of Robinson Crusoe contains 'all the essential determinants of value'. (*Capital*, I, p. 170), but he quite clearly does not mean that Robinson Crusoe's labour is objectified as value. In fact, Marx goes further and claims that the determinants of value 'necessarily concern mankind' 'in all situations' (*Capital*, I, p. 164); but he quite clearly does not mean that value is eternally present. The point is that the determinants are not independent variables, but are simply aspects, one-sided abstractions singled out as a way of analysing the form.

The analysis of a form into its determinants is, however, only the first phase of the investigation. After this phase of individuation of a moment from the historical process, and dissection of the tendencies or aspects counterposed in it, comes the phase of synthesis, of reconstitution of the appearance of the form, and of re-immersing it in process (see Banaji, this volume, p. 28). This second phase does not simply take us back to where we began, but beyond it, because it enables us to understand our starting point in a different light, as predicated on other aspects of a continuous material process. It suggests new abstractions which need to be made from a different angle, in order to capture more of the process. The phase of synthesis brings us back to continuities which the phase of analysis has deliberately severed. The whole method moves in an ever-widening spiral, taking account of more and more aspects of the historical process from which the starting point was individuated and detached.

What kind of knowledge does this method give? It cannot give a Cartesian Absolute Knowledge of the world, its status as true knowledge validated by some epistemological principle. Rather it is based upon a rejection of that aspiration as a form of idealism (see Ruben, 1977, especially p. 99). It is taken for granted, in this method, that the world has a material existence outside our attempts to understand it; and that any category we use to cut up the continuum of the material world can only capture a partial knowledge, a particular aspect seen from a certain vantage point. This is explicitly recognised in the discussion of method in the *1857 Introduction*:

'for example, the simplest economic category, say e.g. exchange value, pre-supposes population, moreover a population producing in specific relations; as well as a certain kind of family, or commune, or state, etc. It can never exist other than as *an abstract, one-sided relation within an already given, concrete, living whole*.' (*1875 Introduction*, p. 101, emphasis added.)

The second phase of the investigation, the phase of synthesis helps to correct the one-sidedness intrinsic to the first phase of analysis, by suggesting other perspectives which must be investigated; new, inter-related ways of cutting up the continuum. These in turn are necessarily one-sided, but the phase of synthesis based on them again helps to correct their one-sidedness. So by following this procedure a more and more complete understanding of the material world can be gained 'in which thought appropriates the concrete'. But there remains always a necessary distance between our understanding of the world, and the world itself:

'The totality as it appears in the head, as a totality of thoughts, is a product of a thinking head, which appropriates the world in the only way it can, a way different from artistic, religious, practical and mental appropriation of this world. The real subject retains its autonomous existence outside the head just as before.' (*1857 Introduction*, p. 101.)

The appropriation of the world can never be completed in thought; it requires practical action.

We must now examine this method at work in Marx's theory of

value. None of the argument so far entails that there are no ambiguities and inconsistencies in that theory, for we have not yet subjected Marx's theory of value to critical scrutiny. There is certainly a danger in using this method of analysis, a danger which Marx explicitly recognised, that 'the movement of the categories appears as the real act of production' (*1857 Introduction*, p. 101). That is, a category of analysis, which as such is a one-sided abstraction, becomes transformed into a self-developing entity; and the historical process becomes transformed into the expression of this entity. The categories of analysis produce our knowledge of the world: but they do not produce the world itself. Marx argues that Hegel

> 'fell into the illusion of conceiving the real as the product of thought concentrating itself, probing its own depths, and unfolding itself out of itself, by itself.' (*1857 Introduction*, p. 101.)

In my view the 'capital-logic' approach[9] falls into the same illusion, taking capital not as a one-sided abstraction, a category of analysis, but as an entity; and understanding the historical process of form determination as the product of the self-development of this entity. One of the key questions considered in the next Section is how far Marx himself succumbed to this illusion.

MARX'S VALUE THEORY OF LABOUR

1. Aspects of labour: social and private, abstract and concrete

In analysing the form of labour in capitalist society, Marx made use of four categories of labour, the opposing pair, abstract and concrete; and the opposing pair, social and private. He did not begin the argument of *Capital* (or *Critique of Political Economy*) from these categories, but I think it is easier to evaluate his argument if we first consider what these categories mean; and what Marx claimed to have established about the relation between these aspects of labour in capitalist society, as determinants of the form of labour.

The first point I want to make is that these are *not* concepts of different *types* of labour. It is not that some labour is private and some social; some concrete and some abstract. Or that labour is at some stage private, and becomes at another stage social; or at some stage concrete, and becomes at another stage abstract. They are concepts of different *aspects* of labour (cf. the 'two-fold nature' or 'dual character' of labour embodied in commodities); and as such they are all one-sided abstractions.

The second point is that they are concepts pertaining to all epochs of history. They are concepts of some of those 'determinations which belong to all epochs . . . No production will be thinkable without them'. (*1857 Introduction*, p. 85.) Where historical epochs differ is the way that these aspects are represented, i.e. the way they appear. Here we need to distinguish between 'formless' appearance as scattered, seemingly unconnected symptoms, and crystallisation into a distinct form of appearance, a representation which enables the aspect to be grasped as a unity: and which gives what Marx calls 'a practical truth' to the abstraction (cf. *1857 Introduction*, p. 105). Marx did *not* regard abstractions which do not have such a 'practical truth' as invalid (cf. *1857 Introduction*, p. 85, p. 105). The criterion Marx put forward for a valid abstraction was that it should be 'a rational abstraction in so far as it really brings out and fixes the common element and thus saves us repetition'. (*1857 Introduction*, p. 85.) What he suggested was that such valid abstractions do not have the same status for all historical epochs: they have a different significance in epochs in which they have a 'practical truth'. In such circumstances, the process bringing to light the common aspect is not only a mental process. The mental process has its correlate in a real social process which gives the common aspect a distinct form of appearance, albeit quite possibly a fetishised form of appearance, so that the common aspect represented may be misrecognised if we go only by appearances.

The third point is that the two pairs of abstractions (abstract/ concrete; social/private) must not be collapsed into one. There is a tendency to suggest that 'abstract' means the same as 'social', and 'concrete' the same as 'private'. (See Kay, this volume, p. 56; and Hussain, this volume, p. 95). There *is* some overlapping in meaning, but the two pairs, as concepts, are nevertheless distinct. What Marx argues is that in the specific conditions of capitalism, the distinctions between the two pairs tend, as a practical reality, to be obliterated: the concrete aspect of labour is 'privatised', and the social aspect of labour is 'abstracted'. These points are not uncontroversial, so it is necessary to deal with them in more depth.

There is a tendency to suppose that Marx analysed capitalism as a form of production in which labour starts off as 'concrete' and 'private'; in the process of exchange this labour, by now embodied in products, is then transformed into a different type of labour 'abstract' and 'social' (cf. in particular Rubin, 1973, p. 70; also Arthur, 1978, p. 93-5). Certainly Marx does refer to commodities as 'the products of private individuals who work independently of each other'. (*Capital*, I, p. 165); and claims that 'Universal social labour is consequently not a ready made pre-requisite but an emerging result.' (*Critique of Political Economy*, p. 45.) And he does discuss the labour process 'independently of any specific social formation'. (*Capital*, I, p. 283.) But this does not signify a departure from his position that

> 'Individuals producing in society – hence socially determined individual production – is, of course, the point of departure'. (*1857 Introduction*, p. 83.)

Rather, it signifies his analysis of the problem that

> 'in this society of free competition, the individual appears detached from the natural bonds etc. which in earlier historical periods make him the accessory of a definite and limited human conglomerate'. (*1857 Introduction*, p. 83.)

In *Capital*, Marx continued to begin from the position that

> 'as soon as men start to work for each other in any way, their labour also assumes a social form'. (*Capital*, I, p. 164.)

The problem was to locate this social form in a capitalist society, where it appeared that men as producers are private individuals free from social forms; or rather that social forms have no independent effectivity and are simply the result of private decisions, individual choices; the cash nexus simply a way of aggregating and reconciling these choices. Marx contrasted this form of appearance with examples of pre-capitalist societies, in which the social forms constraining individuals in production were immediately apparent: the patriarchal family, feudal rights and duties etc. (See *Critique of Political Economy*, p. 32-4; *Capital*, I, p. 169-171.) When Marx refers to 'private individuals' in *Capital*, he is referring precisely to this appearance:

> 'Since the producers do not come into social contact until they exchange the products of their labour, the specific social characteristics of their private labour appear only within this exchange.' (*Capital*, I, p. 165.)

(We should perhaps note that Marx is at this stage of the discussion abstracting from the *internal* organisation of each producing unit.) What Marx means is that capitalist production is private in the sense that the social relation of each producing unit to all others is *latent*, hidden; not in the sense that labour as an activity has no social character, and only acquires one *after* its embodiment in commodities. Marx's argument is not that the process of exchange *confers* a social form on hitherto private labour – but that it brings out the social character which is already latent, albeit bringing it out in a fetishised form, as a 'social relation between things'.

The concept of 'concrete labour' overlaps with the concept of 'private labour', since it is a concept of subjective human activity 'determined by its aim, mode of operation, object, means and result' (*Capital*, I, p. 132). What it adds to the notion of the individual, subjective aspects of human labour is the notion of labour as 'a process between man and nature' (*Capital*, I, p. 283) in which labour takes many different, specific forms: tailoring, weaving, spinning etc. etc. It is the concept of diversity and heterogeneity of labour. The 'private' and 'concrete' aspects of labour are in fact coincidental in capitalist societies, where the different kinds of labour appear to be undertaken as a result of the choices made by the individuals doing them (even if very constrained choices). This is not the case in pre-capitalist forms of production, where,

> 'The natural form of labour, its particularity . . . is here its immediate social form.' (*Capital*, I, p. 170);

and individuals appear to have little choice about the kind of work they do.

The term 'concrete labour' is rather unfortunate, in that it is a hindrance to our recognition that 'concrete labour' is a one-sided abstraction, the concept *not* of labour as 'the concentration of many determinations', as a living whole, a determinate form, (which is how Marx uses the term 'concrete' in the *1857 Introduction*); but rather the concept of certain aspects of labour (*one* of the 'many determinations'). The concept of concrete labour abstracts from labour as a living whole its subjective, qualitative, diverse aspects, which are in all epochs reflected as characteristics of the product in terms of its use-value.

Marx's discussion of the labour process 'independently of any specific social formation' (*Capital*, I, p. 283) does not license us to take concrete labour as the concept of a 'given', determinate reality upon which social relations are superimposed. He specifically mentions that this is a presentation of 'simple and abstract elements' (*Capital*, I, p. 290), and that 'labour process' and 'valorisation process' are 'two *aspects* of the production process' of commodities. (*Capital* I, p. 304, emphasis added). Failure to take note of this tends to lead either in the direction of technological determinism (cf. Rubin, 1973), or to posing the socialist project in terms of the impossible task of removing *any* social mediation between the individual and her work (cf. Colletti, 1976, especially p. 66).

It is generally accepted that concrete labour is a category pertinent to all epochs; but the same is not accepted of abstract labour. (Hussain, this volume, and Itoh, 1976, are exceptions).[10] Generally writers who stress the importance of abstract labour insist that it is a category pertinent only to commodity production (cf. Rubin, 1973; Arthur, 1976 and 1978). To argue otherwise, it is suggested, makes the theory of value an 'eternal' theory, true of all societies, and not specific to capitalism. But this implication does not seem to me to follow from the proposition that abstract labour is a category pertinent to all epochs. The belief that it does possibly stems from a misreading of Marx's claim that it is abstract labour which forms the substance of value as a definition of abstract labour, or the assumption that abstract labour is the concept of a type of labour, and must therefore produce *something*, a something which Marx calls 'value'. But as we shall presently see, the categories of value and abstract labour are arrived at independently, not derived from one another.

At this point we simply note that abstract labour, like concrete labour, is not the concept of a *type* of labour, but of certain aspects of human labour. This is certainly indicated by the phrase 'the dual character of the labour embodied in commodities'. In *Capital* these aspects are at first defined only negatively, as aspects which remain when we disregard the particular, useful, aspect of labour (*Capital*, I, p. 128), and this has perhaps contributed to the confusion. But these aspects are subsequently characterised as those of 'quantities of homogeneous human labour' (op. cit., p. 128), and of 'human labour pure and simple, the expenditure of human labour in general' (op. cit., p. 135). In other words, it is the concept of the unity or similarity of human labour, differentiated simply in terms of quantity, duration. It is *not* an assumption that all work is physiologically identical. Rather, it draws attention to the fact that all work takes time and effort, irrespective of what kind of work it is. Marx specifically claims that this aspect of labour 'in all situations . . . must necessarily concern mankind, although not to the same degree at different stages of development' (*Capital*, I, p. 164), and offers a brief discussion of the way it is of concern in the case of Robinson Crusoe, European feudalism, peasant family production and communal production (*Capital*, I, p. 169-72).

The concept of abstract labour overlaps somewhat with the concept of social labour, in that both view the activity of labour 'objectively' in detachment from particular individuals. Both investigate labour from the point of view of the collectivity, looking at any particular expenditure of labour-power not as an isolated self-generating activity, but as part of a collective effort. What the concept of abstract labour adds to the concept of social labour is the idea of *quantity*, labour is viewed not simply as part of a collective effort, but as a definite fraction of a quantitatively specified total.

The four categories that we have been discussing are thus concepts of four *potentia*, which can never exist on their own as determinate forms of labour. Labour always has its abstract and concrete, its social and private aspects. Marx poses any particular determinate form of labour as a precipitate of these four different aspects of labour. What is specific to a particular kind of society is the relation of these aspects to one another and the way in which they are represented in the precipitated forms. Marx concludes that in capitalist society the abstract aspect is *dominant*. The social character of labour is established precisely through the representation of the abstract aspect of labour:

'Only because the labour-time of the spinner and the labour-time of the weaver represent universal labour-time . . . is the social aspect of the labour of the two individuals represented for each of them. . .' (*Critique of Political Economy*, p. 33).

'the specific social character of private labours carried on independently of each other consists in their equality as human labour.' (*Capital*, I, p. 167).

The concrete and private aspects of labour are mediated by the abstract aspect. The labour of the individual producer

'can satisfy the manifold needs of the individual producer himself only in so far as every particular kind of useful private labour can be exchanged with i.e. counts as the equal of, every other kind of useful private labour. Equality in the full sense between different kinds of labour can be arrived at only if we abstract from their real inequality, if we reduce them to the characteristic they have in common, that of being the expenditure of human labour-power, of human labour in the abstract.' (*Capital*, I, p. 166).

A useful summary of Marx's conclusion, that in the determination of the form of labour in capitalist society it is the abstract aspect which is dominant, can be found in *Results of the Immediate Process of Production*, originally planned as Part Seven of Volume I of *Capital*, and serving both as a summary of Volume I and a bridge to Volume II. Here Marx writes that, in the social terms of a capitalist society,

'labour does not count as a productive activity with specific utility, but simply as a value-creating substance, as social labour

in general which is in the act of objectifying itself, and whose sole
feature of interest is its *quantity*.' (*Results* . . ., p. 1012).

This does not mean that the particular useful qualities of labour, its
concrete aspect, do not matter, but rather thay they matter only in so
far as they affect the quantity of human labour expended in production. The domination of abstract labour signifies 'a social formation
in which the process of production has mastery over man, instead of
the opposite' (*Capital*, I, p. 175). For Marx, money and capital are both
forms of this domination. The theory of value is the foundation for this
conclusion.

Thus, Marx's argument is not that the abstract aspect of labour is
the product of capitalist social relations, but that the latter are characterised by the dominance of the abstract aspect over other aspects of
labour. In these conditions, abstract labour comes to have a 'practical
truth' because the unity of human labour, its differentiation simply
in terms of quantity of labour, is not simply recognised in a mental
process, but has a correlate in a real social process, that goes on quite
independently of how we reason about it. Marx argues, not that some
particular type of labour can in capitalist society be identified as purely
abstract labour, but that the abstract aspect of labour is 'objectified'
or 'crystallised'; that 'the equality of the kinds of human labour takes
on a physical form' (*Capital*, I, p. 164). The objectification of the concrete aspect of labour is universal, but the objectification of the
abstract aspect of labour is not: it is specific to capitalist social
relations. This objectification at some stages in accumulation of capital
may take the form of 'Labour in the form of standardised motion
patterns', labour as 'an interchangeable part' and 'in this form come
ever closer to corresponding, in life, to the abstraction employed by
Marx in analysis of the capitalist mode of production' (Braverman,
1974, p. 182). It may take the form of mobility of labour: (cf. *Results*
. . ., p. 1013-4; this is also stressed by Arthur, 1978). But its most basic
and simplest form is the objectification of abstract labour as a characteristic of the product of labour, reflected in its exchange value. And
for this reason Marx begins the exposition of *Capital* with

'the simplest social form in which the labour product is represented in contemporary society, and this is the *'commodity'* '
(*Marginal Notes on Wagner*, p. 50).

We must now consider the argument by which he tries to establish that
the abstract aspect of labour is objectified, and the way in which this
establishes the domination of abstract labour.

2. The phase of analysis: from the commodity to value

The first phase of Marx's theory of value begins from the commodity[11] and proceeds to value, the substance of which is argued to be objectified abstract labour. The commodity is analysed dialectically as a moment of co-existence of two opposed aspects, use value and exchange value; and then exchange value, as the aspect specific to capitalism is subject to further scrutiny. The movement of the argument from exchange value to value and its substance does present some problems, and has provoked charges from Bohm-Bawerk[12] to Cutler et al., that the conclusions Marx draws cannot legitimately be drawn.

The problem is two-fold: the status of the argument that in exchange commodities are made equivalent to one another, signifying that 'a common element of identical magnitude exists in two different things.' (*Capital*, I, p. 127), and the argument that this common element is an objectification of abstract labour. We might note that the questionable status of Marx's arguments here has largely been overlooked by the 'labour theory of value' tradition of interpretation, because it has ignored the structure of Marx's own argument, and argued from pre-given quantities of labour to prices. I think there is undoubtedly a problem in the way Marx presents his argument, so that some results quite easily appear to be deductions from a formalist and ahistorical concept of exchange. But in my view the analysis is not inherently formalist, and formalist elements in its presentation can be replaced with more satisfactory arguments, some of which Marx develops elsewhere, particularly in *Theories of Surplus Value*.

Let us first consider the argument about exchange, equivalence and the 'common element'.

'Let us now take two commodities, for example corn and iron. Whatever their exchange relation may be, it can always be represented by an equation in which a given quantity of corn is equated to some quantity of iron, for instance 1 quarter of corn = x cwt. of iron. What does this equation signify? It signifies that a common element of identical magnitude exists in two different things, in 1 quarter of corn and similarly in x cwt. of iron. Both are therefore equal to a third thing, which in itself is neither the one nor the other. Each of them, so far as it is exchange value, must therefore be reducible to this third thing.' (*Capital*, I, p. 127).

The above passage does tend to suggest that (as Cutler et al., 1977, claim) Marx regards exchange *per se* as an act which reduces the goods exchanged to instantiations of a common element, *equates* them, and deduces his results from this formal concept of exchange. This impression is reinforced by a later passage where Marx approvingly quotes Aristotle's dictum:

> 'There can be no exchange without equality, and no equality without commensurability.' (*Capital*, I, p. 151.)

The objection that Cutler et al. raise is that while for a transaction to be an exchange, it is necessary that both parties to it agree to the terms of the exchange, there is no necessity for this to entail the reduction of the goods exchanged to a common element (op. cit., p. 14). It is not hard to find examples of exchange where such a reduction is absent, even in developed capitalist societies—for example, the exchange of gifts at Christmas; the exchange of the products of domestic labour in the household. (See also Arthur, this volume, p. 71.) The exchanges here depend very specifically on the kind of goods exchanged, and upon particular relations of personal obligation and reciprocity. In such exchanges the goods exchanged are not reduced to a common element, are not made equivalents; they are not commensurated, though they may be compared. Such exchanges are not, however, accomplished by buying and selling. Clearly, in considering the exchange of commodities, Marx *is* considering a process of sale and purchase, even if he does not emphasise this at this particular point in the argument. Moreover, the example of exchange of corn and iron, cited above, is simply *one* instance of exchange abstracted from a very large number of exchanges, as Marx's preceding paragraph makes clear (*Capital*, I, p. 127). The characteristics of the exchange of corn and iron are not held to depend simply on that one exchange, considered in isolation, but on the whole process of exchange from which this one example has been abstracted. Although Marx does not make the point very clearly, I think we can conclude that he is not considering exchange *per se*, but a particular form of exchange, capitalist commodity exchange. His argument that such exchange is a process of equation, of reduction of the goods exchanged to equivalence is not an argument from a formal, a-historical concept of exchange, but from a *specific* social relation, capitalist commodity exchange.

This reading is supported by Marx's much more explicit discussion of this point in the course of his critique of Bailey, in *Theories of Surplus Value*, Part 3. Here Marx specifically argues *against* the idea that a single act of exchange in itself reduces the goods exchanged to equivalence (see *Theories of Surplus Value*, Part 3, p. 132; p. 142; p. 144). Rather he argues that reduction to equivalence depends upon the general exchangeability, through the market, of every commodity with every other commodity:

> 'the commodity has a thousand different kinds of value . . . as

many kinds of value as there are commodities in existence, all these thousand expressions always express *the same value*. The best proof of this is that all these different expressions are *equivalents* which not only can replace one another in this expression, but do replace one another in exchange itself.' (*Theories of Surplus Value*, Part 3, p. 147).

The same point is made in *Critique of Political Economy*:

'A commodity functions as an exchange value if it can freely take the place of a definite quantity of any other commodity, irrespective of whether or not it constitutes a use-value for the owner of the other commodity.' (Op. cit., p. 44).

This general exchangeability does not simply depend on the individual characteristics of the owners of the goods, or of the goods themselves, for the rates at which the goods in any particular exchange are exchanged depend not only on the parties to that transaction, but upon all the other exchanges simultaneously taking place. This kind of exchange is a social, not an individual process. The abstraction of *a* commodity with *an* exchange value can only be made on the presupposition that this commodity is simply one of a very large number of interchangeable commodities, a presupposition that Marx has made clear in the opening sentence of *Capital*.

'The wealth of societies in which the capitalist mode of production prevails appears as an 'immense collection of commodities'.' (*Capital*, I, p. 125).

In fact, as will later emerge, this kind of general interchangeability of goods can only become the dominant form of exchange on the basis of capitalist relations of production, in which labour is separated from the means of production. (See Brenner, 1977, especially p. 51). But in Chapter 1, the categories for analysing capitalist relations of production have not been elaborated, so this point is not explicitly made. (Although it is clear from *Grundrisse*, p. 509, that Marx was well aware of it.) To summarise: Marx's claim that exchange of commodities entails their equivalence does not derive from an ahistorical and formal *concept* of exchange, but from observation of a specific, capitalist process of exchange, in which goods actually *are* socially commensurated, the visible expression of which is their prices.

Marx is not alone in describing this kind of exchange in terms of equivalence: it is a general feature of the work of economists of all kinds.[13] Where Marx differs is in arguing that such equivalence needs a separate concept, 'value'. Why, for instance, can we not treat this equivalence simply by selecting one commodity as the numeraire in terms of which the exchange values of all other commodities are presented? Does not this correspond to the capitalist economy in which the money commodity serves as numeraire? And if so, surely we must agree with Bailey that value is a 'scholastic invention' (*Theories of Surplus Value*, Part 3, p. 137).

The argument about the 'common element' that Marx gives in *Capital* is quite inadequate to deal with the above point. In the first section of Chapter 1 he gives the famous 'simple geometrical example':

'In order to determine and compare the areas of all rectilinear figures we split them up into triangles. Then the triangle itself is reduced to an expression totally different from its visible shape: half the product of the base and the altitude. In the same way the exchange values of commodities must be reduced to a common element, of which they represent a greater or lesser quantity.' (Op. cit., p. 127).

But this fails to indicate why we should not follow the numeraire approach. Indeed it even encourages the latter, because it poses the question in terms of a process of reasoning and measurement that takes place in our heads. But, as Marx stresses in Section 4 of Chapter 1, the equivalence of commodities is not established in the same way as the equivalence of triangles, but as the result of a social process. The agents in this process do not seek to establish the interchangeability of all products, but simply to exchange their own products. The exchange ratios are formed as a result of an iterative, competitive process, not on the basis of rationally deduced formulae. Money emerges as universal equivalent, not as the result of a rational social convention, but from an unplanned historical process.

The critical point is that if we treat the equivalence of commodities in terms of a numeraire commodity, we must presuppose the equivalence of commodities, but we have still not answered the question 'As what do they become exchangeable?' In what relation do they stand in the social process that enables one commodity to become the numeraire? This point emerges much more clearly from Marx's discussion of Bailey in *Theories of Surplus Value*, Part 3, (p. 133-47) than it does in *Capital*. Much of the most sophisticated modern economics, whether of the Sraffian or neo-classical variety, prefers to side-step this question by not treating the formation of exchange-values as a social process at all. It assumes exchangeability and focuses almost exclusively on the question of consistency. The central question it asks is whether a set of exchange-values (prices) can be deduced from given premises which will be consistent with some criterion set by the economist, such as the reproduction of the structure of production, or the attainment by each consumer of his 'preferred' consumption bundle, given the assumptions about how economic agents react to prices. Finding such a consistent set of exchange-values is called proving the 'existence' of an equilibrium set of exchange-values. But it is a very attenuated concept of existence, referring to the formal solution of an arithmomorphic model, not to the real world process of exchange.

An earlier generation of neo-classical economists were more robust; and so are many policy-orientated neo-classical economists today, who must eschew the theoretical rigour and purity of general equilibrium models if they are to be able to make policy prescriptions. They give the same answer to the question 'As what do commodities become exchangeable?' as was given by Bohm-Bawerk: commodities become equivalents as yielders of utility, of satisfaction. The exchange process is explained in terms of commodity owners commensurating different commodities in terms of the satisfaction they bring. Marx rejects this view, but does not set out very clearly the reasons why, quite possibly because although this has come to be the dominant view among economists, it was not so in Marx's day.

Some of the argument of the first chapter of *Capital*, I, may give the impression that Marx denied any role to use-value in the process of exchange (cf. 'the exchange relation of commodities is characterised precisely by its abstraction from their use-values', *Capital*, I, p. 127). But as his later argument makes clear, Marx is far from denying that use-value plays an important role in the process of exchange: what he is rejecting is the idea that the *equivalence* of commodities can be explained in terms of use-value. There are, I think, two aspects to this rejection. One is that Marx argued that it is in terms of *difference* that use-value is important, not in terms of *equivalence* (cf. *Capital*, I, p. 259). The other is that Marx argued that a *purely* subjective approach to the exchange process could not capture certain crucial features of it (cf. *Theories of Surplus Value*, Part 3, p. 163).

To argue that commodities are equated as use-values entails the view that commodities are wanted for the utility (or satisfaction) they bring; their characteristics as particular use-values are simply a means to the end of getting satisfaction. Utility or satisfaction represents 'the common essence of all wants, the unique want into which all wants can be merged' (Georgescu-Roegen, 1966, p. 195).[14] Marx, however, rejected this idea of the reducibility of wants to a common want.

> 'As use-values, commodities differ above all in quality, while as
> exchange values they can only differ in quantity, and therefore
> do not contain any atom of use value.' (*Capital*, I, p. 128).

And certainly everyday experience yields much support for the irre-
ducibility of wants—bread cannot save someone dying of thirst.

The reducibility of wants remains inherent in most varieties of
neo-classical price theory,[15] even though the nineteenth century idea
that the satisfaction yielded by a commodity could, in principle, be
measured and the satisfactions yielded by different commodities added
and subtracted, has been abandoned (see Georgescu-Roegen, 1966,
chapter 3).

Marx's rejection of use-value as a basis for the equivalence of
commodities does not mean, contrary to what is sometimes claimed,
that Marx rejects *any* subjective element as a determinant of the exchange process. Marx was prefectly well aware that

> 'Commodities cannot themselves go to market and perform ex-
> changes in their own right. We must, therefore, have recourse to
> their guardians, who are the possessors of commodities.' (*Capital*,
> I, p. 178),

and he recognised that the occasion for exchange is the desire of commodity owners (for whatever reasons) for use values other than the
ones they possess. But he also recognised another aspect of the exchange process, which is that while the formation of exchange-values is
necessarily the result of the actions of commodity owners, to each commodity owner entering the market it appears that the exchange ratios
are already given.[16]

> 'These magnitudes vary continually, independently of the will,
> fore-knowledge and actions of the exchangers. Their own move-
> ment within society has for them the form of a movement made
> by things, and these things, far from being under their control,
> in fact control them.' (*Capital*, I, p. 168).

In so far as each commodity owner wants to exchange his own use-
value for some other use-value, the process of exchange is composed of
individual, subjective acts. But in so far as the exchange-values appear
to be 'given' to each commodity owner it is a general social process
which takes place 'behind the backs' of the commodity owners (cf.
Capital, I, p. 180). Marx wishes to capture in his categories *both* the
subjective, individual and the social, general aspects of the process, to

encompass

> 'the crucial ambivalence of our human presence in our history, part-subjects, part-objects, the voluntary agents of our own involuntary determinations.' (Thompson, 1978, p. 280).

It is, I think, for this reason that he treats the equivalence of commodities in a way that is often found extremely puzzling,[17] as a *substantial* equivalence. That is, Marx does not treat this equivalence as a matter of some common characteristic in terms of which commodities are commensurated by their owners; but in terms of a unifying 'common element' or 'substance' which the commodities themselves embody, and which is designated by the separate category 'value'. The equivalence of commodities is explained in terms of the nature of this substance, not in terms of subjective commensuration by commodity owners (cf. *Capital*, I, p. 166).

Unfortunately, Marx does not explicitly discuss the implications of treating the equivalence of commodities as 'substantial', and the considerations which underlie his treatment are not introduced until Section 4 of Chapter 1, 'The Fetishism of the Commodity and its Secret.' This encourages two kinds of misconception: the misconception that Marx's method is formalist, his 'common element' simply a common characteristic in terms of which we can (subjectively) commensurate commodities; and the misconception that Marx's method is idealist, his value substance an idealist reification of the equivalence or continuity between commodities. It was on the basis of the first misconception that Bohm-Bawerk attacked Marx's argument. (See Kay, this volume, pp.50-54). And certainly if Marx's procedure had been formalist in the manner postulated by Bohm-Bawerk, it would have been totally arbitrary to locate abstract labour as the common characteristic. But Bohm-Bawerk ignores the force of the term 'substance'.

The notion that Marx's use of the term 'substance' signals an idealist, metaphysical approach has more plausibility, for 'substance' is a term with a certain philosophical history. It has frequently been used to designate an absolute entity which underlies and produces all particular forms. Thus in the work of Spinoza, there is a single substance, labelled 'God', and all material things or thoughts are conceived of as the modes of being of this entity. (See Ollman, 1976, p. 30.) Marx himself criticised Hegel for 'comprehending *substance* as *subject*' in *The Holy Family* (1845) (see Arthur, 1978, p. 88); but perhaps his own method in *Capital* is vulnerable to the same criticism, as is argued by Moore, 1971? Marx claims in *Theories of Surplus Value* that value 'is not an absolute, is not conceived as an entity' (op. cit., Part 3, p. 130) but how far is this true?

In my view, Marx poses commodities as substantially equivalent in the same way that in natural science, light, heat and mechanical motion are posed as substantially equivalent, as forms which are interchangeable as embodiments of a common substance, which is self-activating, in the sense of not requiring some outside intervention, some 'prime mover' to sustain it and transform it, i.e. as forms of energy. Similarly different chemicals are posed as substantially equivalent as forms of self-activating matter.[18] Only with such a concept is a materialist account of the process of transformation and conservation of energy and matter possible, an account of this process as one of *natural* history, proceeding with a dynamic internal to it, and requiring no extra-natural 'cause', no *deus ex machina* to sustain it.

There is a danger that 'energy' or 'matter' will be reified into absolute entities; but properly understood, they are not discretely distinct from particular forms of energy or matter, rather they are concepts of the continuity between these different forms. Their self-activity is not posed teleologically, as goal-directed or by design. The concept of the equivalence of forms of energy or matter in terms of the substance of energy or matter is thus a materialist, not an idealist concept.

The transformation of one commodity into another, insofar as the rates of transformation are determined 'behind the backs' of the commodity owners, is akin to a process of natural hstory, a process that seems to have objective 'laws' of its own which operate over and above the volitions of the individuals carrying it out. Hence Marx poses this process in terms of substantial equivalence, but with 'substance' understood in materialist terms—as an abstraction with a practical reality insofar as one form of the substance is actually transformed into another form, and not in idealist terms, as an absolute entity realising its goals.

There is an important difference between the interchangeability of forms of energy, and of commodities. the substance of the equivalence in the latter case must be human. Though value appears as a relation of objects to one another, we know that it cannot be so. As Marx tartly observes:

'No scientist to date has yet discovered what natural qualities make definite proportions of snuff, tobacco and paintings 'equivalents' for one another.' (*Theories of Surplus Value*, Part 3, p. 130).

Marx implicitly rejects the procedure of treating the process of capitalist exchange 'as if' agency could stem from some non-human source, a 'structure' or an 'invisible hand'. Though it does not appear to be so, the equivalence of commodities must essentially be a relation between people, not between the commodities as physical objects. Therefore, though the form of the relation must be posed in terms that capture its naturalistic appearance, the content of the relation must be posed in terms that capture its human essence. Hence the substance of value must be the human self-activity, the human energy, embodied in the commodities; the commodities under consideration are,

> 'products of social activity, the result of expended human energy, *materialised labour*. As objectification of social labour, all commodities are crystallisations of the same substance.' (*Critique of Political Economy*, p. 29).

This all seems to have been so obvious to Marx that he took it for granted without discussion.[19] The underlying consideration, that the equivalence of commodities is

> 'only a representation in objects, an objective expression, of a relation between men, a social relation, the relationship of men to their reciprocal productive activity.' (*Theories of Surplus Value*, Part 3, p. 147)

is not made explicit until Section 4 of Chapter 1 on the fetishism of the commodity, but is, I think, present in the argument from the outset. What Marx was concerned with making explicit was 'the particular form which labour assumes as the substance of value', and he often writes as if this is the major question separating him from Ricardo, rather than more fundamental questions of the object of the theory and the method of investigation (cf. *Theories of Surplus Value*, Part 2, p. 172). The social substance of commodities as values cannot be labour as such, for this has a two-fold nature, a qualitative aspect as concrete labour, as well as a quantitave aspect as abstract labour. As values, commodities differ only quantitatively, they are all interchangeable: their substance must be homogeneous, uniform. Thus we are led to the conclusion that the substance of value must be the abstract aspect of labour. As values, substantial equivalents. commodities must be objectifications of abstract labour.

> 'The product of labour is an object of utility in all states of society; but it is only a historically specific epoch of development

which presents the labour expended in the production of a useful article as an 'objective' property of that article, i.e. as its value.' (*Capital*, I, p. 154).

This conclusion has been reached by starting from the simplest form of the product of labour, the commodity; splitting it into two aspects, use value and exchange-value; further examining exchange-value, as a historically specific form of exchange relation, and establishing what this form of appearance must presuppose as a product of a socio-historical process. The methodological premises required to establish this result are those of historical materialism; the 'real' premises those of capitalist commodity exchange. If they are rejected, then the result cannot be established.

The argument in this phase of analysis concludes that the equivalence of commodities presupposes the objectification of the abstract aspect of labour, but it does not show how such objectification can take place. In fact it is a rather puzzling conclusion, as Marx signals with his use of the phrase 'phantom-like objectivity' (*Capital*, I, p. 128). The next stage of the argument, the phase of synthesis, attempts to show how objectification of abstract labour does take place, and how the abstract aspect of labour becomes dominant. At the same time it shows the problematical character of this domination, its tenuous and transient character, the fact that once achieved it is not immutably fixed, but liable to disintegration as a result of its own internal oppositions.

It has been argued by Itoh, 1976, that there is an inconsistency in the first chapter of *Capital*, I, between Sections I and II (the phase of analysis) and Section III (the phase of synthesis) because the first two sections rest on the assumption of the interchangeability of commodities, and the third points to the difficulties of this interchange, to the fact that the equivalence can break down. For Itoh this implies that there is a Ricardian residual in Marx's argument in the first two sections. I disagree with this conclusion. In my view, there is no inconsistency. It is rather that Marx begins the analysis from the most immediate appearance of the commodity, as a product of labour interchangeable with, in a relation of equivalence to, a multitude of other products; in effect, from a set of equilibrium exchange relations. This appearance does not directly signal the problematical character of the equivalence of commodities, and hence among other things lends plausibility to the idea that aggregate supply is always equal to aggregate demand (Say's Law). Marx was, I think, well aware that this appearance of equilibrium is a one-sided abstraction from a process which is fundamentally one of disequilibrium. The second phase of the argument shows the

contradictions of exchange equivalence, and makes apparent the .
ssity of revising the impressions that stem from the immediate
appearance of exchange-value.

3. The phase of synthesis: from value to price

The phase of synthesis encompasses the whole of the rest of Part
One of *Capital*, I. In it Marx discusses the way that the objectification
of abstract labour occurs and how this entails the dominance of
abstract labour; and also shows the precarious nature of this objectification. It is about the operation of the 'law of value' which fundamentally means the 'law' of the process by which abstract labour is
objectified. The term 'law' and the explicit comparison of the law of
value with 'a regulative law of nature' (cf. *Capital*, I, p. 168) is once
more a reference to the naturalistic aspect of this process, the fact that
it takes place 'behind the backs' of the commodity owners. But it is
important to note that Marx does not have a rigid, 'deterministic'
concept of a 'regulative law'. He criticised such a concept in one of his
earliest writings on political economy:

'. . . Mill succumbs to the error, made by the entire Ricardo
School, of defining *abstract law* without mentioning the fluctuations or the continual suspension by which it comes into being. . .
the monetary co-incidence (of cost of production and price) is
succeeded by the same fluctuations and the same disparity. This
is the *real* movement, then, and the above-mentioned law is no
more than an abstract, contingent and one-sided moment in it.'
('Excerpts from James Mill's Elements of Political Economy',
Early Writings, p. 260.)[20]

And he was careful to avoid such an 'abstract law' in the argument of
Capital:

'Under capitalist production, the general law acts as the pre-
vailing tendency only in a very complicated and approximate
manner, as a never ascertainable average of ceaseless fluctuations.'
(*Capital*, III, p. 161).

The 'law of value' is often posed as a relation between value and price,
but this is because price is the form through which the objectification
of abstract labour is achieved. Establishing this result is the first step
of the phase of syntheses.

The problem is to explain the process by which abstract labour,
an aspect of labour, becomes 'objectified' as the value of a commodity.

Marx's argument is that this requires the abstract labour embodied in a commodity (e.g. linen) to be expressed 'objectively', as a 'thing which is materially different from the linen itself and yet common to the linen and all other commodities' (*Capital*, I, p. 142). This can be done if one commodity functions as the bearer of value (or value-form), and reflects the value of the commodities exchanged with it. Section III of chapter 1, *Capital*, I, is devoted to exploring the implications of this 'determination of reflection' (cf. *Capital*, I, p. 149). The simplest implication is that,

'. . . the natural form of commodity B becomes the value form of commodity A, in other words the physical body of commodity B becomes a mirror for the value of commodity A'. (*Capital*, I, p. 144).

Marx calls the commodity which serves as the bearer of value the equivalent form; and the commodity whose value is being reflected, the relative form. The next implication that Marx draws, is that in order to function as a bearer or representation of value, the equivalent form must be 'directly exchangeable' (*Capital*, I, p. 147). That is, its exchangeability (the possibility of exchanging it) must not depend upon its own use-value, nor on the character of the actual, individual labour embodied in it. In this it must differ from all other commodities, where, as we have already seen, their use-value and the private characteristics of their owners play a role in their exchangeability. In the case of the equivalent form, its exchangeability must instead depend upon its *social* position as equivalent. But this social position 'can only arise as the joint contribution of the whole world of commodities' (*Capital*, I, p. 159). That is, no individual commodity owner can decide to make his commodity an equivalent form: this can only come about as the by-product of the actions of each commodity owner trying to exchange his own commodity for others he would rather have (see also *Capital*, I, p. 180).

Direct exchangeability will remain in only an embryonic form unless the equivalent form is a *universal* equivalent, in which *all* other commodities have their abstract labour objectified, their value reflected. The physical form of such a universal equivalent 'counts as the visible incarnation, the social chrysalis state, of all human labour' (*Capital*, I, p. 159). The full establishment of direct exchangeability requires a further condition that there should be a *unique* universal equivalent, a commodity whose 'specific social function, and consequently its social monopoly (is) to play the part of universal equivalent in the world of commodities' (*Capital*, I, p. 162).

And at this point we can make an empirical check on the line of argument. The argument has implied that in capitalist societies there should be a tendency for one commodity to be excluded from the ranks of all other commodities, to have conferred upon it the social monopoly of direct exchangeability with all other commodities. Can such a commodity be found? If not, then something must be wrong with Marx's argument. On inspection we do find such a commodity: gold-money. The implication is not, of course that the universal equivalent must *always* be gold money. As we have already seen, Marx goes on to note that gold, for some purposes, can be replaced as universal equivalent by symbols of itself, by paper money. The implication is rather, that gold-money as the universal equivalent is a necessary precursor to paper money. At the root of the argument here is Marx's rejection of the view that the universal equivalent can be established 'by a convention', i.e. by a conscious and simultaneous decision of all commodity owners to invest some material form with the properties of universal equivalent. Rather he takes the view that 'Money necessarily crystallises out of the process of exchange' (*Capital*, I, p. 181), and that it certainly cannot be treated 'as if' established 'by a convention'.

The fact that we do find a commodity with the social monopoly of direct exchangeability with all other commodities does not prove the correctness of Marx's argument that such a commodity is the visible expression of objectified abstract labour. Rather it has the negative effect of not disproving it, of not halting the line of argument, but allowing it to proceed. This is all an empirical check on the argument can ever do. The question of when we have sufficiently grasped the real relations under investigation, when we know enough about them to proceed to practical action, is not one that can ever be finally decided by an empirical test. It must always be a matter of judgement.

There is a problem with Marx's exposition of the role of gold-money as universal equivalent, 'direct incarnation of all human labour', in that he does not distinguish sufficiently clearly between money as a medium of exchange and the money form of value (money as universal equivalent). Money in itself is not specific to the capitalist mode of production (see Brenner, 1977), and the fact that money is functioning as a medium of exchange does not mean that it is functioning as an expression of value, the 'direct incarnation of all human labour'. This distinction is ellided in many of the statements made in Chapter 2, 'The Process of Exchange', creating the impression that where there is money, there is also value. Money as medium of exchange is certainly a necessary precursor to the money form of value, but in Chapter 2 Marx overstresses the continuity at the expense of the difference. To recapitulate the argument: beginning from an economy in which the capitalist mode of production is dominant and in which there are capitalist relations of exchange (i.e. the general exchangeability of products of labour through a process of sale and purchase), we arrived through analysis at the conclusion that this presupposes value (i.e. the objectification of abstract labour); we then considered the conditions for the objectification of abstract labour and concluded that this implies a universal equivalent that reflects and is the expression of value. Gold-money in capitalist economies does have the characteristics necessary for being a universal equivalent. But being a universal equivalent is itself predicated upon the social relations of the capitalist mode of production.

Marx's line of argument is not formalist but begins from real premises in the specific social relations of capitalism; and it does survive empirical checks, in that a social phenomenon can be found corresponding to what is posited by the argument of the phase of synthesis. Nevertheless, it leads us to an extraordinary conclusion, the extraordinariness of which Marx notes quite explicitly in the last section of Chapter 1, *Capital*, I:

> 'If I state that work or boots stand in a relation to linen because the latter is the universal incarnation of abstract human labour, the absurdity of the statement is self-evident. Nevertheless, when the producers of coats and boots bring these commodities into a relation with linen, or with gold or silver (and this makes no difference here), as the universal equivalent, the relation between their own private labour and the collective labour of society appears to them in exactly this absurd form'. (*Capital*, I, p. 169).

The point is made even more vividly in a passage included in the First Edition of *Capital*, but not in subsequent editions, and recently brought to our attention by Arthur, 1978. The objectification of abstract labour through its incarnation in the universal equivalent

> '. . . is as if alongside and external to lions, tigers, rabbits and all other actual animals, which form grouped together the various kinds, species, sub-species, families etc. of the animal kingdom, there existed also in addition the *animal*, the individual incarnation of the entire animal kingdom.' (quoted by Arthur, 1978, p. 98).

The objectification of abstract labour entails its dependent expression in a determinate form, the form of the money commodity. But does not this conclusion, that objectified abstract labour (value) has an independent expression, undermine Marx's claim that value is not conceived as an absolute entity? Here it is helpful to bear in mind another little-noticed distinction drawn by Marx, that between 'internal independence' and 'external independence' (cf. *Capital*, I, p. 209). Value lacks the 'internal independence' necessary for it to be an entity because it is always one side of a unity of value and use-value, i.e. the commodity. But the value side of the commodity can be given 'external independence' if the commodity is bought into a relation with another commodity which serves only to reflect value. This produces the illusory appearance that value in its money form *is* an independent entity; but the autonomy it confers on value is only relative. It is this externally independent expression, in objectified form, of a one-sided abstraction, the abstract aspect of labour, which is the fetishism of commodities. Unlike the fetishism of 'the misty realm of religion' it is not an ideological form, a product of our way of looking at things; but a product of the particular form of the determination of labour, of particular relations of production.

In the form of the universal equivalent, abstract labour is not only objectified: it is established as the dominant aspect of labour. The concrete aspect serves only to express the abstract aspect of human labour; for the usefulness of the labour embodied in the universal equivalent consists in 'making a physical object which we at once recognise as value' (*Capital*, I, p. 150). The private aspect of the labour embodied in it serves only to express the social aspect: individual producers cannot decide to produce the universal equivalent until it has already been established as universal equivalent by a 'blind' social process. The social aspect of the labour embodied in it, its social necessity, consists in producing a commodity which functions simply as the incarnation of abstract labour. This does not mean that the private, concrete and social aspects of labour are being extinguished, obliterated; that the labour embodied in the universal equivalent is simply abstract labour. What it means is that other aspects of labour are subsumed as expressions of abstract labour. The form of the universal equivalent reflects only abstract labour.

The argument of *Capital*, I, goes on to show the dominance of the universal equivalent, the money form of value, over other commodities, and how this domination is expressed in the self-expansion of the money form of value i.e. in the capital form of value. Further it shows that the domination of the capital form of value is not confined to labour 'fixed' in products, it extends to the immediate process of production itself, and to the reproduction of that process. The real subsumption of labour as a form of capital (see *Results of Immediate Process of Production*, p. 1019-1038) is a developed form of the real subsumption of the other aspects of labour as expressions of abstract labour in the universal equivalent, the money form of value.

In discussing the domination of objectified abstract aspect of labour, through the capital form of value, Marx refers to value as 'the subject of a process', valorising itself 'independently' (*Capital*, I, p. 255). Here again it seems as if value is being posed as an absolutely independent entity. It is indeed these references which form the point of departure of the capital-logic approach. It does seem as if here is a case where Marx is mistaking 'the movement of the categories' for the 'real act of production'. But we need to recall the distinction, made earlier, between external and internal independence; and the fact that these references occur in a discussion of the circulation of capital, i.e. of the form of appearance of valorisation in money terms. At this level it certainly appears that value is the subject of a process, endowed with a life of its own. But there is more to it than immediately meets the eye; which Marx signals in these ironic words:

> 'By virtue of being value, it has acquired the occult ability to add value to itself. It brings forth living offspring, or at least lays golden eggs.' (*Capital*, I, p. 255.)

We are reminded of the ironical references to the mysterious abilities of the commodity, its 'metaphysical subtleties and theological niceties', at the beginning of the section on the fetishism of commodities (*Capital*, I, p. 162). In my view, value appearing as 'the subject of a process', valorising itself 'independently' is posed by Marx as one more aspect of the fact that,

> 'the commodity reflects the social characteristics of men's own labour as objective characteristics of the products of labour themselves, as the socio-natural properties of these things.' (*Capital*, I, p. 165.)

The 'determination of reflection' whereby the abstract labour of one commodity is objectified by its expression in the money form of value is what underlies Marx's statements about the relation of value to price (exchange-value expressed in the money form). It should be clear from earlier sections of this paper that the references in the first two sections of Chapter 1, Volume I of *Capital* (i.e. the phase of analysis) to the determination of the magnitude of value by labour-time do not constitute an argument about the relation of value and price, but about the relation of value and its internal measure. It is in Sections 3 and 4 of Chapter 1 that we find the first references to value as a regulator of exchange ratios, most notably:

> 'It becomes plain that it is not the exchange of commodities
> which regulates the magnitude of their value, but rather the re-
> verse, the magnitude of the value of commodities which regu-
> lates the proportion in which they exchange.' (*Capital*, I, p. 156.)

and,

> '. . . in the midst of the accidental and ever-fluctuating exchange
> relations between the products, the labour-time socially necessary
> to produce them asserts itself as a regulative law of nature'.
> (*Capital*, I, p. 156.)

It will be apparent from my earlier argument that it would be a
mistake to interpret 'regulate' in terms of a relation between a
dependent and an independent variable. Rather we should understand
it in terms of the way in which the inner character of some form regulates its representation at the level of appearance, its reflection. Thus
the molecular structure of a chemical substance regulates the representation of the substance in the form of a crystal, and the cell-structure
of a living organism regulates the form of the organism's body.

We should note that in the passages quoted above, Marx confines
himself to saying that values 'regulate' exchange ratios. He says nothing
specific about the form of this regulation; in particular, he does not
commit himself to the view that the exchange ratios expressed in the
equivalent form, directly represent the magnitude of values (i.e. that
prices are equal to values). There is a passage in the discussion of the
General Form of Value which is rather more ambiguous:

> 'In this form, when they are all counted as comparable with linen,
> all commodities appear not only as qualitatively equal, as values
> in general, but also as values of quantitatively comparable magni-
> tude. Because the magnitudes of their values are expressed in one
> and the same material, the linen, these magnitudes are now
> reflected in each other. For instance, 10 lb of tea = 20 yards of
> linen, and 40 lb of coffee = 20 yards of linen. Therefore, 10 lb
> of tea = 40 lb of coffee, in other words, 1 lb of coffee contains
> only a quarter as much of the substance of value, that is, labour,
> as 1 lb of tea.' (*Capital*, I, p. 159.)

The last sentence certainly suggests an equality of magnitude of value
and price. (Marx argues that here linen is playing the role of money).

But I think we have to pay particular attention to the unstressed reference to 'appearance'. Marx in this stage of the argument is returning from consideration of the inner substance of the relations between commodities to their appearance. The point is that on the basis of the investigation so far, it appears that commodities exchange in ratios which reflect directly the magnitude of their values, and there is as yet no basis for challenging that appearance. In writing *Capital*, I, Marx was however well aware that at a later stage of the investigation conclusions based on this appearance would have to be challenged. He signals this in his footnote reference to 'the insufficiency of Ricardo's analysis of the magnitude of value' which 'will appear from the third and fourth books of this work' (*Capital*, I, p. 173).

Such an awareness is not to be found in *Critique of Political Economy* published in 1859, eight years before *Capital*, I, and which does not contain the same careful distinction between substance (or inner structure) and appearance, failing, for instance, to make a systematic distinction between value and exchange-value.

In *Capital*, I, Marx takes no steps to dispel the appearance that prices directly represent values as magnitudes. But this is not quite the same as making the assumption that prices are approximately equal to values, and subsequently relaxing it. Rather, in *Capital*, I, the argument abstracts from consideration of the social relations that imply that prices cannot directly represent the magnitude of values. This is often explained in terms of *Capital*, I, dealing with 'capital in general' and *Capital*, III, where the form of representation of the magnitude of value is explicitly considered, dealing with 'many capitals' (cf. Rosdolsky, 1977, p. 41-50). The trouble with this explanation is that it often leads to confusion about competition: to the view, for instance, that *Capital*, I, abstracts from competition. This is clearly not the case: competition is an essential feature of capitalism; capital can only exist in the form of many capitals. It is not competition that Marx abstracts from in Volume I, but the question of the distribution of value between capitals.

More helpful is the distinction that Marx himself makes at the beginning of *Results of the Immediate Process of Production*, a distinction between considering the commodity simply as the product of labour, and considering it as the product of capital (i.e. of self-valorising labour). Marx indicates that his procedure in Volume I is to begin from the commodity viewed simply as the product of labour, because this is its immediate form of appearance. The investigations of Volume I show precisely the superficiality of this immediate appearance of the commodity, revealing that the commodity, as the 'immediate result of the capitalist process of production', embodies not only value, but also surplus value; is represented not only in the price but in the profit form.

This forces a reconsideration of the representation of magnitudes of value by prices, which is undertaken in *Capital*, III, where the concept of price of production is elaborated. A discussion of the adequacy of the conclusions reached is beyond the scope of this paper. Here we need merely note that the analysis of the relation between prices and values presented in Volume III does not rest on different premises from that offered in Volume I, but is a further development of the same analysis, attempting to encompass features of the capitalist mode of production from which Volume I abstracts.

Marx not only claims that values regulate, in the sense explained, prices. He also points to the possibility of breakdown of this regulation. In order for the abstract aspect of the labour embodied in a commodity to be objectified, the commodity must have a price. But this price

'may express both the magnitude of value of the commodity and the greater or lesser quantity of money for which it can be sold under given circumstances. The possibility, therefore, of a quantitative incongruity between price and magnitude of value, i.e. the possibility that the price may diverge from the magnitude of value, is inherent in the price-form itself.' (*Capital*, I, p. 196).

Money as universal equivalent is a necessary condition for the objectification of abstract labour, but not a sufficient condition for its objectification in a quantitatively determinate, socially necessary form. The realisation of the magnitude of value in the price form is precarious because of the relative autonomy of the circulation of money from the production of commodities. In the relation between the two processes,

'commodities as use-values confront money as exchange values. On the other hand, both sides of this opposition are commodities, hence themselves unities of use-value and value. But this unity of differences is expressed at two opposite poles, and at each pole in an opposite way.' (*Capital*, I, p. 199).

There is no necessary relation between relinquishing one's own use-value in the commodity form and acquiring someone else's use-value; for one can choose to hold money, a commodity which, unlike any other, is normally exchangeable at any time for any commodity. But the magnitude of value of money is necessarily indeterminate, for there is no universal equivalent uniquely reflecting its value, but a whole series of reflections in the quantities of all other commodities that a

given amount of money will purchase (see *Capital*, I, p. 147). The
timing and sequence of purchases and sales of different goods can thus
have an independent effect upon prices, and at any moment in time
there is no necessary identity of aggregate sales and aggregate purchases.

But if the assertion of the relative autonomy of the circulation of
money from the production of commodities

> 'proceeds to a certain critical point, their unity violently makes
> itself felt by producing—a crisis. There is an antithesis, immanent
> in the commodity, between use-value and value, between private
> labour, which must simultaneously manifest itself as directly
> social labour, and a particular concrete kind of labour, which
> simultaneously counts as merely abstract universal labour, be-
> tween the conversion of things into persons and the conversion of
> persons into things; the antithetical phases of the metamorphosis
> of the commodity are the developed forms of motion of this
> immanent contradiction. These forms therefore imply the possi-
> bility of crises, though no more than the possibility. For the
> development of this possibility into a reality a whole series of
> conditions is required, which do not yet exist from the stand-
> point of the simple circulation of commodities.' (*Capital*, I,
> p. 209.)

Our observations of capitalist economies tell us that not only is this
possibility of crisis realised, it is also—temporarily—resolved, in the
sense that restructuring takes place and there is recovery from the
crisis. Thus there are clearly limits to the extent to which the circulation of money departs from the production of commodities; or, in
other words, to the extent to which price departs from the magnitude
of value. What sets these limits can only be established after a good deal
more investigation. Given the categories of analysis established so far,
all that we can say is that these limits must take the form of some
pressure on commodity producers to represent labour-time expended in
production in money terms, to account in money terms for every
moment.[21] To establish how such pressure is brought to bear requires
an analysis of capitalist production. It is quite illegitimate to argue that
the pressure must come from capital's 'need' to reproduce itself. Here
I am in agreement with Cutler et al. who reject such reasoning as
functionalist and economistic (op. cit. 1977, p. 71). But I would also
stress that nowhere does Marx present an argument of this type.

It is true that the investigations of *Capital*, I, proceed for the
most part on the assumption of equilibrium—the reflection of the magnitude of value in the price of commodities (exchange of equivalents)—

rather than on the assumption of disequilibrium – the failure of this reflection to be quantitatively determinate (exchange of non-equivalents). But this is because the assertion of the relative autonomy of the circulation of money from the production of commodities shows up in terms of the distribution of profit between capitals (see *Capital*, I, p. 262-6 for a preliminary indication of this), precisely the question from which Marx abstracts in Volume I. The major concern of Volume I is to establish how it is that labour comes to count 'simply as a value-creating substance', how this entails the subsumption of labour as a form of capital. In doing this Marx follows the procedure of first examining the equilibrium aspect of the process he is considering, its 'law', but he also indicates that this is merely one side of the process, and that the forms of the process of the determination of labour in capitalist economies imply disequilibrium and crisis, just as much as equilibrium and 'law'

4. The political implications of Marx's value analysis

We began by rejecting the view that Marx's value analysis constitutes a proof of exploitation, but argued that such a rejection did not necessarily lead to a de-politicisation of that analysis. We must now briefly return to the question of politics; briefly, because any attempt to treat this question in depth would require at least another essay. In my view the political merit of Marx's theory of value, the reason why it is helpful for socialists, is that it gives us a tool for analysing how capitalist exploitation works, and changes and develops; for understanding capitalist exploitation in process. And as such, it gives us a way of exploring where there might be openings for a materialist political practice, a practice which in Colletti's words 'subverts and subordinates to itself the conditions from which it stems' (Colletti, 1976, p. 69).

In support of this view I will make just three short points: firstly, the theory of value enables us to analyse capitalist exploitation in a way that overcomes the fragmentation of the experience of that exploitation; secondly, it enables us to grasp capitalist exploitation as a contradictory, crisis-ridden process, subject to continual change; thirdly, it builds into our understanding of how the process of exploitation works, the possibility of action to end it.

The first point stems from the premise that those who experience capitalist exploitation do not need a theory to tell that something is wrong. The problem is that the experience of capitalist exploitation is fragmentary and disconnected, so that it is difficult to tell exactly what is wrong, and what can be done to change it. In particular, there is a problem of a bifurcation of money relations and labour process relations, so that exploitation appears to take two separate forms: 'unfair' money wages or prices, and/or arduous work with long hours and poor conditions. The politics that tend to arise spontaneously from this fragmented experience is in turn bifurcated: it is a politics of circulation and/or a politics of production. By a politics of circulation I mean a politics that concentrates on trying to change money relations in a way thought to be advantageous to the working class. Examples are struggles to raise money wages, control money prices; control and remove the malign influence of the operation of the financial system, direct flows of investment funds; make transfers of money income through a welfare state, etc. By a politics of production, I mean a politics that concentrates on trying to improve conditions of production; shorten the working day, organise worker resistance on the shop-floor; build up workers' co-operatives, produce an 'alternative plan' (cf. Lucas Aerospace Workers Plan), etc. Both these kinds of politics have been pursued by the labour movement in both Marx's day and ours. The point is not that these kinds of politics are in themselves wrong, but that they have been pursued in isolation from one another (even when pursued at the same time by the same organisation), as if there were two separate arenas of struggle, circulation and production; money relations and labour process relations.

What Marx's theory of value does is provide a basis for showing the link between money relations and labour process relations in the process of exploitation. The process of exploitation is actually a unity; and the money relations and labour process relations which are experienced as two discretely distinct kinds of relation, are in fact one-sided reflections of particular aspects of this unity. Neither money relations nor labour process relations in themselves constitute capitalist exploitation; and neither one can be changed very much without accompanying changes in the other. (For examples of Marx's argument on this point, see 'Wages, Price and Profit' in Marx-Engels, *Selected Works*, Vol. 2; and *Critique of Political Economy*, p. 83-6). Marx's theory of value is able to show this unity of money and labour process because it does not pose production and circulation as two separate, discretely distinct spheres, does not pose value and price as discretely distinct variables.

The importance of the second point, that capitalist exploitation is analysed as a contradictory process, not a static 'fact', is that it enables us to grasp both how exploitation survives, despite the many changes in its form, changes which the politics of circulation and the politics of production have helped to bring about; and also how it has an inbuilt tendency to disintegrate in the form in which it exists at any moment, and to be constituted in another form. The key to understanding this contradictory process is that although money relations and labour process relations are aspects of the same unity, internally dependent on other, they are nevertheless relatively autonomous from one another. In that relative autonomy lie the seeds of potential crisis. This is important politically, not because such a crisis in itself constitutes the breakdown of capitalism – it clearly does not – but because it indicates a potential space for political action; for the self conscious collective regulation of the processes of production and distribution, rather than their regulation through 'blind' market forces.

But Marx's theory of value does not simply analyse the determination of labour in capitalist society in a way that indicates potential space for political action. Its third virtue is that it also builds into the analysis, not only potential space for political action, but the possibility of taking political action. Now the possibility of taking political action against the capitalist form of the determination of labour, against capitalist exploitation, is taken for granted by all socialists. But the strange thing is that this possibility has all too often not been built into the concepts with which socialists have analysed the process of exploitation. Instead exploitation has been analysed as a closed system, and political action against it – class struggle – has been introduced, to impinge upon this system, from the outside. It may impinge as 'the motor of history' pushing the system on over time, at a slower or more rapid pace; or as the independent variable determining the level of wages, or the length of the working day, or the particular form or tempo of the restructuring of capital after crisis. Whatever formula is used, the same drawback is there: class struggle only enters the analysis as a *deus ex machina*. This leaves us unable to think of the transition from capitalism to socialism as an historical process, a metamorphosis consciously brought about by collective action; rather than as a leap between two fixed, pre-given structures, or as a simple extension of socialist forms considered as already co-existing with capitalist ones (for a longer discussion of this point, see Elson, 1979).

Edward Thompson has recently presented an impassioned critique of Althusserian Marxism on this very point (Thompson, 1978), and it seems to me that his critique is equally applicable to the model-building of most Marxist economics; and to the relentlessly unfolding dialectic of the capital-logic school. All of them analyse capitalist exploitation without using concepts which contain *within them* the recognition of the possibility of conscious collective action against that exploitation. There is a bifurcation between their analysis of what capitalist exploitation is, and their analysis of the politics of ending it. If the 'structure' really is 'in dominance'; if the independent variables are simply 'given', and the dependent variables uniquely determined by them; of capital really is 'dominant subject'; then we are left without a material basis for political action.

In my view, and here I differ from Thompson, the same bifurcation does not occur in Marx's *Capital*. This offers us neither a structure in dominance, nor a model of political economy, nor a self-developing, all-enveloping entity. Rather it analyses, for societies in which the capitalist mode of production prevails, the determination of labour as an historical process of forming what is intrinsically unformed; arguing that what is specific to capitalism is the domination of one aspect of labour, abstract labour, objectified as value. On this basis it is possible to understand why capital can appear to be the dominant subject, and individuals simply bearers of capitalist relations of production; but it is also possible to establish why this is only half the truth. For Marx's analysis also recognises the *limits* to the tendency to reduce individuals to bearers of value-forms. It does this by incorporating into the analysis the subjective, conscious, particular aspects of labour in the concepts of private and concrete labour; and the collective aspect of labour in the concept of social labour. The domination of the abstract aspect of labour, in the forms of value, is analysed, not in terms of the obliteration of other aspects of labour, but in terms of the subsumption of these other aspects to the abstract aspect. That subsumption is understood in terms of the mediation of the other aspects by the abstract aspect, the translation of the other aspects of labour into money form. But the subjective, conscious and collective aspects of labour are accorded, in the analysis, a relative autonomy. In this way the argument of *Capital* does incorporate a material basis for political action. Subjective, conscious and collective aspects of human activity are accorded recognition. The political problem is to bring together these private, concrete and social aspects of labour without the mediation of the value forms, so as to create particular, conscious collective activity directed against exploitation. Marx's theory of value has, built into it, this possibility.

Its realisation, in my view, would be helped if socialists were to use the tools which Marx's theory of value provides to analyse the particular forms of determination of labour which prevail in capitalist countries today. This essay is offered as a contribution to the restoration to working condition of those tools.

Notes

I should like to thank the many comrades in Brighton and Manchester with whom I have discussed value theory over the last few years; and in particular Ian Steedman for reading and commenting on the manuscript of this essay. The responsibility for its idiosyncracies remains mine alone. I would welcome comments from readers via CSE Books

1. Hereafter referred to as *Critique of Political Economy*.
2. As Steedman, 1976, has pointed out, Morishima's 'Generalised Fundamental Marxian Theorem' in fact incorporates a concept of value rather different from that of Marx.
3. A notable exception is the sexual division of labour. The impression that this is determined by 'natural' biological factors is not completely undermined.
4. In the technical analysis of choice theory, an individual chooses from within the choice set, but does not choose the choice set itself. The question of who chooses the choice set, or more strictly speaking, of how the choice set comes to be delineated, is a serious problem generally assumed away by exponents of choice-logic.
5. As Georgescu-Roegen puts it, *'discrete* distinction constitutes the very essence of logic.' (Op. cit., 1966, p. 21). This interesting writer, who may be unfamiliar to CSE members, is an unconventional economist, who is well acquainted with the works of Hegel and Marx; and who critises the arithmomorphism of neo-classical economics from the stronghold of a wide knowledge of mathematics and philosophy.
6. 'Value, therefore, does not have its description branded on its forehead; rather it transforms every product into a social hieroglyphic.' (*Capital*, I, p. 167).
7. John Gray (1799-1850) was an economic pamphleteer and utopian socialist. His scheme has many similarities to the one later put forward by Proudhon.
8. Boisguillebert (1646-1714) was a Frenchman, one of the first writers in the tradition of classical political economy.
9. By the 'capital-logic' approach, I mean the approach which one-sidedly emphasises capital (or value in process, self-expanding value) as the 'dominant subject' (cf. *Capital*, I, p. 255). Rosdolsky, 1977, is a prominant example, and the point of departure for much other 'capital-logic' writing.
10. Although I agree with Hussain and Itoh that abstract labour is a concept pertinent to all epochs, I differ in my interpretation of what it means.
11. But not from 'simple commodity production'. As may already be apparent from my remarks on Marx's rejection of the sequential method of investigation I do not think that Marx followed Adam Smith and postulated some pre-capitalist mode of simple commodity production as the starting point for his theory of value. For a detailed treatment of this point, see Banaji, this volume, p. 14-45.
12. See Kay, this volume, for a discussion of Bohm-Bawerk's critique of Marx.

13. Cutler et al., 1977, are wrong to argue (p. 14) that marginal utility theories of commodity exchange do not explain exchange in terms of equivalence. It is perfectly true that the act of exchange is explained in terms of a *difference* in *total* utility: each commodity owner would get greater utility from some different combination of goods than the one he possesses, and hence enters into exchange. But the quantities exchanged and hence the rate of exchange, are explained precisely in terms of *equivalence* of *marginal* utility. (See for instance, Dobb, 1973, p. 183-4; Georgescu-Roegen, 1966, p. 191.)

14. Georgescu-Roegen, 1966, Chapter 3, has a useful discussion of the fundamental issue at stake here: that of the commensurability of commodities as use-values. Unfortunately, most of his argument is probably inaccessible to the non-economist.

15. Such a reduction can be avoided by postulating a lexicographic preference ordering of commodities (i.e. an ordering made on the same basis as the ordering of words in a dictionary). This gives an order of priority in which wants are to be satisfied, and entails comparability, but not commensurability, of commodities as use-values. This postulate is not the one normally adopted in proving the existence theorems of neo-classical general equilibrium theory, but I am assured that these theorems could be proved, even for lexicographic preference orderings, and hence do not depend on the reducibility of wants. I find it harder to see how the process of formation of exchange values can be explained on this basis, where the process of comparing quantities of commodities in terms of quantities of a common satisfaction is ruled out. The postulate of lexicographic preference ordering seems to me much more suited to a different task: that of explaining the choices of an individual faced with a given set of prices.

16. This 'givenness' of prices is recognised in the general equilibrium theorems of neo-classical economics. But the question of *how* the prices are given seems no longer to be raised. An earlier generation of neo-classical economists did try to tackle this problem. For instance Walras offered an explanation in terms of *cries au hasard*, and Edgeworth in terms of 'recontracting'. (See Schumpeter, 1963, p. 1002). Both of these are subjective explanations, in which prices are determined directly by producers, and not 'behind their backs'.

17. Cf. 'the "substance of value"—a phrase that has puzzled many modern readers', Dobb, 1971, p. 10.

18. Marx uses the term 'substance' in a chemical context in his example of the relation between butyric acid and propyl formate.

(*Capital*, I, p. 141.) Both are forms of the same underlying chemical substance, $C_4H_8O_2$. They are equivalent substances in their chemical composition as $C_4H_8O_2$ but different arrangements of the atoms in the molecule give them different physical properties; but that does not mean that $C_4H_8O_2$ is discretely distinct from either butyric acid or propyl formate – it is their essence, as opposed to their form of appearance.

19. At least I have not yet come across any explicit discussion by Marx of what he means by 'substance'; nor have I found any helpful secondary literature on this point. Perhaps any reader who has found such material would let me know.

20. Mill and Ricardo did, of course, recognise that prices in the market fluctuate considerably. But this was regarded as surface 'noise' which masked rather than manifested the underlying relations. (See Banaji, this volume, p. 14-45 for a further discussion of the relation between underlying relations and appearances in classical political economy).

21. This does not mean that every hour of labour is objectified as the same quantity of value and represented by the same quantity of money. Hours of different kinds of labour may be objectified as different quantities of value, and represented by different quantities of money. Marx deals with this question in terms of the relation between skilled and unskilled labour. It is beyond the scope of this paper to discuss the adequacy of Marx's treatment of this point, but we may note that the literature commenting specifically upon it is as full of misconceptions as the more general writings on Marx's theory of value

Nor does this mean that the purpose of value theory is to generate pricing rules by which the representation of labour-time in money must be governed to secure the reproduction of a particular pattern of labour-time expenditure. The fact that no consistent rules can be generated, in the case of joint production to link the labour-time socially necessary for the production of an individual commodity and the price of that commodity does not, therefore, invalidate Marx's value theory (for an amplification of this point see Himmelweit and Mohun, 1978, Sections 4 and 5).

Rather, Marx's value theory provides us with a tool for analysing why the elaboration of pricing rules becomes necessary in the development of capitalism, giving rise to the whole modern panoply of accountants, capital budgeting experts and value analysts (sic), and also to the concern of modern economists with finding the 'optimum' pricing rules. It also provides us with the tools to investigate a phenomenon with which Marx was little concerned, perhaps because in his day it was of little practical relevance, the *contradictions* inherent in such pricing rules, of which the contradictions of attempts to account for the labour·time spent in joint production are a good example.

Bibliography

Althusser, L (1975), *Reading Capital*, New Left Books, London.

Althusser, L (1977), *Lenin and Philosophy and Other Essays*, New Left Books, London.

Armstrong, P, Glyn, A and Harrison, J (1978), 'In Defence of Value', *Capital and Class*, No. 5.

Arthur, C J (1976), 'The Concept of Abstract Labour', *CSE Bulletin*, No. 14.

Arthur, C J (1978), 'Labour: Marx's Concrete Universal', *Inquiry*, No. 2.

Arthur, C J (1979), 'Dialectic of the Value-Form', in Elson, D (ed.), *Value: the representation of labour in capitalist economy*, CSE Books, London.

Aumeeruddy, A and Tortajada, R (1979), 'Reading Marx on Value: A Note on the Basic Texts' in Elson, D (ed.) op. cit.

Banaji, J (1976), 'Marx, Ricardo and the Theory of the Value-Form. Prelude to a Critique of Positive Marxism', *Marxistisk Antropologi*, 2, 2-3.

Banaji, J (1977), 'Modes of Production in a Materialist Conception of History', *Capital & Class*, No. 3.

Banaji, J (1979), 'From the Commodity to Capital: Hegel's Dialectic in Marx's *Capital*' in Elson, D (ed.), op. cit.

Braverman, H (1974), *Labour and Monopoly Capital*, Monthly Review Press, New York and London.

Brenner, R (1977), 'The Origins of Capitalist Development – A Critique of Neo-Smithian Marxism', *New Left Review*, No. 104.

Colletti, L (1976), *From Rousseau to Lenin*, New Left Books, London.

Cutler, A, Hindess, B, Hirst, P and Hussain, A (1977), *Marx's Capital and Capitalism Today*, Vol. I, Routledge and Kegan Paul, London.

Dobb, M (1971), Introduction to Marx's *A Contribution to the Critique of Political Economy*, Lawrence and Wishart, London.

Dobb, M (1973), *Theories of Value and Distribution since Adam Smith*, Cambridge University Press, Cambridge.

Elson, D (1979), 'Which Way "Out of the Ghetto"?', *Capital & Class*, No. 9.

Engels, F (1962), *Anti-Duhring*, Lawrence and Wishart, London.

Fine, B and Harris, L (1976), 'Controversial Issues in Marxist Economic Theory' in Miliband, R and Saville, J (eds.), *Socialist Register*,

Merlin Press, London.

Georgescu-Roegen, N (1966), *Analytical Economics*, Harvard University Press, Cambridge, Massachusetts.

Himmelweit, S and Mohun, S (1978), 'The Anomalies of Capital', *Capital & Class* No. 6.

Hodgson, G (1976), 'Exploitation and Embodied Labour Time', *CSE Bulletin*, No. 13.

Hussain, A (1979), 'Misreading Marx's Theory of Value: Marx's Marginal Notes on Wagner', in Elson, D (ed.), op. cit.

Itoh, M (1976), 'A Study of Marx's Theory of Value', *Science and Society*, Fall.

Kay, G (1976), 'A Note on Abstract Labour', *CSE Bulletin*, No. 13.

Kay, G (1979), 'Why Labour is the starting point of Capital', in Elson, D (ed.), op. cit.

Marx, K (1969-72), *Theories of Surplus Value*, Parts One, Two and Three, Lawrence and Wishart, London.

Marx, K (1971), *A Contribution to the Critique of Political Economy*, Lawrence and Wishart, London.

Marx, K (1972), Marginal Notes on Adolph Wagner's 'Lehrbuch der politischen Okonomie', translated in *Theoretical Practice*, Issue 5.

Marx, K (1973), *Grundrisse*, translated by M Nicolaus, Penguin Books, London.

Marx, K (1973), *1857 Introduction*, included in *Grundrisse*, pp. 83-111, Penguin Books, London.

Marx, K (1974), *Capital*, translated by Moore and Aveling in three volumes, Lawrence and Wishart, London.

Marx, K (1975), *Early Writings*, Penguin Books, London.

Marx, K (1976), *Capital*, Vol. I, translated by Ben Fowkes, Penguin Books, London.

Marx, K (1976), *Results of the Immediate Process of Production*, Appendix to *Capital*, I, Penguin Books, London.

Marx, K and Engels, F (n.d.), *Selected Correspondence*, Foreign Languages Publishing House, Moscow.

Marx, K and Engels, F (1973), *Selected Works*, Vols. II and III, Progress Publishers, Moscow.

Marx, K and Engels, F (1974), *The German Ideology*, Lawrence and Wishart, London.

Meek, R L (1967), *Economics and Ideology and other Essays*, Chapman and Hall, London.

Meek, R L (1977), *Smith, Marx and After*, Chapman and Hall, London.

Moore, S (1971), 'Marx and the Origins of Dialectical Materialism', *Inquiry*, Vol. 14.

Morishima, M (1973), *Marx's Economics*, Cambridge University Press,

Cambridge.

Ohlin Wright, E (1979), 'The Value Controversy and Social Research', *New Left Review*, No. 116.

Ollman, B (1976), *Alienation* (Second Edition), Cambridge University Press, Cambridge.

Pilling, G (1972), 'The Law of Value in Ricardo and Marx', *Economy and Society*, Vol I, No. 3.

Rosdolsky, R (1977), *The Making of Marx's Capital*, Pluto Press, London.

Rowthorn, R (1974), 'Neo-Classicism, Neo-Ricardianism and Marxism', *New Left Review*, No. 86.

Ruben, D-H (1977), *Marxism and Materialism: A Study in Marxist Theory of Knowledge*, Harvester Press, Hassocks, Sussex.

Rubin, I I (1973), *Essays on Marx's Theory of Value*, Black Rose Books, Montreal.

Schumpeter, J A (1963), *History of Economic Analysis*, Allen and Unwin, London.

Steedman, I (1975a), 'Value, Price and Profit', *New Left Review*, No. 90.

Steedman, I (1975b), 'Positive Profits with Negative Surplus Value', *Economic Journal*, March.

Steedman, I, (1976), 'Positive Profits with Negative Surplus Value: A Reply', *Economic Journal*, September.

Steedman, I (1977), *Marx after Sraffa*, New Left Books, London.

Sweezy, P (1962), *The Theory of Capitalist Development*, Dennis Dobson Ltd, London.

Sweezy, P (ed.) (1975), *Karl Marx and the Close of his System*, by E von Bohm-Bawerk and *Bohm-Bawerk's criticism of Marx*, by R Hilferding, Merlin Press, London.

Thompson, E P (1978), *The Poverty of Theory*, Merlin Press, London.

Printed in the United States
by Baker & Taylor Publisher Services